ISLAM : CHALLENGES IN TWENTY-FIRST CENTURY

ISLAM: Challenges in Twenty-first Century

Dr. Asghar Ali Engineer

GYAN PUBLISHING HOUSE
NEW DELHI-110002

ISLAM: Challenges in Twenty-first Century

ISBN: 978-81-212-0854-3

Price: ₹ 750

Reprinted 2014 in India by
Gyan Publishing House
23, Main Ansari Road, Daryaganj,
New Delhi - 110002
Phones : 23282060, 23261060
Fax : (011) 23285914
E-mail : books@gyanbooks.com
website: gyanbooks.com

Printed at: G. Print Process, Delhi

Contents

Introduction

These essays on Islam were written from time to time both on topical and theoretical aspects. Islam has been under cloud, especially in the world media because of certain events one of which is the one that took place on 9/11 in the USA. In Indian media too number of questions keep on arising about Islam and Muslims. Also, modernity itself has become a problem as far as Muslims are concerned, some adjusting to it and others reacting adversely to it.

All these problems need to be analysed and understood properly. Any religion does not work in vacuum; it has to root itself in the society and has to confront social problems whose nature keeps on changing. No society can remain immobile for long and social change throws up ever-new problems. The orthodox theologians often remain oblivious of these changes taking place around them and stick fast to earlier formulations. Change is seen as evil by them and they refuse to re-think issues arising there from.

Every change is seen as *bid'ah* (innovation) and *bid'ah* is sin. This did have some relevance in the initial period of Islam. *Bid'ah* was then defined as deviation from the teachings of the Qur'an and *sunnah* (practices) of the Prophet. Thus any innovation or deviation from it was strongly denounced and this denunciation had its own justification at the time.

Now one has to re-examine the concept of *bid'ah* since we are far removed from that initial period and also the locale. The Prophet was enacting the Qur'anic teachings in his own time and was providing guidance to his people in the light of society he was living in and problems arising therein. The context should never be ignored. The Holy Prophet (PBUH) was man of great vision and also received revelation from Allah and he tried to construct a just and humane order.

If we want to benefit from the teachings of the Prophet we should understand the principles he left with us both in the form of Qur'an and hadith but equally important, we should also understand his actions and his sayings in the light of his context. The principle and values remain but context changes. It is therefore, our duty to reapply these principles and values in the light of our own context. The problem is with traditional theologians. They are not prepared to re-think or re-apply the fundamental values in our own time. They prefer to stick to the words rather than understand its spirit.

Thus to them tradition is sacred, not its message. Islam was a great revolution of its time. It changed the face of the world. It gave sense of dignity to the weak and oppressed. Women were empowered and given equal status. There was great emphasis on equity and justice. However, soon a new ruling class emerged with conquests of powerful Roman and Sassanid empires. This ruling class adopted ways of these empires and abandoned Islamic emphasis on equality, dignity and justice and seep concern for the weak and oppressed.

The Islamic jurisprudence was also developed under the changed conditions and the *shari'ah* reflected new values of the ruling classes rather than the Qur'anic injunctions and Prophet's *sunnah.* Prophet's sunnah emphasized simplicity and need-based life. However, when Umayyad and Abbasid Empires came into existence the value-orientation changed. The schools of jurisprudence were developed under new political and social dispensation and hence *shari'ah* formulations became more formal and lost earlier revolutionary élan of Qur'anic Islam.

These essays collected in this book and written from time to time are an attempt to understand the original simpler and direct message of the Qur'an and the Prophet's *sunnah* and apply Qur'anic values to modern day realities. Qur'anic message is surprisingly modern and would remain ever fresh. What is needed is proper vision. There is great need to develop new theology, a theology more fitting for our own times and dealing with our own issues. It is not an easy task. One should have thorough knowledge of the Qur'an and *sunnah* and Islamic history, on one hand, and of social and natural sciences of our own times, on the other and also sincere commitment to Islam.

These essays are an elementary attempt to develop new theology for our own times. A theologian not only needs new knowledge and thorough commitment but also a future vision. I fervently hope this book will be a first step in that direction. If it inspires some readers to fulfill the task my objective will be achieved. One may not agree with all that I have to say but if we can agree on the need to develop new theology it will be more than an achievement.

Asghar Ali Engineer
5-5-2004

1
Islam and the Challenge of Poverty

Religion according to its Latin origin *religio* means consciousness and piety on one hand, and to tie, or to bind on the other. Religion, in other words, can be defined as a set of spiritual and metaphysical doctrines binding together all those who subscribe to them. Religion also becomes, over a period of time, a system of significations symbols and rituals providing a deep sense of identity in a complex world to exist where in it self is an existential challenge. Also, religion in the history of human beings, had its origin as a project of quest of life, truth and ultimate destiny. However, and it is negative side of religion, this quest for truth often loses its dynamism and gets crystallised in the form of immutable dogmas. Soon a set of complex rituals arise around these dogmas providing psychological solace and a sense of symbolic fulfillment for the faithfuls.

A few privileged casuists on the other hand, pursue metaphysical questions so abstract in nature that neither do they have any links with existential human problems nor with any sublime human destiny. Religion for them becomes a sterile intellectual exercise. Religion thus neither serves as a dynamic ethical and moral code inspiring its followers to lead spiritually meaningful life within the space of essential material needs nor does it provide guidance for sublimating human destiny and integrating it with the cosmogenic process. In other words religion becomes it set of dead rituals for the masses on one hand, and, a set of abstract, incomprehensible metaphysical doctrines, on the other.

If religion has to be meaningful project, closely integrated with human destiny, both in its mundane and sublime sense, it will have to be liberated from sterile rituals and theological casuistry. However this task is not easy to accomplish. Masses, at the most primitive level of existence, materially as well as intellectually need ritualised religion; oppressed and persecuted, they cling to it for mental solace. They dive into it to drink nectar but remained drowned in a sea of misery. The privileged casuists and theologians on the other extreme are intoxicated with their intellectual abstractions, enjoying full patronage of the established order and mortally afraid of disturbing it. Their jargonised metaphysical abstractions fill in the interstices of the hollow establishment and try to save it from final collapse.

A religion, if it has to ensure social health, and avoid becoming merely a source of mental solace and acceptance of miserable existence, it will have to transform itself into a powerful instrument of social change, an active agent challenging the decripit social order having inbuilt socio-legal and politico-economic mechanism to perpetuate privileges and powers of a few upper castes and classes. The fundamental question, therefore, is: Can religion lend itself to playing such a role without violating the real spirit and legitimate role? My answer is in the affirmative, though often a contrary view has been held by religionists and theologians. I however, in my opinion certain major historical religions like Buddhism, Christianity and Islam are imminently suited to play this role. The theologies of these religions, due mainly to the circumstances of their origin. These religions were, to begin with, powerful protest movements 'not only against established religions but also against, prevailing power-structure. While the Buddhist philosophy (Buddha's proclaimed agnosticism and his this-wordly pragmatic approach did not lend Buddhism to evolving a theology in the traditional sense) stressed abolition of *dukkha,* Christian and Islamic theologies, in their early non-speculative phases, identified themselves with the oppressed. It was only much later that these the logics became part of powerful established empires and began to lose their militant character.

Here I wish to make another important point. A theology, even if derived from revealed scriptural text, partly situational-contextual in character and partly normative-metaphysical. The militant lighting character predominates when theology remains identified with the oppressed masses and speculative metaphysical elements begin to predominate as it begins to identify itself with the establishment which becomes into existence with the religious movement in the later phase. Christian and Islamic theologies both suffered the same fate over a period of time. Both the theologies came under the shadow of neo-platonian speculative philosophy and became highly metaphysical in character. These theologies lost contact with the common people and hence lost contact with the common people and hence lost militancy and dynamism in the process.

In order to meaningfully discuss the problem of ISLAM AND THE CHALLENGE POVERTY it is important to understand the Quranic approach to certain related problems, The Quranic prophets, as the Iranian Islamic thinker 'Ali Shari'ati rightly points out, are part of the masses, not of any ruling establishment or ruling chieftains (with a few exceptions like David and Solomon). The holy Quran clearly states that "He it is who has sent a messenger amongst the masses *from among them*" (6 .2. Emphasis supplied). Thus it would be seen that the Quran emphasises the fact that God sends His messengers to the people and from amongst them. These messengers stand by the people and never identify themselves with the rulers or with the ruling classes (*mala*, ruling chiefs).

When the prophet Nuh (Noah) began to preach among his people the arrogant chieftains rejected his message and ridiculed him. "The chieftains of his people' (*Qaum*) says the Quran, "who disbelieved, said: We see you but a mortal like us, and we see that the lowliest amongst us follow you without deep thinking. We see no merit in you above us and we deem you liars." (11:27). Again in yet another chapter the Quran says: "And we sent not unto any township a warner, but its affluent ones declared: Lo ! we are disbelievers in that which you bring unto us. And they say: We are more (than you) in wealth and children. We are not punished. (34:33.36).

The Quran, in keeping with its approach, describes the rulers, chieftains and those who stand by them as *mustakbirin* (arrogant, drunk with power) and the ruled, or, the masses of people as *mustad'ifin* (weakened, oppressed). The messengers of God naturally arise from amongst the weak and fight for their liberation from the clutches of the oppressors. Prophet Moses fought against the mighty Pharaoh for liberating Israelites who were being oppressed at his hands. Pharaoh was thus *mustakbir* (arrogant oppressor) and the Israelis *mustad'ifin* the weak and the-oppressed). The entire ruling class supported the Pharaoh in this struggle, according to the Quran. "The chiefs of Pharaoh's people said: (O King), will thou suffer Moses and his people to make mischief (the ruling classes always dub any flight for justice as mischief, sedition or rebellion in the land, and flout thee and thy gods? He said: "We slay their sons and spare their women, for lo! we are in power over them." (7:127).

Thus the Quran clearly and unambiguously stands with the weak in their struggle against their oppressors. It also laments, even reprimands those who do not come to the rescue of those who are being persecuted. Reprimanding them the Quran says: "Why should you not fight for the cause of Allah and the weak among men and of the women and the children who are saying: Our

Lord! bring us forth from out of this town of which the people are oppressors ! Oh give us from Thy presence some protecting friend ! O give us from Thy presence some defender !" (4:75).

The Quranic theology thus not only strongly condemns exploitation, arrogance of power and oppression, it also enjoins upon the faithfuls to fight against these evils and come to the rescue of the weak and the oppressed as the above verse categorically indicates. Not only this: the Quran goes a step further and states its intention to put the weak and the oppressed in the decisive leadership position. It says "And We desired to show favour unto those who were oppressed in the earth, and to make them leaders and make them inheritors." (28:5).

Also, according to the Quran no township based on injustice and exploitation, can survive long. "How many a township", says the Quran, "have we destroyed while it was oppressive, 'so that it lieth (to this day) in ruins and (how many) a deserted well and lofty tower." (22:45).

Many more such verses can be quoted from the Quran which strongly condemn oppression and injustice. A tradition ascribed to the Prophet puts unbelief lower down the scale than oppression and injustice. This tradition says that a country can survive with its unbelief (Kufr) but not with its oppression (zulm). It is highly regrettable that later theological development completely overshadowed this noble spirit of Islamic theology. We shall throw some light on this aspect a little later.

Mecca was experiencing acute social tension when the Prophet began to preach there. Apart from inter tribal conflicts and rivalries, Meccan society was dogged with tensions caused by accumulation of wealth in a few hands and lack of distributive justice. Breaking the barrier of tribal structure, a powerful class of mercantile bourgeoisie was emerging in Mecca. The tribal relations of production, in other words, were giving way to mercantile economy base on exchange. There of course continued handicraft production by individual artisans or groups of them. There also continued traces of pastoral economy of which we have evidence in the holy Quran, as well as in the early history of Islam However, the commercial economy was becoming predominant.

The merchants began to accumulate wealth neglecting the tribal norms. The mercantile culture casts its shadow over the tribal one. The poor, needy and orphans began to be neglected giving rise to social tensions. There developed acute discontent among these weaker sections of the Meccan society. The Prophet felt deeply distressed at this state of affairs. We can clearly sense deep concern for destitutes of the society in some of the early Meccan verses which strongly condemn arrogance of the Meccan rich and their neglect of the poor, needy and orphans. "Hast thou observed him who belies religion? That is he who repells the orphan. And urges not the feeding of the needy." (107:1-3) Here it should be noted that believing of religion has been equaled with repelling the orphan and denying food to the needy, fins is very important social dimension of Quranic theology and the one very useful for meeting the challenge of poverty.

The Quran also condemns, in no uncertain terms, accumulation of wealth and arrogance generated thereby. The Quran says in no uncertain terms, "Woe unto every slandering traducer. Who hath gathered wealth and counts it. He thinks that his wealth will render him immortal. Nay, but verily he will be flung to the Consuming One. Ah what will convey unto thee what the Consuming One is! (It is) the fire of Allah kindled, which leapeth up over the hearts (of men). Lo! it is closed in on them. In outstretched columns" (104).

Here the whole imagery is worth noting. The one who accumulates wealth and counts it (without distributing it judiciously) will be thrown into the Consuming One which is defined as the fire kindled by Allah. The traditional theologians mean hell fire thereby in the world hereafter. But one can hardly miss its immediate social context. One needs to evolve what I would like to call socio-theological approach to the Quranic verses in order to understand their correct import. The Meccan society, on account of fast developing disparities of wealth, was on the verge of getting caught into social turmoil. The Prophet with his acute sense of social concern had clearly sensed the gathering storm. 'Through the revealed verses, this situation was depicted in appropriate divine imagery. Thus the kindled fire of Allah would also mean the social turmoil into which the Meccan society could have been caught due to the disparities of wealth. Seen in this context we can better appreciate all such verses in the Quran revealed specially in the early Meccan period. It became an integral part of the Quranic theology that the wealth be justly distributed and should not remain concentrated in the hands of the rich. "That it (i.e. wealth) should not circulate between the rich among you." (57:7) "This Quranic approach remained unchanged even in the later Medinese period. There is strong denunciation of concentration of wealth in the Medineese chapter *Al-Taubah* (Repentance). "They who hoard up gold and silver and spend it not in the way of Allah, unto them give tidings (O Muhammad) of a painful punishment." (9:34).

Needless to say if the challenge of poverty is to be met social structure free from exploitation: oppression and concentration of wealth in a few hands will have to be built. Another kingpin of such a society is justice in social, economic, legal and political sense. The Quran lays great stress on justice and uses terms like 'adl and qist for the purpose. Also, 'adl and ihsan (justice and benevolence) are again the two key terms employed by the Quran for stressing the need for economic justice. One also has to be just in economic transactions. "That you not the measure. But observe the measure strictly." (55:8-9). It is also necessary to achieve economic justice and balance that while reasonable needs for food, shelter, etc. be met, the tendency for extravagance be curbed.

The Quran requires the faithfuls to avoid extravagance. "O children of Adam", says the Quran. "Look to your adornment at every place of worship and cut and drink, but be not prodigal. Lo! He loves not the prodigals." (7:31). We now that the advanced capitalist societies of the West based on structures of oppression and exploitation are affluent and plunder the economic resources of the third world for their prodigious expenditure and maintain unreasonably rich standards of living at the cost of the poorest in Africa. Asia and Latin America The ostentatious consumerist culture of the west in proving to be the greatest curse for the poor of the world. The socialist economies, on the other hand, while ensuring reasonable level of basic necessities, positively discourage ostentatious consumerism. The stress in such economies is on production of wage goods rather than luxury goods. The world economy can achieve balance only if the western economies avoid extravagance and plundering the resources of the third world perpetuating poverty therein. But as we know the North-South dialogue has not succeeded despite repeated attempts on the part of developing countries of the South. The countries of the North refuse to give substantial aide to boost the economies of the countries of the South. They refuse to commit even 2 per cent of the gross product by way of aid these under-developed countries. The challenge of poverty cannot be met if such an imbalance continues in the economies of the North and the South.

Looking to the complex problems of world economy today, economic justice can be established in order to fight the challenge of poverty only if the concept of justice is treated not only in, economic, but also in social and political sense. The concept of justice should be as comprehensive as possible. The Quranic concept of justice, it would be seen on a careful study of its verses, is quite comprehensive in this sense, After saying that say: My Lord enjoineth justice" (7:29), it goes on to say,

"O you who believe! Be you staunch injustice, witnesses for Allah, even though it be-against yourselves or (your) parents or (your) kindred whichever (the ease be of) a rich man or poor man, for Allah is nearer unto both (than you are). So follow not passion lest you lapse (from truth). . . (4:135).

In yet another verse the Quran requires of the faithfuls, ""O you who believe! Be steadfast witnesses for Allah in equity, and let not hatred of any people seduce you that you deal not justly. *Deal justly, that is nearer to piety.* Observe your duty to Allah. . ." (5:8).

From the verses quoted above it would be seen that the 'doctrine of justice propounded by the Quran is not only comprehensive but also quite rigorous. It requires of the faithfuls that even the hatred of other people should not come in their way of dispensing justice. One has to be just even if it goes against oneself, against one's parents and relations and that justice is an integral part of *tuowah* (i.e. piety). Piety does not lie merely in praying and fasting and abstinence but also in being rigorously just. And it is obvious that the battle against poverty cannot be fought without being just in its most rigorous sense.

The modern capitalist system is highly exploitative and so perpetrates unjust socio-economic structures. Within its framework neither social, nor economic nor political justice is conceivable, specially of the Quranic variety discussed above. Even if the political rule does not precisely correspond to the class rule in the Marxist sense in the modern democratic societies due mainly to mass pressure, one can hardly deny the hegemony of capitalist class and their exploitative practices. Any form of exploitation of one human being by another human being is an acute form of injustice and cannot square with the Islamic doctrine of justice. There are other reasons as well why modern capitalist society cannot keep pace with the Islamic *Weltanschauung.*

Islam, as pointed out above, is opposed to extravagance and lays stress on keeping needs under control (it should not be, under any circumstances, construed to mean renunciation as the same has been positively disapproved of by Islam). The Quran also requires of the faithfuls to give away what is super-flous (after meeting one's controlled needs). The capitalist sodiety, on the other hand, perpetuates itself by creating artificial needs through high pressure publicity. The noted American sociologist Vance Packard in his books like *Hidden Persuaders* has systematically exposed the working of advertising agencies and their methodologies. He shows how, based on false claims, high pressure publicity, persuades in very subtle ways, the people to buy. Most sophisticated techniques are used by the advertising industry to create artificial needs so that the products, primarily aimed at making profit, can sell well in the market. It becomes the very rationale of the capitalist society.

It can also be very well understood by the perceptive observers that to high pressure publicity techniques, work much more efficiently in affluent societies of the west which owe their affluence to the plunder of the third world, as already pointed out. Thus the injustice of the capitalist economy gets compounded. Creating artificial needs among affluent people (who owe their affluence to exploitation of the poor) is injustice compounded. The affluent north refuses to render economic help to the poor and undeveloped south because it does not want to cut into the artificially maintained high standard of living thus endangering capitalist profits. The holy Quran, on the other hand, exhorts its followers to control the needs and give away the superllous for those who are deprived and dispossessed. And, for the reasons explained, this is not possible within the frame-work of a capitalist society and hence it cannot meet the challenge of poverty.

Vance Packard, in his another equally remarkable book, *The Waste Makers* shows convincingly how waste making is an integral part of American capitalism. In fact without waste making on colossal scale the wheels of industries in capitalist societies cannot run. Again-the greater the affluence the higher is the degree of waste in the economy. The usable products are destroyed so that the new products might sell in the market under the label of new 'models' without increased use-values, as is convincingly shown by Vance packard in his series of books referred to above. This tog is an unpardonable crime as far as Islamic ethics is concerned. Islam neither approves of extravagance nor of wasting valuable resources. Western affluence, generated by capitalist exploitation of the third world, perpetuates both the crimes against humanity and its future generations who would also be deprived of these unreplenishable resources due to their colossal waste by the present generation. Thus war against poverty would be very difficult to win for the future generations, if capitalism is left unleashed.

The Prophet of Islam hated poverty and starvation. There are number of hadith (traditions) ascribed to him to this effect. A tradition reported by Nissi says, "O Lord I seek refuge in Thee from poverty, scarcity and indignity and I seek refuge in Thee from being oppressed and from oppressing (others)." It is very significant tradition as it links poverty, scarcity, indignity and oppression, one aids and abets the other. The Prophet, by seeking refuge from all this makes it incumbent on all the Muslims to declare war against poverty. Another tradition reported by Abu Daud says, "O Lord I seek refuge in Thee from Kufr (unbelief) and poverty." Thus it is made unmistakably clear that kufr and faqr (unbelief and poverty); both are equally condemnable. Yet another tradition reported by Baihaqi and Tibrani says, "Poverty, in all probability, leads to unbelief (kufr)."

All these traditions ascribed to the Prophet make it clear that a Muslim must declare war against poverty. Poverty is as condemnable as unbelief and as a Muslim should fight against kufr he should fight against poverty. Perpetuating poverty amounts to perpetuating unbelief. Any ism or system which seeks to thrive on perpetuating poverty, starvation and need, must be fought against, be it feudalism or capitalism. Thus war against poverty becomes an integral part of Islamic faith.

There are several related questions as far as Islam and war against poverty is concerned. Some of these questions have been hotly debated and have raised storm of controversy. One of the fundamental questions in this regard is that of property Another important question, though of different nature, is pertaining to ribn' i.e. interest. It is important to throw some light on these fundamental questions, if we want to grapple with the problem of poverty and war against it in the light of Islamic ideology.

Before launching out on discussion of these fundamental problems, it is necessary to make one thing clear, I do not consider the concept "Islamic economics" as valid. Islam is religion whereas economics is a positive science. Islam, as a religion, provides us with a set of norms and values, not with scientific analysis or system. 'Islamic economics, if at all such a term would be used only in a normative sense, not in a positive sense of scientific and conceptual analysis. There have been of late some serious attempts at developing the concept of 'Islamic economies' both in a normative and positive sense. But it is difficult to accept this concept in the latter sense scientifically speaking.

Syed Nawab Haider Naqvi, in his book *Ethics and Economics—An Islamic Synthesis* (The Islamic Found. U.K., 1981) points four axioms of Islamic system namely Unity, Equilibrium, Free Will and Responsibility which are obviously all normauve and value-oriented. He also points out in this connection. "It is important to note that the fundamental axioms themselves are derived not through any logical process, but through observations or by positing a value judgement about their universality."

(pp. 31).

We will discuss the question of property, riba' etc. keeping this distinction between the normative and positive in mind and that the Islamic teachings and doctrines are normative and do not constitute any positive science.

Property or Poverty

The traditional theologians have steadfastly maintained that the right to property is sacrosanct in Islam and cannot be tampered with. The Sa'udi theologians even took the view that nationalisation is not permitted in Islam in view of this right to property. But, on a deeper view of the problem, this position is hardly sustainable. We have already seen that the Quran not only makes strong plea for taking care of the poor and needy, it intends to make the *mustad'ifin* (the weaker sections) inherit the earth and also the leadership of the man- kind. The case of helping the needy and poor constituting the weaker sections of the society has been repeatedly emphasised (though certainly not deemed) but has been subjected to the rights of the deprived sections of the society.

The Quran states categorically, "And in, their wealth the beggar (or needy) and the deprived (who does not beg but nevertheless is needy) had due share." (31:19). This verse thus makes it very clear that the right to wealth or property is not absolute but is subject to the share of weaker sections of the society. We have also seen in the foregoing discussion that where there is accumulation of properly among a small section of a society, poverty is bound to result in the larger section of that society (unless that society, like the western capitalist society keeps itself affluent by plundering other less developed societies). This applies much more to industrial society which is based on production and appropriation of surplus value than to a commercial society which is based on appropriation of exchange value.

Thus one has to decide between property and poverty. The crucial question is Property or Poverty? As far as Islam is concerned, the Quranic verses and the prophetic traditions make it abundantly clear that in the war against poverty, the right to property cannot be treated as inviolable. In fact due share will have to be apportioned for the needy and the deprived. It is also important to discuss here the question of property in an industrial economy. The extent of the property owned by individuals in mercantile economy differs quantitatively as well as qualitatively from the one owned by huge cartels, corporations and multinationals in a modern industrial economy.

The economic might of huge multinational corporations owned by Americans greater than the combined economies of some of the smaller Asian and African countries. The appropriation of the surplus produced by the sweat and toil of the workers keeps on adding to the economic might of these monopolies and multinational corporations. Those corporations, using their strangulating hold over economies of the poorer nations, dictate terms and unreasonable prices and are thus largely responsible for perpetuating poverty in these countries. One can quote here the most recent example of Nigeria. Its economy has been nearly ruined as it refused to bow down to the dictates of the multinational oil corporations.

Islam was confronted with mercantile economy when the Prophet was preaching. It opposed and strongly attacked concentration of wealth even in a mercantile economy. How could it, then allow right to private property remain inviolable in an industrial era? How nationalization could be ruled out, if it becomes necessary for supporting the cause of weaker sections of Society? But either the theologians do not under stand the intricacies of industrial economy or support the status quo themselves depend on it We will throw some more light on the question of nationlization a little later.

Charity or Sharing of Wealth ?

The traditional theologians have argued that Islam wants to meet the challenge of poverty by encouraging charity called *sadaqah.* It is true the Quran talks of *Sadaqah.* Charity was one of the ways of combatting poverty or reducing its rigours in a mercantile economy in those days. However, it was and is not the only way. The Quran, as already pointed out, talks of the share of the needy and the deprived in the wealth and share is much more than charity, a right, not mere supplication . The Quran was also aware of the limitations of charity. The sense of superiority of the giver and that of indignity of the taker often makes it less than worthwhile.

The Quran uses an appropriate simile to explain the inherent shortcoming of such a charity. It goes on to say: "O you who believe! Render not vain your alms giving by reproach and injury like him who spends his wealth only to be seen of-men and believes not in Allah and the Last Day. His likeness is as the likeness of a rock whereupon is dust of earth; a rainstorm smites it, leaving it smooth and bare. They have no control of aught of that which they have gained. Allah guides not the disbelieving folk," (2:264).

Thus the Quran emphasizes the clement of reproach and injury involved in charily and that such a charity is washed away as the dust from the rock in a rainstorm as the same is without any roofs. From this verse the Quran's attitude to charity is very obvious. It often carries the danger of reproach and injury to human dignity and hence cannot strike any firm roots in society. The limited effects, produced if any, by charitable acts, are destroyed through angry uprisings of the deprived sections of society (rainstorm is metaphorical expression for angry uprising).

The next verse following the one quoted above is also quite meaningful in this respect. Mere is its text: "And the likeness of those who spend their wealth in search of Allah's pleasure and for the strengthening of their souls is the likeness of a garden on a height. I he rainstorm smites it and it brings forth its fruit twofold. And if rainstorm smites it not, then the shower. Allah is seer of what you do." (2:265)

The verse could mean to refer to true charity which is done to earn Allah's pleasure. It is likened to a garden which brings forth twofold fruit. It could also mean to signify of wealth through social institutions which does away with any possibility of reproach and injury, since charity in true spirit is so rare in view of human nature. If redistribution of wealth is brought about through well-devised socio-economic institutions, it would generate mass enthusiasm resulting in redoubled efforts and increase in production twofold.

Trusteeship or Social Ownership ?

Some theologians and modernists have also argued in favour of theory of trusteeship. This theory has been propounded as, according to the Quran, Allah is the real owner of all that is between heaven and earth. It is, therefore, argued that man is not the owner of his wealth but holds in it trust. God has entrusted wealth to him to spend on the needy and the poor. He only possesses wealth for the welfare of others. Tolstoy, Mahatma Gandhi and several others have also propounded similar theory. It seems to be a splendid in theory. However, it assumes that man is motivated in his actions by idealism alone. It is far from true. The whole history negates this assumption. Had the man been motivated by idealism alone, the whole history of mankind would have been very much different. The earth would have long been a paradise, Human beings have a highly complex nature.

They are motivated by ideals but not always so; they are motivated by selfish desires more than the ideal motives.

There are very few examples, besides that of the Prophet and few of his companions, in the entire history of Islam, of Muslim individuals and rulers who can be said to have held political powers or wealth as a real trustee of God. The very early history of Islam is full of bloody is rife both for political power and possession of wealth. It was for nothing that Abu Dhar Al-Chifari, that eminent companion of the Prophet had to fight against all those companions of the Prophet and other Muslims who had begun to misuse political power for amassing wealth and its ostensible display. But Abu Dhar met with a tragic end. He was exiled and died a lonely man. His fervent protests proved to be ineffective and amassing of wealth began on a large scale.

While advocating any idealist theory like that of trusteeship one will have to bear all these complexities in mind. What is happening in the Islamic world today should also serve as in eye opener to the advocates of such theories. Despite so much talk of Islamization in several Islamic countries no serious attempt has been made in any one of them for establishing just socio-economic structures. Disparities of wealth so fervently denounced by the Quran continue and the upper classes indulge in conspicuous consumption while the poorer sections continue to suffer. The ruling classes who are the main beneficiaries of the status quo have not accorded any priority to the economic questions in their Islamization programme. Only a half-hearted attempt is made to establish interest free banks keeping the present economic structure intact. We will discuss the question of interest-free economy presently.

What could be the alternative to the trusteeship theory? Does the theory of social ownership fit into the Quranic framework? Let it be clearly understood that the Quran, as explained earlier, does not advocate any specific theory; it only lays down certain norms and emphasizes some-values. It condemns oppression and exploitation and makes justice obligatory on its followers. What is therefore .primary in Islam is putting an end to all forms of oppression and exploitation and establishing a just society by evolving suitable socio-economic formations. It is from here that the boundary of scientific approach to the economic problem begins. The nature of theory should be such as to take Islamic value system into account on one hand, and, should result in mitigating socio-economic injustices in the society, on the other.

It should also be borne in mind that the nature of socio-economic institutions, theories and practical measures would vary with the nature of socio-economic formations. What is valid or efficacious in a tribal, feudal or mercantile economy may not necessarily be valid in an industrial economy. While the fundamental values should not be tampered with (what we can term as hudud Allah i.e. limits of God in the Quranic parlance) the socio-economic institutions must be reconstructed or changed into in order to retain the ellicacy of the values divinely inspired or intuitively gained. I would like to elaborate with reference to the point under discussion.

The institution of *sadaqah* (charity) could serve the end of mitigating the rigours of economic injustice in am emerging mercantile society or in a feudal society. While the overall spirit of the Quranic concept of socio-economic justice is much more radical it could not have been realizable to the same degree in a tribal-cum-mercantile society. It has to be tempered suitably in the prevailing socio-economic milieu. The institutions had to be so devised as to meet the demands of the situation. Much too great a degree of radicalism in non-congenial milieu can defeat the very purpose sought to be achieved. Advocacy of non-pragmatic radicalism has often been the bane of many revolutions. Even a revolutionary like Lenin had to condemn certain measures advocated by a section of Bolsheviks as 'infantile communism'.

The concept of *sadaqah* in the Quran must be seen in this light rather than a permanent institution as sought to be done by theologians and others averse to any change. Only values are permanent, not the social institutions which serve those values in particular circumstances. It would be unfortunate to treat institutions as permanent at the cost of those fundamental values. The Quran was not satisfied, even in those circumstances with the concept of voluntary charity. It categorically states, "Takes alms from their wealth wherewith you may, purify them and may make them grow ..." (9:103). Thus *zakah* is to be taken from their wealth so that the needy and the poor may be taken care of and the wealth and society may grow in harmony.

It does not require much argument to conclude that traditional institution of charily can not meet the challenge of poverty in the industrial economy, especially in the third world which includes India. New socio-economic institutions will have to be fashioned to meet this formidable challenge. Private property cannot be left untouched in the hands of few, if the Quranic spirit is to be upheld. One will have to choose between property and poverty and the Quranic choice is abundantly clear. Private property cannot be treated as sacred and inviolable although it does not mean abolishing private property altogether.

Thus Mr. S.N.H. Naqvi also maintains, ". . . it should be clear-that a substantial dilution, through direct and indirect policies, of the institution of private property must form the kingpin of any egalitarian Islamizaiton programme. This is particularly true to those Muslim countries that live under oppressive feudalistic systems. The most objectionable element of the private property system is landed property, which serves no useful economic functions whatsover. No economic harm will be done, indeed, great social benefits will flow—if all landed property were to be confiscated by the State in one clean sweep and cultivated on its behalf." (*Ethics and Economic*,. Ibid, pp. 149)

In fact Mr. Naqvi raises important question here. In the countries "of the third world there cannot be any effective solution of the problem of poverty without implementing land reforms. However, it is hardly on the agenda of any Islamic country publicising, its "Islamization" programme. Pakistan for example, very badly needs implementation of land reforms. The big landlords are very powerful and no government enjoying their support can dare touch their lands. Zia's "Islamization" does not make even an indirect reference to any such programme. The committee of expert economists appointed by the Zia regime stressed the urgent need for such reforms but the report was shelved.

The Committee, in its report, advocating land reform, says; "In addition to this land reforms should be introduced to reduce the size of the *family holding* of land. Steps should also be taken to promote the Islamic system of partnership tenancy in place of the wide spread practice of hiring out bare land for fixed rent which according to some *Fuqaho* (theologians), is formally equivalent to *ribah.* Furthermore, there is, the explicit Islamic position that land not cultivated for three consecutive years should be taken away by the State, without paying any compensation to their owners, and given to those who can cultivate it." (*An Agenda for Islamic Economic Reforms*, mimeographed report prepared by the Pakistan Institute of Development Economics, Islamabad).

Needless to say no such radical land reforms are cultivated by the Zia regime. Its Islamization programme does not go beyond imposing certain Islamic punishments for theft and adultery and in the economic field beyond establishing interest-free banks which any way do not harm powerful vested interest reponsible for perpetuating poverty. This clearly betrays the class character of the Zia regime. The other Islamic regimes have been no less than guilty in this respect.

As far as the Islamic value-system is concerned, one will have to give altogether a new interpretation to the idea of trusteeship of wealth. If an individual possessor of wealth is considered as its trustee, the desired result is not obtained. It becomes very difficult to demarcate between the rights of a possessor and an owner. In fact the possessors and owners can and do exercise virtually all the rights of owners. It is a well known fact that in high taxation economics, trusts are created by the rich and the wealthy, not to dispense benefits to the needy but to avoid taxes. They, at the same time, continue to exercise all the rights of ownership by retaining their control over the trusts. The government has to further legislate to curb such malpractices.

It would thus be seen that the concept of individual trusteeship of wealth is not adequate to meet the requirements of judicious distribution of social wealth in the society. The problem can be adequately grappled with only *if the society as a whole is treated as a trustee of Allah* and the social wealth is owned by it, including the means of production, in an industrial economy. The society as a whole should hold social wealth in good trust and develop and spend it in keeping with the objectives laid down by Allah. There is nothing wrong even if this happens to be in conformity to the socialist doctrine of social ownership of means of production. The Prophet is reported to have said that "Wisdom if the lost property of the faithful; he should acquire it whatever he finds it."

Another important dimension of social trusteeship of wealth is ecological in nature. The capitalist development, due to its greed for profit and accumulation, often ignores ecological considerations while ruthlessly exploiting natural resources. Ecology must be treated seriously while working out the strategy of economic development. Also, the imperialist countries have shown very scant regard for ecology in the third world in their greed to exploit it for keeping their standards of living very high. If the natural resources and means of production are controlled by the society as a whole, it would not be possible to do so. Yet another dimension of the problem is intergenerational use of the natural resources. The society must hold natural resources in trust for the coming generations too. They should not be exhausted for maintaining high standards of a few generations only. This is precisely what is happening with the oil resources of the Arab world. The ruling classes in the Arab world are selling millions of barrels of oil every year to the industrialised world of the west and themselves appropriating the revenues earned. The life styles of these ruling classes arc becoming almost legendary. An aver age family in Jeddah (Saudi Arabia) owns four cars. The institution of social trusteeship would ensure that coining generations are not deprived of the benefits of natural wealth. The oil resources of the Arabs, it is estimated by the noted economists like Samir Arnin, may be exhausted within 30 years, if oil production is not curtailed. One must also bear another fact in mind that those who talk of the concept of Islamic and reject the concept of nationlization atleast, inclined to share their wealth with the poorer Islamic nations like Bangladesh which is one of the poorest nation in the world. Thus Islamic utnmuh remains purely religious concept which is exploited politically by the rulers of the Islamic world but refuse to dispense economic benefits to the poor and needy of the ummah in other countries, symbolic financial aids apart.

One of the most fundamental doctrines of Islam is *tawhid* (unity of God). Traditional theologians have mostly concerned themselves to explaining its religious aspects. The socio-economic aspects of their far-reaching doctrine have not received any serious attention so far. Unity of God should not be treated merely as a theological concept but also a sociological concept. It is precisely for this reason that the Quran opposed all distinctions based on tribes, races and nations and established the brotherhood of faithfuls. Also, divisions in a society are not merely ethnic in nature, they are also economic. They are termed as class divisions in the economic terminology. The latter divisions cause serious tensions and conflict in the society and no meaningful unity can be achieved if these-divisions persist and keep on widening. If the divine unity reflects social unity—and it should, as per the Quranic spirit- then the *tachiai iqtisadiyat* (what could be roughly, termed as Islamic economics) must minimize these economic disparities. Only a society free of ethnic, national, linguistic and class divisions can be an ideal tawhidi society.

I would also like to emphasize here that social situations are normally highly complex and human behaviour is not motivated by ideals alone but is governed by social situation also. Any theory which fails to take this fact into account cannot come to grips with social and human realities. Whatever the ideals, theological or metaphysical, ethnic, national and class divisions cannot be washed away very easily. The Quran is also fully aware of these social complexities and declares: 'Had Allah willed, He could have made them one community, but Allah bringeth whom He will into His mercy. And the wrongdoers have no friend nor helper." (42:8)

This is very significant verse. It clearly implies the prevailing ethnic and other divisions and tensions and the problems of bringing about unity. "Had Allah willed He could have made them one community" is quite meaningful statement, i e., if only ideal could bring about unity, they could have because one community but Allah guides his servants and leaves them with their social realities (of their own making) and to desire His mercy. Thus it is for the human beings to take initiative and seek His mercy i.e., strive to create a society free of these divisions and ensuring unity. Only those who try to mitigate these divisions and tensions caused by them deserve His mercy. Those who cause these divisions to persist and tensions to be aggravated are wrong-doers and "wrong-doers have no friend nor helper". Thus the (Quran's verdict is clear: it is not Allah's responsibility to forge unity and make them one community; it is for human beings, under His guidance, to strive to achieve this objective by minimizing these divisions and thus deserve His mercy. If they cause these divisions to persist they will face the consequences and will have no friends and helpers.

The question of property and poverty should also be looked into in this light. The right of property is not absolute, but neither can it be easily done away with. It poses numerous problems. The existing class divisions are very sharp. Concentration of property in a few hands undoubtedly aggravates the problem of poverty among the masses but abolition of right to property can also not be achieved in one go. One may have to evolve, through trial and error, in right spirit and inspired by one's ideals, solutions to this problem in keeping with ones situation. Ncilher the abolition of right to property right away nor retaining it as absolute one can meet all possible situations. Both the solutions being extreme, do not take entire complexity of social situation into account. Extreme solutions are workable only in extreme situations, not in existing 'normal' situations.

Sudden abolition of right to property can throw up very complex problems severely affecting the economy. Immediately after the October Revolution in Russia severe restrictions on right to property were applied but after the days of war communism—extreme situation a new economic policy (NFP) had to be adopted reversing sonic of these curbs. The economy would have otherwise been severely affected, even on the question of the pace of collectiviation there was bitter controversy among the Bolsheviks. Also, Mao Ze Dong's advocacy of establishing communes in one go met with severe resistance from other leaders and created serious economic as well as political problems. After his death the new leadership reversed many of these measures and permitted, under the label of modernization, restoration of private plots on limited scale and also adopted 'responsibility' system both in fields and factories in order to boost production.

Thus it would be seen that the question of poverty can not be set led in a simplistic way. From this one should not conclude, as opponents of socialism often do, that tampering with the right to own property is against human nature and that there would be no incentive for production without it. All I intend to emphasize here is that much would depend on the prevailing situation. It is for this reason that the Quran neither upholds right to property as sacrosanct nor rejects it altogether. While opposing exploitation and oppression and emphazing socio-economic justice in no uncertain terms, it leaves concrete modalities of individual and social properties to be worked out in concrete situation.

It would be seen from the foregoing discussion that *adl* (justice) is the cornerstone of an economy based on Islamic values. To realize this concretely in a modern industrial economy it is not enough to establish interest free banks, collect *Zakah* and *Ushr* (on agricultural income) and emphasize charity. These measures are not enough to meet the challenge of poverty and establish social justice important though they are. The socio-economic institutions will have to be re-fashioned in order to establish distributive justice. The first important requirement is that one will have to view the problem in the context of totality of economy, not in piecemeal fashion. Production in modern economy is as important as distributive justice.

It has been argued that profit motive leads to maximizing of production and it also constitutes a just reward for the entrepreneur. And that just reward is in keeping with the Islamic principle. Those who know the working of modern industrial economy and its scale of operation would hardly be taken in by such arguments which used to be advanced century. Giant corporations and multinationals, are not owned by an individual entrepreneur and his work ethics and his profit motive as was the case in the early stages of capitalism. These giant corporations are owned and manipulated by the powerful groups of super rich through the mechanism of buying controlling shares. The huge among of profit are pocketed by those whose skillfully maneuver these controlling shares. The profit thus assured is neither the result of hard work, nor that of proportionate investment. Such a profit is, therefore a result of speculation on the stock exchange and is *haram* (illegitimate), prohibited by Islam. It should also be borne in mind that the profit obtained through commercial exchange, in which the individual owner and investor plays personal role through direct operations is not comparable with the profit obtained through production by workers and appropriated by remote entrepreneurs who do not play any direct role in its generation.

In a mercantile economy on the other hand profit is generated (rather distribute) through commercial transactions carried out by the investor himself. The prophet was faced with this situation in Meccan mercantile economy and it was the profit of this sort was legitimized with a proviso that no speculation or other forms of malpractices like shortweighting, short-measuring or advance trading are not resorted. Thus the two categories of profits should not be confused together. Here we would like to throw some light on the meaning and concept of *riha'* itself. *Riha'* should not be understood in the context of modern industrial economy only as interest; its scope should be widened to include all the exploitative practices. Industrial profit would also fall in this category. Thus abolition of *riha'* should mean banning all exploitative practices including the profit earned by large scale modern industrial establishments. It is only then that the workers and other weaker sections of society would benefit. It is also a point to be noted that free enterprise-oriented industries in their hunt for profit are more interested in producing consumer goods for upper classes including consumer durables rather than wage-goods for the workers and other weaker sections which have much low profitability.

It becomes the responsibility of the society as a whole or the state to produce and supply such goods to the weaker sections of the society. Needless to say this role can be effectively played by the nationalized sector. Large-scale industries will have to be nationalized both for curbing unethical consumerism as well as for establishing social justice, a cornerstone of an Islamic society.

2
The Political Universe of Islam

I

The political universe of Islam has never been a fixed entity. It has been continuously changing depending on locale and time. Also, it is difficult to trace any fixed notion of Islamic state either in the Qur'an, in hadith literature or in any political theory propounded by any Muslim theologian. Popularly it is believed that in Islam, state and religion cannot be separated. It is more of a theological and historical construct rather than a scriptural injunction. It is true in the sense of Islamic values, which must be associated with the state.

It is a well-known fact that there was no state structure in pre-Islamic Arabia. The tribal chiefs in Mecca led by the tribe of Quraysh made all important decisions. These tribal chiefs constituted a council of their own called *mala'* (senate) and all decisions had to be unanimous, else they could not be implemented by dissenting tribal chiefs. Also, there were no institutions like the police or the army for law enforcement as only the tribal customs prevailed. In pre-Islamic Arabia all the wars were inter-tribal and all adult male members of the tribe participated in it. There were no wars with other countries outside *Jaziarat al-Arab* i.e. Arabian peninsula.

The outside rulers had to deal with tribal chiefs as there was no head of the state. Also, for outside rulers no need arose for invasion of this area and hence no army was needed. Thus both the institution of army as well as that of police (*shurta*) came into existence only in the post-Islamic period when a primitive state structure came into existence. The state structure which, came into existence after the death of the Holy Prophet could be described as proto-democratic. As long as the Prophet was alive all decisions were made by him be they political or civil in nature. He of course consulted his companions when the need arose. The Qur'an also exhorts him to consult his companions (see 3:159)

On the death of the Holy prophet of Islam, Muslims differed on the issue of succession, Sunnis maintaining he left no successor or any will to that effect. The Shi'ahs, on the other hand, maintained that he did appoint his successor and that both in spiritual and political sense the successor ship will continue in the progeny of Ali, the Prophet's son-in-law and Fatima, his daughter.

Thus it would be seen there were no agreed views about the successor, much less on its mode. There was no pre-Islamic model to follow. The Sunnis followed the pre-Islamic tribal tradition and elected the chief of the state as tribals used to elect a successor to the deceased chief. But that election was also not smooth there being many claimants and each claimant laying claim on some or the other merit. The Quraysh laid their claim on the basis that theirs was the most experienced tribe in diplomatic sense and that the Prophet was from amongst them. The Ansar, on the other hand maintained that they were the first to help the Prophet and thus had greater claim to being his successor. Some even suggested that let there be one co-ruler from the Quraysh and one from the Ansar.

Since there was no institution of monarchy in pre-Islamic Arabia and all decisions were taken with mutual consultation, and there being no authority like the Prophet any more, all decisions were taken by the succeeding caliphs through mutual consultations with the senior companions of the Prophet. There was no clarity about the powers of the caliph and also about duration of his regime. However, one thing was clear that the caliphs had to rule according to the Qur'an and Sunnah and prophet's companions had to assist him in discharging these duties.

Both the Qur'an and Sunnah were the most progressive and liberative sources of legislation at the time. Islam came as a liberating religion for the weaker sections of society including women. No doubt the people embraced in large numbers. Not only this history tells us that the poor and unprivileged people of Roman and Sassanid empires even welcomed Muslims as conquerors. They opened the doors of the forts and even guided them through secret routes to enter into the city. Thus the Islamic State of the time was a revolutionary state.

Even the first Caliph Abu Bakr is reported to have said while assuming the charge of caliphate, "O people! Behold me – charged with the cares of Government, I am not the best among you; I need all your advice and all your help. If I do well, support me; if I mistake, correct me. To tell the truth to a person commissioned to rule is faithful allegiance; to conceal it, is treason. In my sight, the powerful and weak are alike; and to both I wish to render justice. As I obey God and His Prophet obey me; and if I neglect the law of God and the Prophet, I have no more right to your obedience." (Syed Athar Husain, *The Glorious Caliphate*, Lucknow, 1947, p-19)

This was an excellent doctrine of governance for a revolutionary state. To dispense justice to the weak and powerful alike and to ask the governed to speak truth to the ruler and to treat it as a true allegiance. The Qur'an laid maximum emphasis on justice to the weak, to bring about redistribution of wealth in favour of the poor and the needy and to create the institution of *bait al-mal* (state treasury) to achieve such redistribution. And these caliphs tried to follow the spirit of the Qur'an as rigorously as they could.

However, it was possible within smaller area and more or less homogenous population of Mecca and Medina (though it was not as homogenous as one would like to believe). But as the Islamic empire spread to Egypt, Syria, Palestine and other parts of Roman Empire on one hand, and Iran and Central Asia, on the other, diversity increased tremendously and size of population too. Also, there were diverse customs and traditions and liberative aspects of Islamic teachings were not acceptable to all, particularly to the former ruling classes.

Thus it was no longer possible to enforce the Islamic doctrine of justice and redistribution of wealth in favour of the weak as rigorously as it was possible within a small area with a more homogenous population. The fissures began to develop with the increase in size of the Islamic Empire. Here before we proceed, we would like to deal with an important issue for a, Islamic state.

Those ideologues of Islamic state who fervently advocate its establishment has to seriously reflect on the question whether it is possible to establish an Islamic state like the one which was established immediately after the death of the Holy Prophet? Firstly, there was no unanimity among the Muslims as to the question of succession as pointed out above. The Muslims were vertically divided on the question of succession. Secondly, within less than thirty years of establishment of caliphate, civil war broke out among the Muslims leading to great deal of bloodshed.

The first Caliph Hazrat Abu Bakr had clearly stated the principles of transparent governance which could be applied for a very limited area and limited period. Also, all the present rulers who claim to establish an Islamic state never refer to the principles laid down by the first Caliph for governance. They only apply certain parts of Shari'ah law that too as it was developed during medieval ages without re-thinking it. Such mechanical application of the law creates anomalies difficult to resolve. No rulers of the present day Islamic state follows the Qur'anic values of *'adl, ihsan, rahmah and hikmah* (justice, benevolence, compassion and wisdom) besides those of equality, human dignity and brotherhood. It is these values which are more fundamental to the Islamic state than any thing else. No Islamic State in contemporary period has established a welfare state, let alone brought about distribution of wealth among the poor and the needy. (59:7)

An Islamic state cannot be merely based on some selected aspects of Shari'ah law like dress code for women and other restrictions on them, *hudud laws* (laws of punishments), blasphemy law, personal law and so on. These laws were based on the interpretation of the Qur'anic verses in the then prevailing cultural ethos and hence need to be rethought to accommodate modern problems.

Also, in the medieval political theory there was no concept of citizenship, let alone citizens' rights. The values of governance as developed by the first Caliph on the basis of the Qur'an and Sunnah were soon abandoned by the Muslim rulers. The third Caliph was murdered apparently because he did not apply the principles of justice very rigorously and the fourth caliph because he applied them too rigorously. The character of the Muslim ummah had drastically changed due to conquests of large areas of Roman and Sassanid empires and it was very difficult in these circumstances to apply any coherent political theory, let alone the fundamental principles and values.

Here we would also like to deal with the concept of ummah. This concept of Muslim ummah has also undergone change from its early usage in the Islamic history. According to Imam Raghib any community whether based on religion or geography and contemporaneity, be it optional or non-optional, it is not even limited to human community, even the birds belonging to same group can constitute ummah (6:38). The Qur'an describes entire humanity as one *ummah wahidah* (2:213) (i.e. one human community). (See *Mufradat al-Qur'an*, Lahore, 1971, under *ummah*)

The Qur'an also expresses in the verse 5:48 that if Allah so desired He could have created all human beings as one community and the Qur'an also says that from amongst you, should be a group (ummah) who should become role model for goodness to others (3:104). Thus we see that the Qur'anic usage for ummah is not only for Muslims but much wider in its scope.

Ummah in the sense of Muslim community alone became current much later. The Prophet of Islam drew up *Mithaq-i-Madina* which included various Jewish and pagan tribes besides Muslim tribes and this conglomeration was also referred to as *Ummah wahiday* i.e. one community. It is important to note that Maulana Husain Ahmed Madani of Jami'at al-Ulama-i-Hind opposed two nation theory on the basis of this Medinese covenant saying when the Prophet of Islam called the composite community as Ummah Wahidah, how can Jinnah describe Hindus and Muslims as two separate nations.

Thus it is only in spiritual and religious sense that Muslims can be described as one ummah, not in political sense. In political sense Muslims constitute ummah separately in every country along with others, may they be Hindus or Christians or Buddhists. Today majority of Muslims lives as minorities in various Asian, African and western countries including Europe and North America. How can these desperate groups of Muslims living in these countries constitute one ummah in political sense? Culturally, linguistically and ethnically they are much closer to those non-Muslim groups with whom they live in those countries.

In medieval ages, countries were not divided into nations. Today's political realities are very different from those of medieval period. And even during medieval period all Muslims were not under one caliph. Earlier political theory of Islam had proposed only one caliph but this state of affairs did not last more than a century. Gradually number of rulers came into existence in the Muslim world and that reality had to be accepted by the Islamic theorists.

Also, there was no single method by which even the first four caliphs – called *khulafa-i-rashidun* could be elected. And after the fourth caliph Mu'awiyah, belonging to the Umayyad clan, seized power even without popular sanction and he nominated his son Yazid to succeed him thus introducing the monarchical institution in the world of Islam. Many prominent companions of the Prophet (PBUH) refused to acknowledge Yazid as a legitimate successor and the Prophet's grand son Imam Husain gave his life but not his hand into the hand of Yazid. He became the great martyr in the cause of Islam.

Thus we see that no single political theory worked in the world of Islam. Drastic changes have taken place in political institutions from caliphate to monarchy to army dictatorship to democratically elected governments. Of all these, one can say that democratically elected governments can be said to be closest to the spirit of Islam.

II

The contemporary scenario in the world of Islam has no uniformity either. There are all forms of governments in the Islamic world today from monarchy to military dictatorship to controlled democracy. No Muslim country has free democracy. It is also true that in these countries traditional and orthodox 'ulama, wield tremendous influence. They strongly resist any attempt at modern legislation. They represent orthodoxy and dogmatism. The noted Urdu poet Iqbal describes Islamic shari'ah as dynamic and names one of the chapter of his book *The Reconstruction of Religious Thought in Islam as* "The Principle of Movement in the Structure of Islam".

However, we hardly see this in practice in Islamic countries. What we see in these countries is stagnation and opposition to meaningful change. The women continue to suffer sexual discrimination. Any progressive legislation giving even Islamic rights to women is fiercely opposed by the conservative 'ulama. The latest example can be given from Egypt. When the Hasni Mubarak Government in Egypt introduced a legislation for giving women right to divorce (which is sanctioned by the Qur'an) the Islamic clergy opposed it on the grounds that women are hasty in decision making and any such right given to them would destabilise the family life.

Thus the shari'ah law has become totally stagnant in the hands of these conservative sections of 'ulama and its dynamic spirit has been totally lost. What is needed today is progressive changes in the shari'ah law in keeping with the spirit and fundamental values embodied in the Qur'an. The Qur'an lays so much emphasis on justice and equality but these values are not reflected in the shari'ah law in the sense in which these values are understood today. In all Muslim countries (with the exception of Pakistan and Bangla Desh) on the other hand, there is great emphasis on *hijab* for women. Wearing *hijab* has been made compulsory in almost all Muslims countries.

What is very interesting to note in this respect is that there is no uniform application of shari'ah law in these Muslim countries. There is great deal of differences in interpretation of these laws. As for example in Kuwait women are not allowed to vote as it is considered against Islamic law. The Kuwaiti women have been struggling for right to vote for a long time. But no luck so far. On the other hand, in Pakistan and Bangla Desh they are not only allowed to vote they became even prime ministers of the two countries. And in Bangla Desh women hold both positions that of prime minister ship and that of leader of opposition.

In Saudi Arabia women cannot drive cars whereas in other Islamic countries they are free to do so. The Taliban in Afghanistan when they were in power, did not allow women to come out of their houses and go for education. In some Islamic countries women are not allowed to go to market or any other public place without being accompanied by a male relative, even in the case of emergency. And all this is done in the name of Islam.

There is no possibility of change unless there is democratisation of these regimes. The colonial legacy is still going strong in these Muslim countries. The colonial powers had propped up some monarch or sheikh or even military strongman in power to serve their political hegemony. They are still propped up by these western powers. These rulers frustrate any attempt at democratisation of their regimes and seek Islamic legitimation through the conservative 'ulama. It is these 'ulama who provide support to these rulers and these rulers in turn wield tremendous political clout and resist any change in the Shari'ah law.

Thus conservative ethos rule the roost in most of the Islamic countries. Secularism and democracy are considered anti-Islam in such atmosphere. The earlier military regime in Pakistan is a good example of this politically created religious conservatism in an otherwise a modern state. Thus there is great need for thorough democratisation in all these Muslim countries.

It is only through democratisation that peoples of these countries will enjoy democratic freedoms and only through democratisation that these countries will get rid of pro-western regimes. These regimes cause so much anger among the people who are even unable to express their opinions freely and the pent up feelings lead to acts of terrorism as in the case of Usama bin Laden and his al-Qa'ida group. One can usher in modern secular polity with the concept of citizenship and respect for human rights only through democratisation of these regimes.

And when the rulers do not depend on the support of 'ulama they will be able to, with the help of popular support, bring about modern legislation making the shari'ah law really dynamic that it was in its earlier days. Shari'ah law can respond to the needs of modern times only in a democratic regime. Islam permits *ijtihad* (dynamic and creative interpretation of Islamic law) and it is conservative 'ulama who do not permit carrying out of *ijtihad*. In a democratic regime popularly elected parliament can appoint expert committees to examine the orthodox law and the much needed changes to make it respond to present times. And on recommendations of these committees the parliament can enact necessary legislation.

Not only that the Islamic teachings do not come in the way of democratisation it is in fact very much in keeping with the spirit of Islam to bring about democratisation in the Islamic world. In fact all the modern changes depend on that. Also, the institution of caliphate represented, as pointed out earlier, proto-democracy. If Mu'awiyah had not interrupted the process and introduced the institution of monarchy full-fledged democracy could have flowered in the Islamic world much earlier.

Now the time has come that what was interrupted should be re-introduced and thus democracy can fructify in Islamic world. It is feudalism and colonialism, which robbed Islam of its dynamism. Unfortunately Islamic world is still labouring under feudalism and semi-colonialism. There was time when Islam had come as a liberating religion. However, it lost its liberating thrust altogether in the last one thousand years and much more so during the colonial period. It is high time that Islam re-appropriates its liberative role.

With democratisation the political universe of Islam will undergo a through change and whereas it is stagnating today, it will acquire much needed spirit of dynamism and change.

3

The Tragedy of Karbala and Its Implications

Every year Muslims throughout the world observe with great solemnity the 10th of Muharram as a day of great tragedy. It was on this day that Imam Husain, along with his 72 relatives and friends and supporters were martyred in Kerbala (Iraq) in 61 A.H. (Islamic calendar). For last 1400 years Muslims have been mourning this tragedy. And for Shi'ah Muslims this day of Muharram known as *'Ashura* has even greater significance. Sunni Muslims too observe this day with great solemnity.

What is the significance of this day? Why Muslims observe 10th of Muharram with such solemnity and so much mourn the death of Husain, the grandson of the Prophet of Islam? What is important to note that all Muslims across sectarian lines (except perhaps the Kharijites) accept the significance of the tragedy of Karbala. It is maintained, and rightly so that it was martyrdom of Husain which gave new lease of life to Islam. Khwaja Moinuddin Chishti, the great sufi saint from India says in one of his *ruba'i* (quatrain) that 'so much so that Husain is the very foundation of *la ilah* (*hatta ki bina'i la ilah ast Husain*)

In order to understand this we have to go to the very background of this tragedy and for that we will have to understand the significance of Islamic revolution itself. The Arab society before Islam, as endlessly has been pointed out by many scholars and historians of Islam, was a tribal society without any higher civilisation or culture and without any written tradition, much less any religious scripture or literature. It is said by Tabari, and other historians that there were on 13 persons in Mecca who could read and write. There was no tradition of learning in Meccan society of the time. However, there was strong oral tradition as also of oral poetry as in most of the tribal societies. And this poetry amounted to much more than folk songs. This could be rated as higher genre of poetry.

The pre-Islamic Arabs were hardly interested in seeking knowledge. In fact they took pride in being illiterate. There was no tradition of meditative or reflective knowledge also. However, a great change was taking place in the Meccan society. It was not merely a static tribal society but a dynamic society with emerging international trade relations and Mecca being in route to borders of Roman Empire, had also emerged as an international finance centre of significant proportions.

Thus there was a sharp social contradiction emerging in the society: a primitive tribal social structure with no traditions of higher learning was moving in higher gear of international trade and finance. This contradiction, though motive force, was also causing a social malaise. Mecca, in other words, was in great need of a socio-religious revolution, a moral revolution and a revolution of knowledge and ethics.

It was this socio-religious backdrop for appearance of Islam on the Meccan scene. It was a great revolution, revolution of knowledge, of ethics and morality, of great social, economic, political and religious significance. W. C. Smith, a great Islamist from Canada says that Islam was the greatest and most systematic effort to usher in social justice before Marxism.

Islam, it is interesting to note, laid great emphasis on acquisition of knowledge, on equality of all human beings and on social justice. Knowledge, *'ilm*, was not only repeatedly emphasised but was equated with light and ignorance – jahl – with darkness and posed the question 'Can darkness be equated with light'? One who is ignorant is like blind and one who acquires knowledge like one who can see. Thus Qur'an brought the revolutionary message of knowledge – *'ilm*. In twenty-first century it might not appear of such gigantic proportion but in 6th Century Mecca, such fundamental emphasis on knowledge was no mean revolution.

Also, in that world of sixth century which was socially deeply hierarchical such emphasis on equality of all human beings and equality of dignity for all children of Adam – something which we have not achieved even in twenty first century – was, to say the least, was of utmost significance. Needless to say, the world then could hardly appreciate significance of the concept of equality of all human beings white or black, rich or poor, Arab or non-Arab, Muslim or non-Muslim.

Also, today in the post-modern world we have begun to understand the importance of plurality of cultures and religions. The Qur'an declared then, more than fourteen hundred years ago, the importance of plurality and taught respect for all the prophets and religious guides, *hadis*. In fact the Qur'an says that if Allah desired he could have created one *ummah*, one religious community but he created plurality in order to test us whether we can live in peace with each other. (5:48) The Qur'an, while doing away with all differences of caste, creed and colour emphasised the message of *istibaq al-khayrat* i.e. vie one with the other in virtuous deeds rather than quarrel about superiority of one's own faith.

The Qur'an also laid emphasis on distribution of wealth equitably. It warned against wealth circulating only among the rich and being accumulated by the few depriving others of their basic livelihood. The importance of this message was also realised only in twentieth century. No one in those days had thought of equitable distribution of wealth. Today it is duty of every state to ensure welfare of weaker sections of society. In the world then weaker sections counted for nothing. At the most they were object of charity and could not think of rights.

Islam did not make weaker sections only object of charity but gave them rights. The concept of zakat is not the concept of charity. It is tax on the wealthy, a share of weaker sections in the wealth of rich, a tax even to pay debt of indebted and to free the slaves in addition to take care of widows, orphans and the poor (9:60). It denounced concentration of wealth (9:34).

Not only this: it took another revolutionary step. It empowered women and gave them equal rights (2:228) and 33:35). It even gave women right to earn and own properties besides right in inheritance as daughter, as wife and as mother. This was very revolutionary step which Muslims of that time also could not appreciate, much less practice it honestly. The prophet of Islam (PBUH) made acquisition of knowledge for women as obligatory as for men. Groups of women used to go to the Prophet to acquire knowledge, ask him questions and many female companions of the Prophet became source of narrating Prophet's tradition and important source of knowledge for scholars of subsequent generations.

Women played very important role in Islamic history until they were confined again in the four walls of their houses by the society ironically in the name of Islam. In Karbala too, as we will see, Susain's sister Syeda Zainab, played very important role. The concept of equality of sexes was most revolutionary one and ahead of time by centuries and hence could not be practised by Muslims of that time and even today Muslims, mostly living in feudal societies, are not able to realise its significance.

Thus Islam came to Arabs and non-Arabs as a liberative religion, a transformative movement and hence the rich unbelievers of Mecca opposed it as they had powerful vested interest in maintaining the status quo.

They believed in continuing uninterrupted accumulation of wealth, enjoying all pleasures of life without realising the significance of spiritual side of life. In other words it was crass materialism for limited few and unending suffering for the people at the bottom of economic and social hierarchy. The powerful rich of Mecca opposed Muhammad (PBUH), not so much because of his doctrine of unity of God *(tawhid)* as for revolutionary implications of his teachings on their wealth and prestige. Islam gave the poorest and slaves equal rights, and demanded judicious distribution of wealth, something the rich of Mecca would never accept.

But all those who were suffering and all those who realised the importance of spiritual side of life and significance of social justice rallied round the Prophet and suffered all persecution and indignities in order to make Islam successful. Many of them happily courted martyrdom in various battles fought by the Prophet so that Islamic revolution succeeds. It is interesting to note that the word for martyrdom in Qur'anic terminology is *shahadah* which means witness.

Thus martyr *shahid* is one who witnesses, at the cost of his/her life, the end result of his/her martyrdom. The moment of *shahadah* is the moment of witnessing, witnessing what is one dying for. Thus they die in order to live permanently in the form of social revolution they help usher in. It is in this sense that Qur'an says, "And think not of those who are killed in Allah's way as dead. Nay, they are alive being provided sustenance from their Lord." (3:168) Thus it is in this sense that a martyr lives permanently by giving his life so that others can live. They make humanity permanent, sustenance of human life permanent by giving their own life. It is living through others. It is permanently witnessing fruits of ones own sacrifice.

If martyrdom of any believer is so significant the martyrdom of Husain, the grand son of the Prophet himself, is even more significant. We will throw light on the significance of Husain's martyrdom (*shahadah*) below as to why it has such special significance in the history of Islam that he is referred to as *shahid-e-a'azam* i.e. the greatest martyr.

The period after the demise of the Holy Prophet was not an easy period. The period saw many controversies, of succession to the Prophet, share in power by different tribes, clans and regional groups and about method of appointments of caliphs. The period of 30 years – the period for which the Caliphate lasted was full of turmoil, violence and civil war. More than hundred thousand people are reported to have been killed during this period. This period also was the period of major conquests. It was during this period that major parts of Roman and Sassanid empires came under Muslims.

These conquests not only brought great deal of wealth but also created new power equations and political conflicts. The Islamic shura' (consultation) system also came under great stress. Ali, in order of elected caliphs was the last caliph. His standards of justice and his enforcement of Islamic ideals was very rigorous and now the new class of governors and power brokers which was coming into existence, resented these rigorous enforcement of standards of honesty and integrity and began to create other power centres. Ali's letter to one of his governors Malik Ushter, bears witness to the rigorous standards Ali wanted to follow in his administration. This created many enemies for Ali.

Thus the power centre began to shift to those who were hardly committed to Islamic ideals and revolutionary goals of Islam. They were interested more in either capturing power or enhancing their share in it. Ali was martyred by Kharijites (seceders) as a result of conspiracy while he was praying in the mosque of Kufa early in the morning. After Ali's martyrdom his elder son Imam Hasan was elected but the people of Kufa were enticed by the new ruling class in Damascus, Syria and was forced to abdicate in favour of Mu'awiyah. Thus now a new centre of power came into existence away from Islamic centre of power.

This shift was very fundamental and had far reaching consequences in Islamic world and in the history of Islam. It was, in fact a paradigm shift and Maulana Maududi, a theologian and political theorist of Islam from Pakistan, termed it a shift from *Khilafat to Mulukiyyat* (i.e. from caliphate to monarchy) (See his book *Khilafat se Mulukiyyat*). This shift created new political tensions in Islamic world. As far as Caliphate was concerned, it was far more democratic and Muslims of different origins had say in it and Caliph used to consult prominent Muslims before any policy decision.

However, due to this paradigmatic shift in politics, power was concentrated in the hands of one person. There was no consultation for major policy decision. The Islamic caliphs had not allowed any change in their style of living and had tried to stick to the simplicity advocated by Islam and practised rigorously by the Prophet (PBUH). The caliphs used to consult companions of the Prophet before taking all major policy decisions or before laying down Islamic law. Successor was not appointed from caliph's own family or matter left to the Muslims.

Now all this changed forever. Damascus was far away from centre of Islam and much closer to Roman Empire. And this was not symbolic but substantive. The new power centre was much closer to Roman imperial ways than to Islamic ideals. Mu'awiyah now created atmosphere of Roman court, put on expensive silken robes considered prohibited for men in Islam and constructed a palace to live in. Now imperial orders were issued and the rich and powerful were favoured and companions of the Prophet had no role in shaping the policies of the state. This was a big difference from the Caliphate period.

The change was not limited to this. The question of succession also underwent a radical change. When Imam Hasan abdicated in favour of Mu'awiyah one of the conditions of the agreement signed was that Mu'awiyah will not appoint his successor and leave the question of successor to the Muslims. However, Mu'awiyah did not fulfil this condition and appointed his son Yazid as his successor. Thus shift to monarchical model of rule was complete.

After the death of Mu'awiyah Yazid took over reigns of power. This shocked all the important companions of the Prophet. Even a person like Abdullah bin 'Umar, son of Hazrat Umar, the 2nd Caliph who was not much interested in political matters, refused to recognise Yazid as a legitimate successor of Islamic Caliphate. Imam Husain of course refused to accept Yazid as legitimate successor for two reasons: Firstly, he became successor in violation of the agreement between Imam Hasan and Mu'awiyah as the agreement stipulated that the matter of succession would be left to the Muslims to decide. And, secondly, Yazid's personal conduct was totally unacceptable to any pious Muslim, let alone to Imam Husain.

Yazid was neither a companion of the Prophet nor he had cared to imbibe any of the ideals of the Islamic revolution. He was brought up as a prince rather than an Islamic revolutionary or activist. He adopted all the ways of pre-Islamic Arabian society, drinking, enjoying all the material pleasures without any ethical or moral considerations. Also, many historian of Islam tell us that the Umayyads (Banu Umayyah) had never accepted Islamic principles and Islamic morality. Arab paganism ran through their blood (with some exceptions, of course). Yazid even ridiculed teachings of Islam.

Naturally Imam Husain strongly disapproved of all this. He was brought up not only in Islamic atmosphere but was brought up by Fatima and Ali. Fatima was the dearest daughter of the Prophet who had spent every moment of her life with the prophet from her childhood until the death of her father. The Prophet himself had shown highest respect for her and for her integrity.

Ali was also under the patronage of the Prophet (PBUH) from his childhood and he had made maximum sacrifices for the sake of Islamic revolution. He was not only the flag bearer of Islamic revolutionary army but one who had deeply imbibed Islamic values. He, after the Prophet, was most knowledgeable about Islam. The Prophet used to say that "I am city of knowledge and Ali is its door." (*Ana madinah al-'ilm wa 'Aliyun babuha*). Thus Imam Husain had imbibed all this and was highly respected by all Muslims. There was no comparison, absolutely not, between Yazid and Imam Husain.

Mu'awiyah, disregarding all this appointed Yazid as his successor which negated all that Islamic revolution stood for. In fact appointment of Yazid, with his un-Islamic conduct, was, what could be called as counter-revolution. Husain, who had lived Islam every moment of his life and had been brought up by parents like Fatima and Ali, could not accept appointment of Yazid as Caliph of Muslims. It meant a counter-revolutionary heading a revolutionary regime. This was just not possible. There was absolutely no place for monarchy in Islam, no place for negation of various ideals of Islam.

Yazid wanted Husain to give *bay'ah* (pledge of loyalty) to him as Husain was person of extra ordinary importance in the Islamic world. His recognition of Yazid would have meant silencing all the critics and would have legitimised his appointment. Yazid thus gave top priority to extracting *bay'ah* from Imam Husain and Imam Husain was determined not to give *bay'ah* to Yazid. Accepting Yzid as legitimate ruler of Muslims would mean endorsing all that Islam stood for.

Islam stood for dignity of all human beings irrespective of caste, creed and colour or social status. Yazid, on the other hand, stood for superiority of one clan over the other, he stood for morality of period of *jahiliyah* (ignorance) when Arabs lived in an era of darkness without higher morality, without any written and codified law. Women had no rights and status and so in Yazid's court also women were an object of pleasure and enjoyment rather than human beings. Brotherhood and equality were replaced by social distinctions and feudal hierarchy. Non-Arabs and non-Umayyads were treated as lesser beings. Piety and fear of Allah (*taqwa*) was at a discount.

Islam, in other words, became merely a powerful political establishment and was losing its revolutionary fervour. Husain, the only true inheritor of Islamic values of equality, justice and brotherhood, refused to legitimise Yazid's regime by pledging political support to him. This incensed Yzid and he ordered his governor in Madina Walid either to take *bay'ah* from him or to behead him. Husain, coming to know of this plot left Madina and went to Mecca. He left Mecca also realising that Yazid was after his blood in the holy city of Mecca also.

Husain then came to Karbala, a city on the bank of river Furat and encamped there as he was prevented from going to Kufa. Imam Husain was invited by people of Kufah to lead them against Yazid but people of Kufa were also silenced by unleashing terror on them through 'Ubaydullah bin Ziyad. Husain's emissary Muslim bin Aquil who was sent to Kufa by Husain to gauge the mood of the people of Kufa was also killed by Ibn Ziyad..

Husain, it is important to note, did not fight Yazid to get political power as alleged by some. He fought Yazid and sacrificed his life and those of his friends and relatives to restore values of Islamic revolution. He could not see Islamic values being trampled underfoot by Yazid and his supporters and era of darkness being restored. The martyrdom of Husain undoubtedly gave a new lease of life to Islam and Islamic values. It is in this sense that Moinuddin Chishti, the Sufi saint of Ajmer, said in his quatrain that Husain is the very basis of *la ilah* which is the founding principle of Islam.

4

Polygamy in Islam - Concept and Practice

Polygamy has been a very controversial issue in Islam. The Orthodox 'Ulama maintain that it is part of Islamic Shari'ah and hence men can take up to four wives, if they want to, without any reasonable cause even. The modernists and champions of women's rights, on the other hand argue that the polygamy is only permissible in certain conditions with the strict provison for equal justice with all the wives. According to the modernists, man just cannot take more than one wife simply because he likes some other woman or gets enamoured of her beauty. They also argue that the Qur'anic norm is monogamy but polygamy is permissible in certain exceptionable circumstances with strictly enforceable condition for justice.

The orthodox 'Ulama justify polygamy on the grounds which have not been stated in the Qur'an. They argue that men's sexual needs are greater than those of women; secondly they argue that women go through periods or give birth to children and it is not possible to have sexual intercourse with them during these periods and hence man needs more than one wife. They also argue that if a woman is terminally ill it is better to marry another woman rather than divorce her and make her psychological wreck. Also, if she is barren and cannot give birth to another child, it is better to take second wife without divorcing her and add to her woes. She already suffers from lack of children.

Of course, as pointed out above, these arguments are not there in Qur'an or sunnah of the Prophet (PBUH). These arguments have been invented by some 'Ulama to justify polygamy. Apart from these arguments, they also argue that there are more women than men and hence polygamy ensures dignified life for women rather than life of infamy and breaching the limits set by Allah.

The modernists and those championing women's rights, on the other hand, rebut all these arguments. They argue that it is not at all biologically and scientifically proven that women's sexual needs are any less than that of man. It is her social conditioning, which makes her sexually less active. Given proper environment a woman will also be equally sexually active.

The champions of women's rights also maintain than man is not created a mere sexual animal that he cannot restrain his sexual activity during menstrual period of his wife or when she gives birth to a child. Thousands of men do so. All men are not prone to polygamous marriages. Most of them, on the contrary, are monogamous. They can restrain themselves from sexual activity even when their wives are ill for long time and cannot cohabit with them.

Even when they are terminally ill, they can go without sexual activity and this sacrifice is worth making for a life time partnership. One cannot sacrifice this companionship just because she is terminally ill or is not capable of cohabitation. Those upholding women's rights argue that marriage is not all about sexual gratification only. The institution of marriage is much more than that. It is for life long partnership between the two, besides creating children and ensuring continuity of human life on earth. This can be ensured with minimum sexual activity. In fact polygamy is a medieval institution which was invented by man to fulfil his sexual lust and to keep women under his authority.

As for barrenness there seems to be some weight in taking another wife to procreate, as procreation is one of the objectives of marriage. But, in our society often blame is foisted on woman for failing to give birth to child. Man can also be barren and man often is. Unless it is medically tested one should not rush to the conclusion that woman is barren and hence man should take another wife to have children. Only and only when it is proved that a wife has medical problem in giving birth to a child or is completely barren she could be responsible for lack of child.

Perhaps then there could be some justification for taking second wife. But thanks to modern scientific advances there are other possibilities: test tube babies. May be there is no *ijma'* so far about Islamic validity of test tube baby. We will have to leave it to the conscience of the persons concerned whether they would like to have test tube bay or not. Similarly adoption is also not permissible in Shari'ah law. Here is some bind for a conscientious Muslim. One can say in such case (i.e. when it is medically certified that wife, and not husband, is barren) husband could be permitted to take second wife. The other alternative is to remain childless. Some might prefer that way. Only when a wife is proved to be medically unfit for conceiving the husband perhaps could seek her permission (without using coercion in any form) to take second wife and provided, he is capable of doing equal justice to both of them, as required by the Qur'an

Another argument for polygamy is that rather than let women lead sinful life it is better that one takes them as co-wives. Firstly there are very few societies wherein there are many more women than men. Even if there are more women, it is marginally so. Only during world wars when millions of people were killed there were substantially more women, than men. But it was a temporary and not lasting period. Perhaps there could have been some justification for polygamy during that period. But it is not correct to say that prostitution is because of more women in society than men. There is prostitution even when there is excess of men over women.

In India, for example, there is excess of men over women there being 1000 men for every 930 women and yet there is widespread prostitution. There are other reasons for prostitution than excess of women over men in a society. Prostitution has been in the world throughout history. In fact it is known as one of the oldest institutions in the world. Uneven distribution of wealth, migration of men to other countries or to urban areas in search of livelihood and extreme poverty in women's families, lax morals and organised crime are some of the factors responsible for prostitution. Mere polygamy, as some knively believe, cannot eradicate prostitution from the society. Even stringent law drives it underground rather than abolish it.

Thus all these arguments in favour of polygamy are hardly valid. These arguments have been invented for justifying polygamy; they hardly explain its existence. There are reasons other than the ones advanced above for persistence of this institution for so long. One must understand those causes and try, as much as possible, to control and regulate the institution of polygamy

THE QUR'AN AND POLYGAMY

Then one can justifiably ask why Qur'an permits it? Or what view the Qur'an takes of polygamy? One must take up the verses on polygamy in the Qur'an and explain them not merely as isolated verses but in the total spirit of the Qur'an. No verse of the Qur'an can be explained as an isolated verse. It is the context (in the light of *asbab al-nuzul* i.e. occasions of revelation) and norms of the Qur'an which have to be taken into account in order to understand the real intention of the Qur'anic verses. Also, it is not enough to refer to one verse on the subject but all concerned verses should be taken into account.

Often one verse is quoted to prove one's point of view. It is not proper.

There are two verses in the Qur'an as far as multiplicity of wives is concerned i.e. 4:3 and 4:129. However, to take an overall view of Qur'anic spirit we will have to take more verses into account besides these two. Those other verses are equally important to determine the Qur'an approach to the controversial issue of polygamy.

First let us take the two verses which make direct pronouncement on polygamy i.e. 4:3 and 4:129. The first verse i.e. 4:3 appears to permit taking up to four wives while 4:129 seems to caution against hazards of multiplicity of wives. Needless to say both the verses must be read together in order to determine Allah's intention. While the first verse takes given context into account and seems to permit multiplicity of wives, the second one takes long term view and also the likely consequences of taking second wife and this verse tends to be more normative than the other.

The first verse says: "And if you have reason to fear that you might not act equitably towards orphans, then marry from among women such as are lawful to you – two or three, or four: but if you have reason to fear that you might not be able to treat them with equal fairness, then (only) one – or those whom you rightfully possess." (4:3). This verse could be interpreted differently. It is not very clear whether it means two or three or four at a time or during ones lifetime. If up to four was meant it could have said "upto four". But the Qur'an rather chooses more complex way of putting it.

Even if what is meant is two or three or four at a time, the Qur'an does not permit it according to the whims of a man. It lays down strict condition for treating all wives with equal fairness and if you have reason to fear that they cannot be treated with equal fairness then marry only one. Thus if one reads even this verse alone literally, it would be obvious that more emphasis is on equal and fair treatment rather than having more than one wife. And this should not be determined by husband alone whether he can treat his wives with equal fairness or not.

Here in this verse the words "if you have reason to fear that you might not be able to treat them with equal fairness" are addressed to whole Muslim society and hence society as represented by its judicial institutions (*'adalah*) will determine whether the person has capability to treat his second or third or fourth wife with equal fairness or not and also whether there is any need for it. Thus it is obvious that taking of more than one wife should be socially regulated and should not be an individual decision. Unfortunately often decision is made individually as if it is personal privilege and no social intervention can be tolerated. The Qur'anic spirit, on the other hand, does require social intervention as equitable and fair treatment of wives is very essential.

There is also debate whether equitable and fair treatment implies only equal maintenance and equal facilities to all the wives or it also includes equal love. Some commentators, especially of the *Mu'tazilah* persuasion insist that equal love is also a necessary condition for all wives. And they argue that since equal love is humanly impossible (a man will always tend to love one of his wives more than the other wife or wives) polygamy is as good as banned by the Qur'an. Justice in treating all the wives equally is so important that the verse ends with the words *alla ta'ulu* (this is more proper that you may not do injustice.

Thus in verse 4:3 fear of injustice is stressed twice. Thus this moral dimension of polygamy cannot be taken lightly. Therefore, either it should be banned or should be strictly regulated and taking of second wife should not be left entirely to an individual. Social intervention is highly needed.

Also, the verse 4:3 should be read in conjunction with

another verse on polygamy i.e. 4:129. This verse states, among other things, "Ye are never able to be fair and just as between women even if it is your ardent desire. But turn not away (from a woman) altogether so as to leave her (as it were) hanging (in the air). If ye come to a friendly understanding, and practice self-restraint, Allah is oft-forgiving and Merciful."

This verse is so clear on the question of justice and fair treatment with all wives that polygamy is almost impossible to practise. The words that you cannot do justice "even if it is your ardent desire" are so clear that there is no need for any further discussion. It is humanly impossible to treat all wives equitably (especially in matters of love) and one should not leave one woman hanging in the air and incline totally towards the other.

Here it is important to point out the Qur'anic methodology in social matters like slavery, polygamy and similar other matters. At the first stage the Qur'an permits an existing practice with proviso for reforms and improvement so as to lessen its negative impact but subsequently it points out in no uncertain language that it is best be abolished. A good example in this respect is of slavery. The Qur'an first requires Muslims to treat slaves in a humane way and also encourages their manumission as compensation for not able to keep obligatory fast or for expiation of sins etc. Bu subsequently it says that "All children of Adam have been honoured equally (*laqad karramna bani Adam*) (17:70). Thus all children of Adam deserve equal dignity and some cannot be slaves and others master. This makes institution of slavery totally redundant. But the Qur'an first accepts institution of slavery with necessary reforms and subsequently makes it clear that it is against human dignity.

Similarly approach has been adopted for the institution of polygamy. First it is permitted with strict proviso for fair and equal treatment and cautioning against injustice against any of the wives. It is also important to note that this verse (i.e.4:3) has been revealed along with the verse pertaining to the problems of widows and orphans (*yatam*). This verse on polygamy begins with the words "If you fear that you shall not be able to deal justly with the orphans, marry women of your choice, two or three or four...."

Thus polygamy was permitted by the Qur'an to do away injustice to orphans and widows (actually the Arabic word *yatama* includes widows also). The Arabs, as per Zamakhshari of Al-Kasshshaf (Vol.I, Beirut, 1977, pp-496), would marry orphans and widows with beauty and wealth (far in excess of four women) and then try to usurp their wealth and do injustice to them in treatment. The Qur'an, in order to save these orphans from such injustices (and hence it begins with the words (If you fear that you shall not be able to deal justly with orphans....) those Arabs were permitted to marry up to four (thus reducing the number of wives one could take drastically) to avoid injustice to the orphans.

Thus polygamy (without any restriction as to the number of wives) already existed in the society and also injustices to the orphans. Thus with this verse (4:3) the Qur'an, which considers justice as most fundamental moral category, tried to stop abuse of orphan girls' properties (and this was vitally necessary) on one hand, and injustices to the women who were taken as wives without restriction to any number, and not treated fairly and equitably. This verse thus accomplished two objectives in one stroke – justice to orphans and justice to helpless wives by restricting their numbers to four and requiring oral responsibility of equal and fair treatment.

But, the Qur'an was aware that this is not the ideal solution as far as women were concerned. Thus in the second verse on polygamy (4:129) it was made clear that it is not possible to do equal justice to all wives even if one ardently desired and so the men were cautioned not to leave the first wife hanging in the air (*fatazaruha kal mu'allaqatin*). Thus, if both the verses are read together

– and one must – monogamy would be the norm and polygamy a merely permitted measure to meet the given situation.

Thus the real intention of the Qur'an, is to ultimately abolish polygamy albeit gradually. It is also to be noted that marrying orphans to misappropriate their properties was peculiarly an Arab phenomenon, not a universal one. And polygamy was permitted by the Qur'an only in that context. It has also been pointed out by some commentators that the verse 4:3 was revealed after the battle of Uhud when more than 10% of Muslim men population was killed and there were many orphans and widows in the society and they had to be taken care of. Perpetuation of polygamy forever was far from the Qur'anic intention.

Thus the noted translator of the Qur'an Abdullah Yusuf Ali also says in the footnote to the above verse (4:3), "The unrestricted number of wives of the 'Times of ignorance' was now strictly limited to a maximum of four, provided you could treat them with perfect equality, in material things as well as in affection and immaterial things. As this condition is most difficult to fulfil, I understand recommendation to be towards monogamy." (The Holy Qur'an, Abdullah Yusuf Ali, Vol. I, Hyderabad, India, n.d.pp-131)

More arguments can be advanced from other verses of the Qur'an if one takes the Qur'anic verses in totality as one must. The Qur'an uses the word *zawj* for husband and wife and *zawj* implies couple. So basically there should be one husband and wife – a couple – and not one husband and several wives. Adam, the first Prophet had one wife Hawwa'. The Qur'an also describes husband and wife as each other's garment (2:187). Also the Qur'an says, "And the believers, men and women, are friends one of another. They enjoin good and forbid evil and keep up prayer and pay the poor-rate and obey Allah and His Messenger." (9:71)

Whole spirit of this verse is of equality and friendship between men and women. Thus this noble spirit of the Qur'an in respect of man and woman does not admit of four women being lorded over by one man. Also the verse 33:35 which makes men and women equal in every respect hardly can admit the institution of polygamy. Also, 2:228 establishes equality between men and women and can hardly admit of the polygamous marriages. Thus it will be seen that all these verses militate against polygamy. Polygamy can at best be an exception rather than a rule.

As for the Holy Prophet's *sunnah* is also concerned he preferred monogamy over polygamy. He remained highly faithful to his first wife Khadija as long as she lived though she was much senior (by fifteen years) to him. He never took second wife in her lifetime. He was a very loyal and devoted husband. He married A'ishah only after the death of his first wife Khadijah. And A'ishah was the only virgin wife he took. All other wives were either divorcees or widows and were more in the nature of political and tribal alliances than marriages for fulfilling sexual needs. Had he so desired he could have taken young women as his wives. But he never did after A'ishah.

He also strongly disapproved of Hazrat Ali, husband of his daughter Fatima, taking second wife during her lifetime. He was very angry when he learnt that Ali wanted to take second wife when Fatima was around. All this goes to show that the Prophet (PBUH) also stressed monogamy and one must follow his *sunnah* in this respect also.

Today's Qur'anic approach to justice and equality is much more relevant than before. Women's rights are being greatly stressed and if their rights to equality are to be respected, and one must, polygamy should be permitted only in highly exceptional circumstances. Actually monogamy should be the rule. The Qur'an foresaw this 1400 years ago and stressed concept of justice in sexual relations also and never accepted woman to be subordinated to man. The Qur'an, in fact gave dignity to woman by accepting her legal entity. However, through the ages she lost out to man in sexual politics. There is great need to restore dignity to her which is fundamental requirement of the Qur'an. She is equal partner to man in every respect.

5
Da'wah or Dialogue ?

Most societies now tend to be highly diverse in many ways –religiously, culturally, racially and linguistically. Even tribal societies tend to be quite diverse with different tribes living together in one geographical area. Today with faster means of migration and communication diversity tends to be almost bewildering. While it is enriching to live with diversity it is quite challenging as well.

In medieval ages religious missions played an important role. The religious authorities worked with missionary spirit (the spirit of *Da'wah*) and spread religions to other nations and other peoples. It was considered as a religious duty to spread ones religion. While Christians called it mission Muslims referred to it as *da'wah. Da'wah* literally means invitation, invitation to join the faith. Both Christianity and Islam spread throughout the world though missionary or *da'wah activities.* Today one finds in these two world religions peoples of different nationalities, races, languages and tribes. Thus in both these religions there is great deal of internal diversity.

Missionary and *da'wah* activities still continue in certain parts of the world, especially Africa and Asia and the two religions compete with each other giving rise to tensions. Today a large number of Muslims of diverse origin have migrated to western countries and are living as religious and racial minorities with the Christian majorities. There is hardly any Western country of Europe or North America where Muslims are not found. Most of them are from Afro-Asian countries.

Both the missionary and *da'wah* activities and Muslims living as religious minorities in Western countries cause religious tensions. In the interest of stability and peace one has to minimise tensions and create inter-religious harmony. These conditions can be created through mutual dialogue. Today dialogue rather than *da'wah* or missionary activities is needed. One has to promote the spirit of dialogue.

As far as Islam is concerned there is no obligation on Muslims to spread one's religion at the cost of peace and mutual good will. Peace is more fundamental to Islam than aggressive *da'wah. Da'wah* is desirable only if it does not lead to loss of peace and harmony. Firstly, the Qur'an, accepts validity of religion preached by all Allah's messengers and a Muslim is required not to discriminate between one and another prophets of Allah. Allah has sent thousands of prophets some of whom have been named in the Qur'an and many have not been even named. The list of the prophets in the Qu'an is illustrative and not exhaustive. The Qur'an not only accepts all Biblical prophets but also adds others like ones from nations of Thamud and 'Aad and others. The Qur'an makes it obligatory on all Muslims to accept all these prophets and not to belie any one from amongst them. Anyone who discriminates, one from the other is true kafir (4-150-51).

Thus to recognise and respect other religions based on revelations from Allah whether mentioned or not mentioned in the Qur'an is part of Islamic faith. It is truly in keeping with the spirit of dialogue. The Islamic thinkers who have imbibed the spirit of dialogue have added prophets, not mentioned in the Qur'an to list of prophets sent by Allah. Some Sufi saints like Mazhar Jan-i-Janan have accepted some Hindu highly revered religious figures like Ram and Krishna as prophets.

The Qur'an does not encourage undesirable methods for *da'wah*, much less aggressive methods or defiling others religious beliefs. The Qur'nic requirement for *da'wah* is wisdom and goodly exhortation. (16:125). Anyone who uses aggressive methods or abusive language deviates from the Qur'anic guidance and exhortations. The Qur'an specifically prohibits offensive or abusive language. (6:109). Instead it encourages what it calls *istibaq al-khyrat* (excelling each other in good deeds). It also makes it clear that diversity or plurality of laws and faith is Allah's own desire (5:48) Thus diversity is a divine destiny and should be respected.

The Qur'anic concept of *da'wah* is more dialogical than an attempt to impose religion of Islam on others. It is a great myth that Islam advocates its spread through sword; nothing can be further from truth and injurious to the spirit of Islam. Even if some conquerors have done it, it was their personal responsibility and not that of Islam.

Islam, in its earliest period had to deal with two major religions, Judaism and Christianity. It not only showed respect for the two and tried to accommodate them but also tried to have dialogue with them on the basis of what was common between them. It is interesting to take note of the following verse (5:82): "Thou wilt certainly find the most violent of people in enmity against the believers to be the Jews and the idolaters; and thou wilt find the nearest in friendship to the believers to be those who say, We are Christians. That is because there are priests and monks among them and because they are not proud."

Here the verse is speaking of people, not faiths. The Qur'an refers to the Jews as people who are violent towards Muslims and Christians as friends. The conflict between Muslims and Jews was not on grounds of their faith. The Qur'an showed highest respect both for Abraham and Moses. The conflict between Muslims and Jews was of supremacy of power and domination. The Jews were dominating Madina before the Prophet of Islam migrated to Madina along with his followers. Though the Jews initially entered into a pact with the Holy Prophet called **Mithaq-i-Madina** (the covenant of Madina) they were not happy with it and inwardly resented it. They clearly saw that the Muslims were an emergent community who will take over reigns of Madina. They, therefore, betrayed the covenant at the first available opportunity and thus violent conflict developed between the followers of two faiths.

There was no such problem with the Christians. Christians had no presence in Madina and there was no conflict of interest between them and Chrsitians in Madina. The Prophet, however, came in contact with the Christian priests and monks who had no ambition for power or domination and hence the Qur'an says "they are not proud". Hence the Christians are "nearest in friendship.

Thus often it is not conflict of faith, which creates problems but conflict of power or domination. The Qur'an was very clear on this count. It does not falsify any faith, Jewish, Christian or any other. The Prophet even extended a hand of friendship towards the followers of the other faiths and looked upon them with respect. However, it is vested interests, which clashed.

And even when it was necessary to argue with the people of the Book i.e. Christians and Jews the Qur'an did not want Muslims to be aggressive at all. Thus for *mujadilah* (mutual arguments) Qur'an lays down clear guide lines. It says , "And argue not with the people of the Book *except by what is best*, save such of them as act unjustly. But say: We believe in that which has been revealed to you, and our God and your God is one, and to Him we submit." (29:46) (emphasis supplied)

Thus Qur'an requires Muslims to argue with the people of the Book in best possible manner. If this is not dialogical spirit what it is? Note that people of the Book include both Christians and Jews It is these two religions, which were present in the immediate environs of the

Qur'an and hence these two religions are repeatedly mentioned in the Qur'an. In fact these are more of principles and guide –lines, which can be applied to other religions as well, including Hinduism in India.

Maulana Muhammad Ali, in his commentary on this verse, tries to explain its spirit. He says, It should be noted that this passage deals only with the mode of controversy to be adopted in inviting those who already had scriptures in their hands – which the Arabs had not – to the truth of Islam and the revelation of the Qur'an. The Qur'an makes its own meaning clear when it explains that it is the broad principles of religion that should demand paramount consideration. The fundamental principle of religion is that God exists and that He reveals Himself to man, and it is common to all revealed religions." He also adds that a Muslim's conception of Divine revelation is wider than that of follower of any other religion, recognising, as it does, that Divine revelation is granted in all ages to all nations. A Muslim, therefore, admits the truth of all prophets and revelations...(*The Holy Qur'an*, Lahore, 1973, pp-769)

Thus a Muslim should not shun dialogue with followers of other religions recognising the basic truth in them. It is not proper for him to denounce other religions as false. It is not disputation but dialogue with others that is in true spirit of Islam. The Qur'anic verse 3:63 represents true spirit of Islam in this respect: "O People of the Book, come to an equitable word between us and you that we shall serve none but Allah and that we shall not associate aught with Him, and that some of us shall not take others for lords besides Allah. But if they turn away, then say: bear witness, we are Muslims." (3:63)

Thus in this verse also the stress is on what is common and not what is contentious. And this is important for carrying on dialogical process. I think when Islam came into being in Arabia in 7th Century this tradition of respecting other religions and stressing what is common in other religions did not exist anywhere. It is Qur'an which accepted truth of other religions and sought their co-operation.

The Muslims, wherever in the world, living in majority or minority, should seek to revive this Qur'anic spirit of dialogue. In medieval ages the whole emphasis was on *da'wah* or conversion in Islam and on missionary activities among the Christians. Now in our times the emphasis is on dialogue i.e. understanding each other and interaction with each other. Globalisation makes it all the more necessary. Globalisation leads to much increased shifting of population and migration. Thus diversity increases and people of different religions and cultures live together. If there is no dialogue among themselves or they emphasise *da'wah* in place of dialogue it would lead to tension, strife and conflict. And social tensions would disturb social stability.

It is, therefore, necessary to promote the spirit of dialogue among people of different faiths. It is, therefore, necessary to throw some light on the methodology of conducting inter-faith dialogue.

The first requirement of the spirit of dialogue is to know the 'other' in faith. No dialogue can ever be successful if this spirit does not prevail. There should not be any attempt to influence, much less convert the other. It is, therefore, very necessary that we cultivate the habit of listening, not of arguing. A successful dialogue can be conducted only if we listen to each other with rapt attention so that we can understand each other. Argumentation should not be there or should be kept at minimum. We can understand the other only if we patiently listen to the other. Listening is the sterling quality in the process of dialogue.

It is also important to develop trust in each other and the process of dialogue should lead to building up trust in each other. If trust is lacking no dialogue can ever succeed. Mutual trust is very basic to any inter-religious dialogue.

It is also necessary for building proper spirit of dialogue to talk to the other to explain and listen to learn and to counter as it often happens.

In the process of dialogue one should know the self in order to know the other. Without knowing the self fully it is not possible to know the other properly. It has been often observed that without knowing ourselves we try to know the other and this will only result in confusion rather than clarification. The first question should be who am I before we ask who the other is?

Also, as quoted from the Qur'anic verse above we should develop the spirit of sharing in common what can be shared in common. The emphasis should be on what is common rather than what is different. The conflict develops when we stress what is different rather than what is common. Not that it is not necessary to know what is different; it is. But first we should build trust in each other by emphasising what is common before we go to differences amongst us. Differences could come last.

It is also important to have dialogue with the inner other before we have dialogue with the external other. Each religious faith is divided in number of sects and schools of thought. Thus dialogue with inner other is as necessary as with the external other. The differences between, for example, Shi'ahs and Sunnis among Muslims and Catholics and Protestants lead to creation of inner other. Some times dialogue with the inner other becomes more necessary than the external other. Here too we should be guided by the principle of what we share in common and what could lead to building up the spirit of trust with the inner other.

We live in democracies today and sometime political differences may override or coincide with religious differences. In a democratic and secular polity often religious differences may become secondary and political unity may override religious differences. Thus the religious other may not necessarily be the political other and political other may not necessarily be the religious other. One may have much in common politically with the religious other. If we share political ideology with the religious other it is likely to reduce religious tensions. One should encourage such processes. Religious polarisation is likely to be more problematic for peace and stability than political polarisation. In a democratic set up followers of different religions may come together politically, resulting in greater religious harmony.

Also, linguistic and cultural otherness might erode 'we' feeling in a religious group. The linguistic and cultural differences can also become as explosive as religious differences. Thus a linguistic other may not be able to have strong 'we' feeling with ones own religious group. It is thus necessary to make dialogues linguistically and culturally inclusive too.

It is also necessary to understand that the identity of 'we' and 'they' also keeps on changing with the context. Identities also cannot be static or may be even multiple. Even religious identities change or evolve. One may have orthodox identity today and liberal one tomorrow or vice versa. Or conversion also leads to change of identity. Even when we emphasise the importance of dialogue conversion cannot be completely ruled out. Conversion is not always the result of da`wah, it can result from inner motivation and conversion through inner motivation and inner feeling is more genuine than through mission or through da`wah. Thus religious identity evolves or changes.

Identity is a sense of belonging and a psychological boundary vis-à-vis other. An identity can be defined only by drawing a line between the self and the other, between one group and the other. There cannot be sense of identity if the other does not exist. It is always with reference to other that I have my identity. And my own identity evolves with my own better understanding of faith from its very elementary understanding to highly specialised knowledge of my faith.

It is also important to note that a liberal Hindu or Christian or Muslim may have more in common than an orthodox and a liberal co-religionists. Thus liberals of two different religions share much more in common than an orthodox and a liberal from the same religion.

One should also keep in mind that a dialogue is an encounter and not a confrontation. Encounter always leads to deeper understanding while confrontation leads to conflict and violence. Quality of dialogue depends on quality of knowledge the partners in dialogue have. Dialogue between ignorant persons will lead to strengthening of prejudices. As pointed out above in globalised world people of diverse religious, linguistic and cultural backgrounds are thrown together some times by choice and some times by compulsion. The peoples of these diverse backgrounds have to live together in a geographical area. This living together should become a commitment and dialogue further strengthens this commitment.

It is generally thought that a homogenous group can live in greater peace and stability. Thus all Muslims or all Hindus or all Christians can live together without problems or tensions. This is not borne out empirically. The so-called homogenous groups soon dissolve into several sub-groups with inner tensions and these tensions can even become explosive. So even a most homogenous group can develop 'we' and 'they' groups and dialogue may become necessary among them.

Thus in modern world commitment to live together with the other is very essential and to make this living together successful knowing the other is highly necessary. Also a dialogue should always create a culture of tolerance and a culture of respecting the other. We often demonise the other and draw a false sense of solace from it as it leads to feeling of self-righteousness in the 'in' group. Such demonisation of other can wreck the process of peace in the society. Some times we even try to overcome inner group tensions by demonising the other.

Islam teaches Muslims to live in peace with others, including religious, linguistic, racial or national other. The Qur'anic verses like 5:48 or 4:35 or 22:40 or 30:22 or 6:109 are very important in this respect. In fact the verse 5:48 throws challenge to us to live with plurality of faith and laws and the Qur'anic emphasis is on excelling the other in good deeds and not competing with the other in religious rituals or ways of worshipping. Thus Qur'an accepts diversity as given, as the Will of Allah rather than rejecting it.

For a good Muslim living with diversity in a spirit of tolerance should be a commitment and he/she should fulfil this commitment for pleasure of Allah. A Muslim should also continuously enter into dialogue with wisdom with the other to promote the Will of Allah. Millions of Muslims today live as religious minority in countries of Asia, Africa, North America and elsewhere. Everywhere, whether in majority or minority they should become active agents of promoting better understanding among diverse faith, linguistic, racial or cultural groups.

If Muslims actively involve themselves in fulfilling this duty world will be much better place to live in. Living in peace and harmony is as important a duty as believing in unity of Allah (*wahdaniyyah*). *Tawhid* (belief in unity of God) is not only a theological concept but it is also a sociological concept. On sociological level the concept of tawhid results in unity of whole humankind as His creation. Qur'an often addresses humankind as *nas* (people) *bani Adam* (children of Adam) which emphasises this sense of human unity. Thus the Qur'anic concept of tawhid is all inclusive concept.

Thus unity and sense of inclusiveness can be promoted only by promoting the spirit of dialogue and spirit of tolerance. It is real spirit of *tawhid*.

6
Islam, Globalisation and Fundamentalism

Is there any relationship between religious fundamentalism, specially Islamic fundamentalism and globalisation? There is no doubt that one witnesses world- wide phenomenon of fundamentalism today. Is it a new phenomenon? If not, why fundamentalism is on the increase? Also, is globalisation a new phenomenon? Or is it a new name for the old phenomenon, which has always existed in the world. Same question can be posed about fundamentalism as well. Is fundamentalism a new phenomenon? Or is it an old one given new name? Also another important question is what is fundamentalism?

First let us answer the question what is fundamentalism? Can it be applied to all religions or only to Christianity? I think the term fundamentalism should not be applied to all religions without proper qualifications. The term fundamentalism was first applied to the Protestant Christian movement in America, which believed that every word of Bible is literally true. It was not used in pejorative sense.

Thus if the word fundamentalism was used in a particular sense for a Christian movement can we use it for other religions, particularly to Islam without proper qualification? I do not think it will be appropriate to do so. The word fundamentalism was applied to Islam for the first time by American media when Islamic revolution was taking place in Iran in late seventies and it was applied in a pejorative sense. Since then the world media has been using it (i.e. Islamic fundamentalism) in a very negative sense. Not only journalists but also academics are using it world-wide pejoratively.

What is Islamic fundamentalism? In fact Islamic fundamentalism has become most widely used term both in media and academia in a very loose sense. The Americans had deliberately coined this term to serve their political agenda. The Shah of Iran served American interests most faithfully in the region. Ayatollah Khomeini who led the Islamic revolution was, on the other hand, very hostile to

America and called it a great Satan. Thus Islamic revolution of Iran dealt a great blow to the American interests in the region and hence America began to denounce Islamic revolution of Iran and applied the term "Islamic fundamentalist" revolution. American media used headlines like "militant soldiers of Allah on march".

Thus it can be seen that the term 'Islamic fundamentalism' is basically a political term rather than a religious one. It basically conveys a sense of political hostility rather than religious rigidity, militancy, conservatism or orthodoxy. American media did not describe Saudi Islam, which is more rigid and orthodox but friendly to America was never condemned by American media as fundamentalist. Thus fundamentalism is basically a political term.

Fundamentalism in this essay, will however, be used to mean religious rigidity, militancy and extremism as well as use of Islam for political ends rather than for spiritual and moral development. Mere dogmatic approach to moral and spiritual questions should not be dubbed as fundamentalism. The term Islamic fundamentalism thus should be used with proper qualification.

Let us now define globalisation. Is globalisation a new

phenomenon? I do not think it is. Globalisation is as old as the human habitation on the earth. Various tribes migrated from one part of the globe to the other in most ancient periods. Globalisation is said to be about connectivity, connectivity with different parts of the globe. It may be said that today all parts of the world are well connected as never before. But connectivity itself is not an entirely new phenomenon.

Does globalisation by itself lead to religious fundamentalism? There is no such evidence in the past though there is some evidence in contemporary period. Thus globalisation per se does not necessarily lead to promotion of fundamentalism. It happens so only if other factors are present. It would be necessary to discuss those factors in order to understand relationship between globalisation and fundamentalism.

Globalisation, as pointed out before, is not a new phenomenon. The silk route connected several parts of the world in old times. Human migrations from one continent to another have been known to anthropologists. It is true means of communications were much slower than today but it is a matter of technology. What technology we possess today may prove to be slower tomorrow. Thus mere technology cannot define globalisation through connectivity and speed is of essence in globalisation. Thus all we can say is that the contemporary globalisation is qualitatively better and faster than that of tomorrow.

After defining the two key terms i.e. fundamentalism and globalisation let us see what is the connection between the two in the contemporary period. Is this relation between the two a dependent relationship? Does globalisation today necessarily leads to fundamentalism i.e. religious militancy and extremism? In the absence of other factors one hardly finds any such dependent relationship between the two. Moreover why one talks of Islamic fundamentalism today? Why western media, particularly American media is full of news and write-ups on Islamic fundamentalism and not Buddhist and Christian fundamentalism? Christianity and Buddhism are also two great religions of the world besides Islam. Then why so much talk of Islamic fundamentalism then?

Thus to understand the relationship between globalisation and Islamic fundamentalism we have to introduce another factor which is political, particularly oil politics in the middle eastern region. Without taking into account this factor of oil politics it will not be possible to understand the phenomenon of fundamentalism and globalisation.

As pointed out above the Islamic revolution in Iran is a watershed as far as Islamic fundamentalism is concerned. One hardly heard about this term before the Islamic revolution in Iran. The revolution in Iran upset the American strategies in this region. America lost the 'valuable' support it had for its oil politics. The Shah of Iran not only supported American interests in the region but also supported Israel and Israeli policies, which strengthened American cause further.

Thus America's perception of Islamic revolution in Iran was highly hostile and it dubbed it as militant and extremist and 'fundamentalist'. It gave a great jolt to American policies in the region. Even the CIA never expected such a revolution to take place in Iran. Shah's highly repressive regime was thought to be impregnable by American rulers. They were totally surprised when the Shah's regime collapsed like a house of cards. In 1952 when Mosaddeg had captured power in Iran and nationalised the oil companies the CIA had managed to stage a coup with the help of some religious leaders on one hand, and, that of lumpen elements, on the other. However, this time the foundations of Islamic revolution were so strong that even CIA could not do anything and remained a mere helpless spectator.

The Islamic revolution also removed the sense of helplessness among the Muslims world over, particularly in the Middle East region, which is so sensitive to American interests. For the first time the Muslims of the region felt that America is not so impregnable after all and that it could be defeated. This further increased American threat perceptions. The other supporters of American policies in the region like the Saudi monarchy or Kuwaiti sheikhdom were also trembling with fear. They thought the people of their respective countries may be inspired by revolutionary ideals and overthrow them. However, it was not to be for reasons not to be discussed here.

But nevertheless threat perceptions remained and American policies were redesigned to fight the 'threat of Islamic fundamentalism'. Iranian Islam had to be fought with the help of Saudi Islam. It is interesting to note that Iranian radical Islam could be countered not with democratic secularism but with more conservative Wahabi Islam.

Whosoever supported Iranian revolution was called 'fundamentalist' and was ridiculed. 'Fundamentalism' became the most widely used but most misunderstood term. The Iranian Islamic revolution also must be understood in all its complexity. The Iranian masses had welcomed the Islamic revolution as it liberated them from Shah's repressive regime and not necessarily because it was 'Islamic'. There were various shades of opinion and different interpretations from liberal to most conservative.

Khomeini himself is difficult to categorise. It is easier to describe him as 'orthodox' but it would not be realistic. His views about Islam and his politics were far more complex. If fundamentalism means, as we have defined above, as representing militancy, extremism and conservatism Khomeini was not fundamentalist in this sense as American media would have us believe.

Khomeini was, undoubtedly a radical. He was greatly concerned with weaker sections of society. He was closer to the left in as much as he championed the cause of weaker sections and denounced western, particularly, American imperialism. His radicalism was of course based on the Qur'an. He repeatedly quoted the Qur'anic verse 28:5 which says, "And We desired to bestow a favour upon those who were weakened in the land, and to make them the leaders and to make them heirs."

According to Ayatollah Khomeini the conflict between the weak and the powerful is eternal and the Qur'an is on the side of the weak (*mustad'ifun*) and opposes the powerful (*mustakbirun*). Thus Khomeini sided with the third world vis-à-vis America though he based his sympathies with the poor not on the basis of any secular but Qur'anic ideology. Khomeini cannot, therefore, be described as "fundamentalist" in usual sense. Even his interpretation of the Qur'an was very different from other orthodox interpreters.

The epithet 'fundamentalist' is often used with political agenda and hence America used it against Khomeini. This is not only in case of America but also others, individuals, parties and groups who accuse others of being fundamentalist. In very few cases the word fundamentalist is used to mean religious orthodoxy, rigidity and inflexibility.

Now coming back to globalisation and fundamentalism whether there is any connection between the two and if so of what nature? Firstly, it should be noted that modern globalisation is qualitatively different from earlier globalisation. The widespread education and information technology makes this qualitative difference. The widespread education has brought tremendous awareness among the people of the developing countries and information technology makes it easier for this awareness to spread. Nothing remains confined to a region or a country. Any major event has global impact. It was not possible in earlier days.

Another important factor is democracy, which empowers people and more often than not, it empowers unevenly. Various collectivities in society, particularly in developing countries where there is so much poverty and backwardness this empowerment is quite uneven. One community or caste or tribe grabs much more share in political power or economic development than other community, caste or tribe. Both then mobilise their fellow community, caste or tribe people – one to retain the privileges and the other to obtain them by using religious, caste or tribal identity.

This mobilisation on the basis of religious, caste or tribal identities leads to extremism depending on the political and social situation. In India community and caste identities have led to growth of religious extremism and fundamentalism. This fundamentalism is further fuelled by globalisation as members of the community settled abroad and comparatively more prosperous finance leaders of these communities.

The growth of Hindu fundamentalism in India and Islamic fundamentalism in Pakistan can be partly explained in this light. It should also be noted that fundamentalism grows more in educated middle classes. These middle classes mobilise poorer members of their community by invoking religion and displaying religious extremism. Hindu religion is quite liberal and has universal outlook but the Sangh Parivar Hinduism is just opposite of that. It is most rigid, extremist and narrow. They distinguish it from Hinduism and call it Hindutva.

Hindutva is basically a political ideology and has nothing to do with spiritual and moral or philosophical aspects of Hindu religion. Hindutva ideology is most combative and aggressive and seeks to mobilise upper caste Hindus for grabbing political power and economic hegemony. The upper caste Hindus, especially those from Gujrat, settled abroad send money to Vishwa Hindu Parishad (VHP) for promoting fundamentalist Hinduism. More the money from abroad greater rigidity and extremism, and more rigidity and extremism more money flows from abroad. Now Bajrang Dal which can be called

Hindu *jihadis* is giving its men and women training in using arms in the name of self defence.

This has gone to such an extent that a leading magazine Outlook in its issue of July 8, 2002 says, in its cover story "The Crisis in Hinduism" "One of the World's most liberal religions is in danger of being perverted. The siege is from within. A way of life has been seized upon as a means to political power and a religion held hostage." In the same cover story Swami Agnivesh, a noted Hindu scholar and human rights activist says, "*Hindutva* is a total perversion of the subtle, profound, enduring qualities of Hinduism."

All this is being done by exponents of Hinduism not to serve any moral, spiritual or philosophical cause but to grab political power. If the *Hindutvawadis* perceive that political power is slipping from their hands, they intensify their *Hindutvawad.* Greater the fear of power slipping from their hands greater the efforts to militarise the Hindus. Communal violence in Gujrat in which more than thousand lives were lost was a direct consequence of fear of losing coming elections. The VHP and Bajrang Dal, with the help of BJP Chief Minister Mr. Narendra Modi, planned and executed most horrid communal carnage in Gujrat.

In Pakistan it is Islamic extremism which plays the same role. The *jihadis* (those who use Islamic term jihad) have a clear political agenda. The Muslim 'Ulama who have tested power and others who see in Islam a great opportunity to come close to power centres, invoke the Islamic concept of jihad and practice most sectarian, extremist kind of Islam. Partly America is responsible for creating fundamentalist Islam in Pakistan.

America was interested in bringing down the left regime in Afghanistan and it trained thousands of Muslims to fight Soviet army in that country and called them 'mujahids' (a laudatory Islamic term which means those who fight bravely). Osama bin Laden was also creation of CIA and was used in Afghanistan to fight the Soviet forces. Religious extremism was deliberately cultivated among the Afghans and Pakistanis. Once Soviet forces withdrew from Afghanistan and Soviet Union collapsed the USA dumped these 'mujahidins'.

However, these Afghan and Arab fighters in Afghanistan had become quite aware of their own rights and their own plight and now decided to fight American power in the region. America, in order to maintain its hegemony in Middle East, backs up Saudi monarchy on one hand, and unconditionally supports Israel, on the other. It also attacked Iraq to serve its own interests in the region. It has maintained its troops in Saudi Arabia for the same purpose. All this created strong resentment among these so called *mujahidins* and they now turned against their old master.

Thus these *jihadi* groups are products of struggle for political power in the region. Zia-ul-Haq, the military dictator of Pakistan also promoted highly narrow and sectarian Islam to seek legitimacy for this power, which had no popular sanction. Thus Zia-ul-Haq greatly contributed to promote Islamic fundamentalism in Pakistan. The ISI of Pakistan is also instrumental in spreading Islamic fundamentalism in South Asia. The military has now permanent stake in power in Pakistan and would keep on strengthening fundamentalist forces in Pakistani society.

It would be really difficult to fight Islamic fundamentalism effectively in Pakistani without strengthening democratic forces in that country. It has become a sort of vicious circle in Pakistan. Greater the power of military more the potentiality of fundamentalism being promoted and if democratic rule comes military, in collaboration with some militant mullahs, intensifies fundamentalism to frustrate democratic aspirations of the people. This has been going on in Pakistan for number of years.

Though president Musharraf is not interested in

promoting fundamentalism and has modern mind set but is now prisoner of the situation. It is not easy for him to defeat the fundamentalist forces. These forces are extremely powerful and can incite a section of people in the name of religion. These forces also do not hesitate to kill or assassinate their foes. Such political assassinations are quite common in Pakistan today. The Saudi and Iranian political interests in Pakistan have also provoked Shia-Sunni militancy. The extremist Sunnis belonging to Lashkar-e-Jhangvi kill Shiahs and Shias, in retaliation kill the Sunni extremists.

Thus it will be seen that religion has become most powerful tool in the hands of politicians and they are using it without any compunction. Religious extremism is being financed from abroad in almost all cases. Sikh fundamentalism also had its source of finance in U.K. and USA, *Hindutvawadis* also get financial support from these countries and Islamic *jihadis* in South Asia, particularly in Kashmir and Afghanistan also have their supporters in these countries.

Thus the migrants to USA and U.K. are providing lot of funds to religious militants in whole of South Asia. Even LTTE militants in Sri Lanka have their sources of funding from U.K. and European countries. These migrants to western countries feel guilty for having left their motherland and also feel alienated in western countries and compensate for their guilt by financing religious militant groups back home. Thus, in a way, globalisation is fuelling religious fundamentalism in Asia, particularly in South Asia.

The interests involved are so powerful that there is no easy solution to this problem of religious militancy. In some countries it is military dictatorship, which fuels it and in some countries it is democratic set up, as in India, which promotes it. Thus democracy by itself is no remedy for fundamentalism unless other factors like justice and morality become integral parts of it. Social, political and economic justice is very essential for fighting religious fundamentalism. Most of the societies are faced with highly unjust and uneven power structures with high rates of poverty and unemployment. These are the breeding grounds for religious fundamentalism coupled with ruling class interests.

7

Intellecutal Approach to Islam

What is intellectual approach to religion? Is intellectual approach possible? Some people maintain that intellectual approach to religion is not possible, as it is basically spiritual experience. The questions religion raises are those which are out of realm of reason. Only spiritual or revelational experience can answer them. This is by and large true from one viewpoint. Then what do we mean by intellectual approach to Islam? Is such an approach desirable?

Before answering this question one has to properly define religion itself. What does one mean by religion? What areas does it embrace? It is often claimed by followers of different religions that it is a way of life which means it embraces all areas of life. No area of life can be excluded. If it is so religion does qualify for intellectual approach in several areas of life.

What we generally mean by religion is quite comprehensive. It includes as it is known in Islamic terminology *'ibadat* and *mu'amalat.* But what common people mean is even more comprehensive. It includes for them all customs, traditions and even superstitious beliefs. All that they have inherited from their forefathers is included in religious beliefs and then one acts according to these beliefs. Any opposition to these beliefs is condemned as unpardonable heresy. Often even primitive knowledge about the universe became part of these religious beliefs Thus both in Christian and Islamic tradition entire Ptolemaic astronomy and Aristotelian observations about the universe became part of religious traditions. In many Islamic institutions of higher education even today Ptolemaic astrology is taught and Aristotelian beliefs are considered part of Islamic teachings. The Christian world has, by and large, changed its outlook in these matters. Islamic institutions and the 'ulama have not.

Thus, if religion is so defined, and made all inclusive, there is great need for intellectual approach to religion else we will become only a backward superstitious community. There is another difficulty here. Any religious community, particularly in Asia and Africa, is highly stratified – economically apart from culturally and educationally. Masses are often poor, illiterate and backward; the elite, on the other hand, are affluent and has higher educational qualifications.

This stratification also affects understanding of religion. There is no uniform understanding of religion and religious beliefs. At one extreme i.e. at the level of poor and illiterate masses, religion is nothing more than superstition and superstitious practices. It is no use condemning such superstitions at the level of extremely poor, illiterate masses. What is needed is to improve their income and literacy rates. Thus actual fight against superstitions is not mere ideological but efforts to improve their living and literary standards.

It does not mean there are no superstitious beliefs at the level of those who are better off in terms of income and education. Often one finds even rich and educated believing in superstitions. Superstitions at such levels are borne out of insecurity, tensions due to unresolvable problems or incurable diseases; not for want of intellectual incapabilities or lack of proper understanding. Such people often expect miracles – miraculous cure, miraculous solution for their problems, and miraculous way of becoming rich.

Religion for most of us, has become short cut to our problems. Belief in God – Allah – is not spiritual relations with the creator but He is looked as problem solver. It is important to note that in the Qur'an Allah is not projected as problem solver but as a Guide – Guide to right path. We are told to invoke Him for guiding to the right path – *sirat al-mustaqim.* Thus Allah is source of values – justice (*'adl*), benevolence (*ihsan*), compassion (*rahmah*) and wisdom (*hikmah*).

Also, He is projected as creator and nourisher (*rabb*). He is creator of all so He is nourisher of all. His guidance is for all, not for selected few. If someone follows His guidance and practices values the kind of problem we face will not arise. There will be no tension if we do no injustice, do not exploit others, show compassion to all, be benevolent to others and exercise wisdom gifted to us by Allah. It is we who create various problems through our wrong doings and then create problems for ourselves and for others. If our behaviour is value-based there would be no need for miracles and for superstitious behaviour. The whole problem is our behaviour is not value-oriented, it is interest-oriented. We act not according to the values of our revealed scripture, but to promote our personal interests

It is for this reason that we behave unjustly, greedily, maliciously, exploitatively, egoistically to promote our interests and in turn create conflict, bloodshed, murders and wars. The rulers wage wars for territorial ambitions and then pray for victory to the Almighty and expect miracles. And by sheer might of physical force if he or she wins the war it is projected as miracle and 'divine sanction'.

Islam is basically defined by what we call *shari'ah* which, as developed by the jurists over a period of time, includes both *`ibadat* (matters relating to spiritual aspects) and *mu`amalat* (matters related to human interaction in this worldly matters). As far as `ibadat are concerned they need not be judged intellectually but they too are not necessarily irrational or based on unreason. They may be beyond reason but not against reason. This distinction is important to make. *'ibadat* have their own rationale whether it is praying, fasting or pilgrimage or some other spiritual practices. They may not be same in all religions as every religion develops its own specific spiritual practices depending on history, culture and traditions.

Qur'an very clearly emphasises this that "And for everyone is goal to which he turns (himself), so vie with one another in good works." (2:148) Thus emphasis is not on method or direction of prayer but on good (value-based) deeds. Again in 5:48 the Qur'an says "For every one of you We appointed a law and a way." The specificity, we should not remember, is not superiority. Much of irrational fights between religions can end if we accept specificities of 'ibadat for every religion and emphasise, as the Qur'an does, the ethical aspects of individual and collective behaviour. Also, it must be borne in mind that *'ibadat* are a way of creating relationship between human being and her/his creator. Through this relationship one orders ones metaphysical aspects of life or builds theories of other worldly life. One also gives meaning to ones existence through spiritual relationship. One cannot lead meaningless life. One must give meaning to ones life through some or the other spiritual system. One thus enriches ones life though metaphysical relation with ones creator. Such an exercise of imparting meaning to ones life cannot be irrational though it may be beyond limitations of ones reason or comprehension.

The role of intellect is very important as far as *mu'amalat* is concerned i.e. the human interactions in social matters of this world. Some religions, depending on historical an cultural reasons, emphasise only spiritual aspects of religion i.e. *`ibadat* and may not directly deal with *mu`amalat* leaving it to customs and traditions or to framing of laws by human beings.

Qur'an, however, deals with legal aspects to i.e. with *mu'amalat*. It does lays down certain laws for marriage, divorce, inheritance, property, theft, rape and so on. The *shari'ah* laws in this respect, are based on the Qur'anic pronouncements. It is in this sense that *shari'ah* is considered divine by Muslims. But it must be understood that Qur'an is much more concerned with justice in human matters (*mu'amalat*) than any thing else.

Justice (*'adl*) is very fundamental to Islamic values. It is most fundamental value and all human relations are to be based on justice. Unjust relationships lead to conflict and violence. But there is problem, defining justice. Throughout human history justice was defined by the powerful. Might was considered as always right. But according to the Qur'an, any relationship based on exploitation of one by the other is unjust, unethical and punishable in this world by worldly laws and by Allah in the world hereafter.

Thus the Qur'anic concept of non-exploitative relationship between human beings is an important contribution to human ethics and in the sphere of *mu'amalat*. This is, it must be admitted, very rational approach to morality and ethics. "Might is right' approach is most irrational and though prevalent even today where intellect is considered most developed, and must be totally rejected.

The Western world where reason is supposedly prevalent in relatively much more than in 'backward' countries of Asia and Africa, justice is often decided through use of might. The inter-human relationship is far from being non-exploitative. The West dominates the world because of its might. Science has not been used rationally to promote common good but to monopolise resources for a few and hence there is so much conflict and violence in the world today.

Today with all human intellectual development it is not difficult to understand that what is just is rational and only what is rational can bring stability on earth. Even the most advanced countries on our planet experience great turmoil because their system is exploitative and not just and what is unjust cannot be stable and hence that system is not rational despite its breath taking progress in science and technology. Science and technology is means to an end, not an end in itself.

It is important to note that intellect is a tool and tool must be used in keeping with certain values to make it a boon for entire humanity. Allah has gifted human beings with two most precious gifts – intellect and compassion and if the two are synthesised humanity will never suffer. We often use our intellect for selfish end and it becomes disaster for humanity. In twentieth century millions of people were killed in two wars with the help of science and technology. The world had never seen such destruction of human life before. Such destruction of human life took place with the help of human intellect as it was used for selfish ends. But if human intellect is used with compassion for human suffering world will turn into paradise.

The Qur'an lays stress on *hikmah* (wisdom) more than anything else as it synthesises both reason (*'aql*) and compassion (*rahmah*). One of Allah's names is Hakim (wise) and if wisdom is exercised there will be no suffering on earth. The power of intellect will be used for doing away with human suffering and never for intensifying it. Unfortunately today power of human intellect is being used more for increasing human suffering than minimising it.

Violence has been with us throughout human history and it is one of the greatest causes of human suffering in the world. With inventions of science and technology the power to perpetuate violence has increased beyond human imagination and this power is utilised by the most powerful nations to subjugate others or dominate others and to exploit the weak. The retaliatory violence on the part of the weak also tends to be horrific claiming innocent lives in the name of justice.

Since the weak cannot match the power possessed by the powerful it adds another dreadful weapon – religious rhetoric to its armoury. 'Jihad' is such a religious rhetoric being employed in the Islamic world. If one exercises wisdom as one of the important Qur'anic value, it will not be difficult to understand that such rhetoric is much more harmful to Muslims themselves. It brings even more disaster and invites self- destruction as it happened in Afghanistan after attack on World Trade Centre, in New York.

One must reflect seriously whether violence will pay to the weak. Violence, it should be obvious on little reflection ultimately benefits the powerful who possess much greater capacity to retaliate. Should one be then permanently subjugated or dominated? Certainly not. The world is increasingly accepting democratic values, human dignity and just governance. It still appears to be an empty rhetoric. But it is acquiring increasing urgency in the modern world. What is needed is ever greater efforts to disseminate these values through modern means of communication. This 'weaponry' of democratic values is far more powerful for the oppressed than arms

However, and it is important to note, before flinging these values i.e. democratic values, human dignity and just governance before the international powers, one has to struggle hard to apply them at home. Today in the entire Islamic world these values have no meaning. In the first place there is no democracy in these countries. The very discourse of human dignity and human rights is rejected as 'western' while the rulers of these countries ironically depend for their very existence on the western powers whose values they reject so contemptuously.

Thus it is quite a challenging job to struggle for political acceptance of these values of democratic governance at home. It is then alone that these Islamic countries will be able to confront the western dominating powers for a dignified and meaningful relationship with these powerful countries. Today the dictatorial governments of Islamic countries dependent for their existence on western powers cannot build any such relations with western countries.

Also, there being no democratic freedom in these countries, a section of the youth uses violence against dominating countries in sheer frustration. And this violence, as pointed out before, proves more disastrous and also brings bad name to Islam. If one tenth of energy is spent on struggle for democratic governance by launching peaceful agitation it will be far more fruitful. Today there is total absence of such democratic movements in the Islamic countries. It is true these movements are ruthlessly suppressed by the governments in Muslim countries but one has to after all fight for these values. This struggle for democratic governance will ultimately help fight for these values internationally.

Peace in Islam, as repeatedly pointed out by this writer, is much more fundamental than 'jihad' and peaceful democratic struggles will earn much greater acceptability and sympathy for the just causes. Violence delegitimises the very cause one is fighting for. Suicide bombing in Palestine does not help the cause much. Israel, which is an aggressor and usurper, earn more sympathy world-wide. Suicide bombing has not earned any support for the cause of Palestinians anywhere, in any quarter. It has brought condemnation.

Suicide bombing cannot be justified on Islamic grounds at all as it kills only innocent people, even school children who do not even understand the issues involved. The Qur'an clearly says "..whoever kills a person, unless it be for manslaughter or for mischief in the land, it is as though he had killed a whole humanity. And whoever saves a life, it is as though one has saved entire humanity.." (5:32)

Thus it will be seen that saving a life is as if one has saved entire humanity but suicide bombing instead of saving a life takes so many innocent lives who are neither responsible for manslaughter nor for mischief in the land.

Suicide bombing is, thus, clear violation of the Qur'anic injunction. Suicide bombing not only kills the person himself which is certainly suicide, and not permissible, but also so many others, even a greater sin.

Compassion for innocent lives is the greatest virtue. Even in jihad one is not permitted to kill women, children and old men whereas suicide bombing kills all without any distinction. How can it be justified? Also, it is no way to humiliate the Israeli Government, which is real culprit. There is no better way of shaming an oppressor than invoking justice and compassion.

A rational approach and not emotional one would help the cause of the oppressor much more than otherwise. If the Palestine movement had stuck to peaceful democratic values it would have won far more sympathisers outside the Islamic world. Today human rights discourse is far more powerful, despite its limitations in the unjust world order. Even in early twentieth century Gandhiji's weapon of non-violence proved to be mightier than the British Empire. The 'naked fakir' proved to be more powerful than the highly armed British Empire.

Non-violent agitation is real combination of reason and compassion and is a great boon. Reason of course tells us that violence cannot help those with few weapons compared to those who have weapons to destroy the world several times over and compassion requires that no innocent life be taken. Jihad had some justification in the days when absolutist power prevailed and there was no acceptability for democratic discourse at all and peaceful and no-violent movement could not be launched.

One who takes cynical view can still insist that 'human rights discourse' is meant for weak and the powerful understand only the language of violence but it is not wise view. If non-violence and discourse of peace is intensely and repeatedly applied it is bound to produce result and it has been tried by many.

A real intellectual approach would reduce bloodshed in the world. A man of religion, a true Muslim, should be full of compassion as he/she worships Allah who is compassionate and merciful. Religion is nothing if not source of values and a religious person will be inspired by these values. Unfortunately religion is also hijacked by the powerful vested interests and rituals, rather than values, occupy the centre stage.

Also, religion has become a source of submission to (unjust) authorities rather than a powerful resource for dissent from it. An intellectual approach will inspire us to be critical of unjust authorities and for submission to justice and compassion. A religious person will negate all that is unjust and will carry on jihad against unjust social structures. Compassion for life, all forms of life, is real submission to its the creator. Any person who destroys life cannot be real worshipper of creator of this world.

Negation of all forms of oppression through sustained peaceful struggle is real iman (faith) and a passionate commitment to justice and peace is real submission to Allah. It is both intellectual and compassionate approach. Not the love of tradition but tradition of love is the way out for suffering humanity. Human intellect and love of humanity and human dignity will redeem humanity.

8
Western Feminism or Rights of Women in Islam

There is strong criticism of those who work for rights of women by conservative Islamists and they are accused of imitating Western feminism. It is debatable whether it is so but even if it is what is wrong with it? Western feminism is based on secular ideology but upholds dignity of women and their rights. If secularism is not always negation of religion (only atheistic secularism negates it, not other forms of secularism) and in most cases it is not, there is no objection to feminism. The Holy Prophet says acquire wisdom (*hikmah*) wherever it is found as it is believer's (*m'umin*'s) property.

It is well known that until sixties even Western societies – despite their secularism – had not accorded equal rights (sexual equality is still not meticulously practised in Western societies) to women. In fact even right to inheritance and property was given to women in Western countries in thirties. In some countries women got right to vote only during the decade of thirties. The women had to struggle, a lot in the West for acquiring these rights, which Islam had given to them centuries ago.

Even in Western countries the debates go on many issues and many women's organisations are not fully satisfied about the women issues. Man's domination continues in most of the spheres including the domestic sphere. Man certainly enjoys more privileges, if not rights, in those western countries. Man still resists performing domestic chores and even wife beating is not unknown.

The fact is that patriarchal structure of society is still going strong and one does not know whether it will disappear in the foreseeable future. It is for this reason that with few exceptions political power rests with man in most of the countries. Again, in most of the western countries representation of women in legislative bodies hardly exceeds 10 per cent though their population is close to fifty per cent in all societies. It is for this reason that the feminists are struggling for equal rights in western countries too. All one can say is that the condition of women is somewhat better compared to third world countries or Islamic countries. Though in western countries equality of sexes has been established theoretically it is far from having been achieved in practice.

And those struggling for women's rights in third world countries in general and, in the Islamic countries in particular have to struggle against much greater odds. These odds remain insurmountable even if these women work within the framework of Islam. Many Muslim countries like Kuwait even refuse to give its women right to vote. The Saudi Government does not allow its women even to drive even when accompanied by their husbands, let alone go out alone in public.

We have such primitive conditions in several Islamic countries and if women protest against such intolerable restrictions they are dubbed as 'western feminists'. The real thing is that such demands of equal rights hurt male ego. Male domination is not at all Islamic, though it is justified in its name. Men use some selective verses from the Qur'an, ignore their social context and use them to perpetuate their domination. They conveniently ignore the verses empowering women or laying down equality of both the sexes. In fact in verses like 2:219, 2:228 and 33:35 there is clear statement about equality of both the sexes and yet they are totally ignored and instead they quote verses like 4:34 to establish their domination. They even distort the meaning of words like *qawwam* used in above verse to retain their hegemony.

They also use several *hadith* (Prophet's sayings) to put undue restrictions on women. It is forgotten that thousands of *ahadith* cannot be even authenticated as many of them were forged by those who had anti-women attitude and these *ahadith* are used as authentic source for legislation about women even when they contradict clear Qur'anic assertions. Thus the Saudi law not allowing women to venture out alone is not Qur'anic but based on a *v* which prohibits women going out alone.

Even if the *hadith* is authentic one totally ignores the social conditions then and now. In those days there was conflict between the Jews and Muslims and the Jews used to tease Muslim women and so in view of this the Prophet might have cautioned women not to venture out alone. Most of the *ahadith* are narrated without mentioning any context or reason and these are followed by the orthodox 'ulama mechanically. And practices like prohibiting to drive does not even have any base in *hadith*. There were no automobiles in those days.

One cannot even derive it by inference or *qiyas* (analogy) as women were not prohibited by the Holy Prophet from riding camels or horses. The women did ride camels and horses and they even drove them by themselves. Such prohibition is nothing more than extreme conservatism of the Saudi 'ulama and their stubborn refusal to concede rights to women. It is interesting to note that while the Saudi Government does not allow women to drive cars the Iranian Government has started exclusive taxi service to be run by women. Thus Iranian women can not only drive private cars but can also be a taxi driver.

Similarly while the Kuwait Government refuses its women to vote other Muslim countries like Pakistan, Bangla Desh, Egypt and other countries allow them to vote. How does one explain these contradictory practices? Are their different Islams or there are differing attitudes towards women? Thus it is not Islamic sources but men's attitude which matters.

And when Muslim women demand their rights – and Islamic rights at that – they are denounced as western feminists. It is a fact that Muslim women enjoy differing degree of rights in different Islamic countries. While in Turkey Mustafa Kemal Pasha introduced secular Swiss code thus according equal rights to both men and women on one hand, and, the total restrictions in Saudi on the other hand. In other Muslim countries like Egypt, Morocco, Algeria, Jordan etc. there is comparatively greater latitude of freedom for women. It is because the rulers in these countries are more liberal towards women.

Thus it is not Islam, which comes in the way but man's attitude which determine the laws of Muslim countries regarding women. But these men in various Muslim countries invoke name of Islam to stem the tide of women's movement for better rights dubbing it as western feminism.

Some Muslim countries like Pakistan and Bangla Desh had or have women prime minister and some Muslim countries like Kuwait do not accord women right to vote. Such gross contradictions are really difficult to gloss over in the name of Islam. It all depends either on social conditions of that country or even on political exigencies.

When Fatima Jinnah tried to contest for the office of President in early sixties against Ayuub Khan, the latter wangled a fatwa from the conservative 'ulama that a woman cannot become head of the state. They quoted a *v* from the Holy Prophet that if a woman becomes head of a nation that nation will face disaster. However, the supporters of Fatima Jinnah which included head of Jama'at-e-Islami Maulana Maududi approved of her contesting the President's election. They also managed to obtain a fatwa to this effect from a prominent 'alim like Maulana Ashraf Ali Thanvi who justified on grounds that in democracy the head of a state does not have absolute powers but depends on votes of members of parliament whose majority is of men.

All these political games are unfortunately played in the name of Islam rather than giving women rights due to them in a modern democratic society and which are not contrary to the teachings of the Qur'an. Most of the Muslim women in Islamic countries are not guilty of following 'western feminism' but are agitating for their Islamic rights. The Taliban regime was the worst offenders in this respect. They not only followed the rigid Saudi laws but put more restriction than the Saudis do.

The Taliban who were essentially following tribal norms justified all that in the name of Islam. They did not even allow women to go out for schools and madrasas totally ignoring the famous *hadith* of the Prophet that seeking knowledge is obligatory both for Muslim men and Muslim women (muslimah). The prophet separately mentioned Muslimah keeping in mind that soon after him the Muslim men would restrict women from acquiring knowledge. The Prophet used the word *'ilm* which includes both religious as well as secular knowledge.

However, with few exceptions throughout medieval ages Muslim women were not allowed to acquire literary skills and reason was cited that learning reading and writing would corrupt them and they might write 'love letters' to strangers which is sin. Today no one argues on these lines and of course Muslim women are acquiring secular as well as religious knowledge in public institutions. And this is no more considered as un-Islamic.

Thus what was considered un-Islamic until yesterday has become perfectly Islamic today and is accepted with good Islamic conscience by men in all Islamic countries. Many Muslim countries even permit co-education, which was great 'sin' until recently. Thus it can be seen that much depends not on Islam but on social dynamics, on medievalism or modernity, on orthodoxy or liberalism.

The man in male-dominated society in Muslim countries forgets that Islam ushered in its days a great revolution, which can be called feminist revolution today. It accorded equality to both man and women in various ways sometimes saying that "women have rights similar to those against them" (2:228) and sometimes saying for everything men and women will be equally rewarded (33:35).

But except for initial period of few decades Muslim women never enjoyed equality in the Islamic world. Soon, for various reasons, more and more restrictions were imposed on them. Though there was absolutely no place for monarchy in Islam, the institution of monarchy developed in the Muslim world within 30 years of the death of the Prophet and all feudal customs and traditions associated with monarchy came to be adopted by Muslim monarchs (though continued to be called caliphs for religious reasons) including severe restrictions on Muslim women. In other words all feudal practices were imposed on women in the Muslim world which continue until today.

Within hundred years after the beginning of the Islamic calendar she almost lost all her Qur'anic rights. Qur'an recognised her as legal entity and gave her all rights including contracting marriage, divorce, right to inherit, to have her own property, to earn and have her own income and to own her own business. But by the time the Umayyads consolidated their rule, all pre-Islamic traditions and customs were revised and also feudal traditions added to them thus completely subjugating women.

The Qur'an had required her to dress in dignified manner and conceal her sexual charms, the Muslim society put her under veil requiring to conceal her face completely. She could only peep though her two holes provided in the veil. This is no where the intention of the Qur'an yet this form of veiling is practised in many Islamic countries today.

She was confined to her house whereas during the Prophet's time and for quite some time thereafter she even took part in battles fought against non-Muslims. It is said that it was Umm Ammarah who saved the Prophet's life in the battle of Uhud. However, from Umayyad period onwards she was not even allowed to go out of home without her husband's permission after marriage and with father's permission before that and that too accompanied by some male relative called *mahram* (a blood relation with whom marriage is not permissible like brother, uncle etc.)

A *hadith* was also invented requiring her to be totally obedient to her husband and that *sajda* before husband would have been ordered had it not been prohibited for anyone except Allah. This *hadith* is reflective of the feudalisation of Islamic ethos. In other words women by then had lost her autonomy and what revolutionary changes and empowerment of women effected by the Qur'an were totally lost.

It would be interesting to quote here from a medieval text to show the concept of an ideal woman prevailing in that society. "An ideal women", according to this medieval writer, "speaks and laughs rarely and never without a reason. She never leaves the house, even to see neighbours or her acquaintance. She has no women friends, gives her confidence to nobody, and her husband is her sole reliance. She accepts nothing from anyone, excepting her husband and her parents. If she sees her relatives she does not meddle in their affairs. She is not treacherous and has no faults to hide, nor bad reasons to proffer. She does not try to entice people. If her husband shows his intention to performing the conjugal rites, she agrees to satisfy his desire and occasionally provokes it. She assists him always in his affairs, and is sparing in complaints and tears; she does not laugh or rejoice when she sees her husband moody or sorrowful but shares his troubles, and wheedles him into good humour till he is quite content again. She does not surrender herself to anybody but her husband, even if abstinence would kill her. Such a woman is cherished by everyone." (See Shaykh Nefzawi, *The Perfumed Garden.* Tr. Richard F. Burton, New York, 1964), p-97). This is how a Muslim woman was pictured in medieval ages.

It is these feudal restrictions that we have inherited from our past and we glorify them as 'Islamic' and any deviation from it is condemned as western feminism. These restrictions are still practised in most of the Muslim countries because they still have not been democratised and women have no access to modern education. There is hardly any Muslim country, which has democratic governance. Either there is monarchy or military dictatorship or controlled democracy.

However, modernisation is also going apace and it is difficult for the rulers in Muslim countries to resist spread of modern education among women. More modern education spread among women and society becomes increasingly democratised, awareness for rights grows among them and they demand their rights either on Islamic or secular grounds.

It is interesting to note that while in several Muslim countries like Saudi Arabia and Kuwait women are demanding modernisation and political and social rights some women in Turkey are keen to go into *hijab*. In many non-Muslim countries also a section of Muslim women are taking to *hijab*. It is important to note the reasons for the same.

Though in general women are demanding their rights in all countries some Muslim women feel proud to observe Islamic dress code. It is more for reasons of identity. Westernisation (which is not necessarily modernisation and one must distinguish between the two) has led to certain excesses in manner of dressing which violate sexual modesty as the whole emphasis is on displaying feminine charms and body line rather than conceal them.

Today there is feeling among the people in developing countries of western culture assuming hegemonising role, which creates resentment. Globalisation has further strengthened the hegemony of western culture and the people of developing countries have become quite conscious of their own culture and cultural practices. The Muslim women are also taking to their own cultural way of dressing to assert their cultural identity. *Hijab* should thus be seen as part of this process rather than a way of restricting women. Thus *hijab* today is part of visible cultural identity than anything else. However, this *hijab* should not be imposed and should not cover face to become restrictive. Wearing scarf or chador as Iranians call it, should suffice.

Such way of dressing should neither be imposed nor should it be opposed. In Turkey, the Member of Parliament was also not allowed to attend the House wearing *hijab*. She was disqualified from membership fearing she represents fundamentalists in Turkey. Such compulsion to wear only western dress is as condemnable as making it compulsory to wear *hijab*. A woman should be free to wear dress the way she likes though within the limits of modesty.

One should not condemn any movement for empowerment of women as western feminism. Women are as much human beings as men and today women's rights are part of human rights. Women have every right to take part in all social, cultural and political movements. They should not be debarred from any arena. There is no sphere of activity in which women have not excelled men. It is only in Muslim countries that she is still restricted from taking part in public sphere.

It is unfortunate that there is even debate whether a woman could pray in the mosque or not. Many Muslim communities still do not permit women to pray inside mosques let alone allow them to take part in public activities. In countries like India now there is reservation in jobs and even in political bodies like *panchayats* and municipalities and municipal corporations. There is reservation for women for posts of *sarpanch* and mayors. Some conservative 'ulama gave *fatwa* that a woman cannot contest elections. Muslim women in India rightly defied such *fatwas* and contested elections.

Such *fatwas* are given more out of ignorance of Islamic jurisprudence. The past traditions should alone cannot be the guide for issuing such *fatwas*. As society is changing social legislation should also change in a healthy way. Such change does not necessarily amount to imitating the west. While we should condemn globalisation in as much as it imposes western hegemony we should not reject modernity per se.

Islamic legislation should be dynamic and the concept of *ijtihad* does provide spirit of dynamism to Islamic shari'ah. It is unfortunate that our 'ulama are quite incompetent to understand modern society. They are totally past oriented and they think everything past is in keeping with Islamic practices. Time has come to critically evaluate all past practices and legislate afresh in many areas in keeping with the Qur'anic values on one hand, and modern spirit on the other.

Our 'ulama laid more emphasis on *v* literature than on the Qur'an, particularly, when it came to legislating about women and the *v* literature reflects medieval feudal ethos than the real Qur'anic spirit. There is, therefore, great need today for women theologian who could properly interpret and appreciate the Qur'anic verses concerning women's rights.

This writer has no hesitation in asserting that Qur'an is very assertive of women's rights and, if read carefully, it accords equal dignity and equal rights to both the sexes. However, this spirit of the Qur'an could be appreciated either by women theologians or men committed to women's rights.

9

Islam and Nationlism

What is relation between Islam and nationalism? Does Islam approve of nationalism or rejects it. Many Muslim theologians and intellectuals maintain that Islam does not approve of nationalism. Islam, they maintain, is an international religion and cannot be confined to any territorial limits. The noted poet from India Muhammad Iqbal said in one of his verses that what is nation (*watan*) is Islam's shroud (*kafan*).

What Iqbal means to say is that nationhood is death of Islam. Muslims constitute an *ummah* and *ummah* cannot be confined to any territorial limit. However, Maulana Husain Ahmed Madani, the eminent Islamic theologian from India, maintained that nation is a geographical concept whereas *ummah* is a religious or spiritual concept. Muslims are *ummah* and are, in that sense, an international community. But, the Maulana says, one should not confuse between the concept of nation and the concept of *ummah*. The former is a political category whereas the latter is a religious category.

Thus it is interesting to note that Maulana Husain Ahmed Madani who was also the president of the Jami'at al-'Ulama-I-Hind', refused to support two nation theory propounded by Jinnah and his Muslim League. He, instead supported the composite nationhood (*Muttahida Qaumiyyat*) and had written a book called *Islam aur Muttahida Qaumiyyat* (i.e. Islam and Composite Nationalism).

It is quite interesting to note that Maulana Husain Ahmed Madani quoted, in his above book, the covenant which the Prophet (PBUH) drew up with people of Madina belonging to different religions and tribes (it is called the *Mithaq-I-Madinah*). The Maulana called it the predecessor of the modern concept of nation. The Prophet drew up the covenant between different religions (Jews, Muslims and pagans) and various tribes (Jewish, Muslim and Pagan) and described this composite community as *ummah wahidah* i.e. one community. Thus the Prophet (PBUH) transcended the boundaries of religion to constitute a geographical community.

Again, the concept of nation is certainly of modern origin. It originated in Europe in 17th century after the Protestant movement challenged the authority of Catholic Church. These nations came into existence on the basis of common language and culture and a sense of shared history. After break up of the Papal authority there was no common religious bond and this religious bond was replaced by common language and culture.

It has also been maintained by many Muslims that in Islam religion cannot be separated from politics thus maintaining unity of religion and politics. These theologians and intellectual thus deny legitimacy of secular nationalism completely. They think that secularism has no place in Islam and secular politics should be completely rejected. Like nationalism, secularism too, is a modern concept and one cannot find any precedence for secularism in the Qur'an and *Sunnah*.

But we find both nationalism and secularism in many Muslim countries. Turkey, for example, is both secular as well as a nation state. Even Indonesia, the largest Muslim country in the world today is a secular nation. Many such examples can be multiplied. It would be very difficult to find unanimity of opinion on such controversial issue. What is needed is *ijtihad* and creative and imaginative thinking which does not clash with fundamentals of Islam.

In fact right in the beginning of Islam there was no political theory. There was, as we have shown in our book *The Islamic State,* there was no concept of state in the Qur'an or in the *hadith* literature. The very concept of state did not exist among the Arabs. It is tribal chiefs who took all decisions in Mecca through a tribal council called *mala'*. There were no state institutions like the police or army even after the Prophet of Islam established a political unit in Madinah. It would be difficult to describe it as a full-fledged 'Islamic State'. Everyone worked voluntarily inspired by moral and spiritual teachings of Islam and under the direct guidance of the Holy Prophet.

There were no defined functions nor there were state functionaries maintained by the state funds. All these functions were purely morally inspired and only reward expected was in *akhirah* i.e. the Hereafter. If one fought against the enemies it was also voluntary courting martyrdom for a moral cause and, if won, could get a share in the defeated enemy property as per the well-established tribal practice.

Similarly, for internal law and order or security there was no police or para- military force. Even the offenders tended to treat their offence as offence against Islamic morality rather than against the state and more often than not, they voluntarily presented themselves for punishment so that they are not punished in the Hereafter by Allah. Obviously such a moral dispensation cannot qualify as a state. It was moral rather than political community.

Since we cannot call it a state it cannot qualify for a term like the Islamic state. This term will not be found even during the Umayyad or Abbasid period. The Umayyad or Abbasid political establishments were known as Caliphate rather than Islamic State. The terms like the Islamic State or Islamic nation are modern day terms. The word *khilafat* also does not connote any concept of state but of succession to the Prophet.

The mode of succession also was full of controversy. There was no unanimity among Muslims as to who or how one would succeed to the Prophet, through nomination or election? It was this question which brought about formal split among the Muslims. Those who are known as Sunnis maintained that succession should be through *bay'ah* (pledge of loyalty) of the believers and those called Shi'ahs maintaining that the Prophet (PBUH) had nominated his successor.

Thus the concept of Islamic state cannot be traced to Qur'an or Sunnah as no such concept existed in those days. The Caliph was treated as the supreme leader of Muslims who led them in religious as well as worldly matters. Again, he was more of a religious and moral leader than a political one. His primary duty was to guide the believers in the light of the Qur'an and Sunnah and by evolving *ijma'* (consensus) among them on controversial matters. The khilafat did have well defined concept of functions, rights and duties. The whole discourse was a moral and not a political discourse. The word siyasah also came into existence much later and was derived from the function of tending and controlling horse. A ruler was also thought of tending and controlling people. There was no such division as the state and civil society.

The concept of civil society is also a modern concept when people got civic rights and the whole political discourse became discourse of rights, not of duties. Those who propound the theory of Islamic state lay stress mainly on duties of believers, not of their rights. One cannot think of modern state without the concept of rights. In the theory of Islamic state the whole discourse – whether it pertains to the rulers or to the people – is a moral discourse and in terms of duties.

Modern democracy cannot function without the concept of, as pointed out, rights. In the Islamic discourse minorities are treated as *dhimmis* i.e. responsibility of the Muslims to protect them and to provide them the security of life and property. Thus Muslims have duty towards minority but there is no concept of minority rights as such. In modern nation state minorities have well defined rights and they can sue the state if these rights are denied to them.

Thus it will be very difficult to talk of Islamic State in the early period in the modern sense. All modern Muslim states are territorial states with well-defined territorial limits whereas we find no such concept in earlier political theories like those of Mawardi who is first major political thinker among the Muslims.

When the khilafat came into existence after the death of Holy Prophet there was no concept of territorial limits. Islam was essentially confined to the Arabian Peninsula. When the first caliph Abu Bakr took over as the first caliph Islam had not spread outside Arabia but then began the Muslim conquests and soon entire Roman (Byzantine) and Iranian (Sassanid) empires were humbled and large parts of their territories became part of Islamic Caliphate.

It was even theorised, after incorporation of these territories that there can only be one caliph, not even one. The caliph was also known as *Amir al-mu'minin* i.e. the leader of the believers and there could be only one leader of all believers, not two. Thus the whole concept was of (religious) belief, not of territory at all. During the Umayyad period this concept of one caliph for entire Islamic world persisted but this became irrelevant when the Abbasids overthrew the Umayyads and Umayyads established a parallel caliphate in Spain. Again this had to be justified that there could be two *Amirs* of believers.

It was just the beginning. Subsequently more and more rulers came into existence and territory rather than religion, became fundamental category. Now each ruler had well defined territory over which he ruled. The moral also began to be overshadowed by the political. The political had of course established its predominance over the moral of early caliphate during the Umayyad period itself. There was hardly any Islamic teaching which was not violated by them. It was far from being an Islamic regime. It was perceived to be quite tyrannical and all prominent companions and companions of the companions of the Prophet were against the Umayyad regime. It was during such regime that a hadith began to be circulated that to be Islamic it was enough if prayer (*salah*) was established which the Umayyads did. All other cardinal principals of Islam like justice, equality, compassion, piety etc. were not necessary. Still the Umayyad rulers claimed to be caliphs. The Umayyads also spread the doctrine of jabr (divine determination) as against that of *qadr* (freedom) to establish that what was happening was inevitable and out of divine will and nothing could be done about it, it being the divine will.

The Abbasid dynasty proved no better. It should also be seen that both Umayyads as well as Abbasids were dynastic rule and had nothing to do with the earlier Caliphate model which was far from being dynastic. The Khilafat was close to elective principle than the dynastic principle. It was because of its elective principle that it was held sacred by Muslims, particularly Sunni Muslims. The Caliphs, unlike the Umayyad and Abbasid rulers, were far more committed to Islam, its values and its teachings. So at all these stages it hardly makes any sense to call these establishments (early Khilafat, Umayyad and Abbasid rules as Islamic State.

In fact, as pointed out before, the very term Islamic State is a modern one coined during the colonial period in nineteenth and twentieth centuries. The medieval period had no concept of state. This concept is fairly modern one. A modern state has a constitution, well - defined powers and a political structure. As against the state there is notion of a civil society which also has its well-defined role and notion of rights. As far as 'Islamic state' is concerned it is very difficult to define its structure.

For example the 'Islamic State' of Saudi Arabia has

no constitution or democracy. The Saudi rulers maintain that the Qur'an is their constitution. There is no concept of civil society in Saudi Arabia as citizens have no rights, they only have duties. Maulana Maududi, on the other hand, talks of 'theo-democracy' rather than democracy. In this 'theo-democracy' too, there is no notion of civil society or human rights. The state cannot even legislate as the Shari'ah is the only legislation and no one has power to alter it. And according to the Islamists, Shari'ah is very comprehensive divine legislation and so there is no need for any legislation except on some subsidiary matters.

Iqbal, the noted poet, was supporter of **ijtihad** and thought that the parliament in an Islamic State would bring about necessary changes in Islamic Shari'ah t6hrough ijtihad i.e. creative interpretation of the Islamic law. Thus as far as Iqbal is concerned, the Parliament shall have legislative powers but as for other Islamic thinkers it will have hardly any legislative powers.

No wonder than that in most of the Islamic countries there is either no democracy, parliament etc. or quite controlled kind of democracy. But all these states in Islamic countries do have well-defined territories and no Islamic country is prepared to cede an inch of its territory. That clearly means that these countries do have well- defined territorial limits. Nation is defined within well-defined territorial limits. Thus nationalism has been accepted by all Islamic countries in the Islamic world. They have also accepted the concept of citizenship as territory alone cannot make a nation.

Thus nationalism is an accepted phenomenon throughout Islamic world. And the nation states exist in all Muslim countries. It is also true that a Muslim from one Muslim country cannot freely go to another Muslim country without valid travel documents and these documents will permit him a limited stay in the host country. This is precisely what Maulana Husain Ahmed Madani points out in his book *Muttahida Qaumiyyat Aur*

Islam that the concept of *ummah* cannot be political but religious and spiritual.

Muslims throughout the world do not constitute a political community. It was possible only in early period of caliphate – during what is called the period of *Khilafat-I-Rashidah* when Muslims could move from one part of the Caliphate to another part. There were no restrictions. But when many Muslim rulers emerged on the scene restrictions began to appear. And now in modern nation-states no Muslim can go and settle in any other Muslim territory unless permitted to do so according to the rules. Thus the concept of the modern nation state has been universally accepted by all Muslims including the Islamists. Ummah, no longer means and Islamic political community.

The religious minorities in these Muslim nation states are no longer treated as per the Shari'ah concept of *dhimmis* but as citizens according to the constitutional provisions of the country. The nation state, be it Muslim or otherwise, is a political and not a religious entity. And citizenship rights are given not on the basis of religion but on the basis of birth in a particular territorial state.

Even Saudi Arabia, which claims that the Qur'an is its constitution, does not allow Muslims from other parts of world to settle in its nationally defined territory. Even for the purpose of Haj one has to obtain visa. Had the Saudi Government followed the Qur'anic model, it should allow all those Muslims, whoever wishes to settle down in its territory as all Muslims are an '*ummah*'. But the Saudi Arabia does not allow any non-Saudi Muslim to settle down in its territory. How can then it claim that Qur'an is its constitution?

Thus in modern times the concept of *ummah* can only be spiritual and religious and not political. Islam, as a religion, is followed by Muslims holding very different nationalities and enjoying different degrees of political rights in their nation states. The territorial spread of these

Muslim states is such that even a confederation is not possible. Also, despite belonging to one religion Islam their mutual relations are not always cordial. In many cases they are hostile and antagonistic.

Let alone all Islamic states, even the Arab states cannot come closer and form a confederation. Iraq invaded Kuwait and Arab states were divided into two hostile camps and even invited the USA to invade Iraq and compel it to vacate Kuwait. Many Arab states support the USA in its campaign against Iraq. Had there been acceptable concept of one *ummah* in political sense such developments would not have occurred. The European nations have created European Union despite different languages and cultures and absence of shared sense of history. But though there is common language Arabic, one religion and one culture, Arabs have not been able to form any such Union of Arab States, let alone of all Muslim countries.

It should also be stressed that except some on the extreme fringe, Muslims generally no longer talk of one *ummah* in political sense. Nationalism and Islamic State has by and large., come to be accepted throughout the Islamic world. Also, despite having common Shari'ah law there are greatly differing political and social needs for legislation and body of legislations in these Islamic countries differ widely form each other. Except a few Muslim countries like the Saudi Arabia Islamic criminal code has been almost abandoned in most of the Muslim countries. It was done so in the colonial period.

It is true that some Muslim countries are trying to bring back the Islamic criminal code but it is more to win political legitimacy by undemocratic rulers than a felt religious need of the Muslim masses. Many Muslim countries like the Sudan and Nigeria have significant proportions of non-Muslim (Christian) population and it creates great difficulties to apply Islamic criminal code to these non-Muslim citizens.

As Muslims have accepted notion of nationalism they should also strive to re-think various connected legal issues through the process of *ijtihad* and evolve new body of legislation fit for modern composite nation states. Today majority of Muslims in the world live as religious minorities in several non-Muslim countries. And, most of them enjoy all citizens' rights (though there may be some or the other difficulties) the Muslim majority countries should also treat their non-Muslim minorities as equal citizens not only as a reciprocal measure but as a matter of principle.

It is true that the concept of *dhimmi* was quite progressive one when Islam established its hegemony in the world in 7th and 8th century but today, with modern concept of citizenship of a nation state, it is certainly inadequate. Thus the concept of dhimmi should be replaced with the concept of citizenship for non-Muslim citizens in all Muslim majority countries.

Also, Islam had evolved the principle of full freedom of conscience and freedom of religion, which was most modern in its content and this should be practised unambiguously by all Muslim political regimes. The Holy Prophet of Islam had given full freedom of faith to not only Jews, but also to pagan Arabs in Madinah through the Covenant of Madinah. This needs to be followed meticulously by the modern political regimes.

Lastly, as nation states have been fully accepted by all Muslim countries they should also accept democratic way of governance which too, is quite in keeping with the Qur'anic spirit and the spirit of Sunnah. Dictatorship, dynastic or military rule is, on the contrary, quite contrary to the spirit of Islam.

10

Shari'ah Punishments (Hudud Laws) and Nation-States

In the last decades of twentieth century many Muslim countries declared themselves as 'Islamic State' and as a proof thereof, enforced the *hudud* laws (the shari`ah laws of punishment for certain crimes) in their countries. It led to much discussion about two things: one, the concept of Islamic state and two, the nature of Islamic laws. The orthodox Muslims and the 'ulama' who absolutise these laws shorn from their context naturally celebrated creation of 'Islamic state' and also enforcement of *hudud* laws.

The very term 'Islamic state' is a modern term. It has nothing to do with the Qur'anic or hadith terminology. While the Qur'an does not mention any form of governance, hadith refers to what is called *'khilafa'* or popularly known as khilafat. The loose governing structure which came into existence after the death of the Prophet (PBUH) was termed as 'Khilafat-i-Rashidah' in the history of Sunni Islam. The Shi`ah, on the other hand, while not accepting the concept of *khilafah*, developed the institute of *imamah*. While the Sunni doctrine of *khilafah* meant a successor to the Prophet (PBUH) had to be elected through the institution of *bay'ah* (i.e. pledge of loyalty) the Shi'ah doctrine upheld the institution of *imamah* through appointment (by the Holy Prophet), and not by election.

Thus the doctrine of *khilafah* became central to Sunni Islam, that of *imamah* became integral part of Shi'ah Islam. But nowhere we find the term 'Islamic state' which a modern political construction in the post-colonial world. To this world neither the concept of *khilafah* could be applied nor that of *imamah*. A modern concept was needed and that was provided by the 'Islamic State'.

There could be endless discussion on the nature and content of Islamic State. Would the Islamic State be run by Parliamentary system or through monarchy or through military establishment? Again it is important to note that these 'Islamic States' were confined to the territorial limits of a nation state unlike *khilafah* or *imamah* which knew no such territorial boundaries. The boundaries of Khilafat-i-Rashidah were in no sense the boundaries of any nation state.

However, what is known as Islamic State today has definite national boundaries and has no single concept or uniform doctrine despite the fact that it is post-colonial human construct. A monarchy, a military dictatorship or a parliamentary form of government, all can claim to an Islamic State. One sees no contradiction in this. Thus the Saudi Arabia, a monarchy, can as much claim to be an Islamic State as Iran or Malaysia, which also claim, with equal validity, to be Islamic States. No one is concerned about the form of government as long as it applies to itself the appellate of 'Islamic State'.

These states generally proclaim Islamic State by proclaiming enforcement of *hudud* laws i.e. the shari'ah laws of punishment for theft, fornication or adultery etc. Besides these *hudud* laws some other shari'ah laws pertaining to personal matters like marriage, divorce, inheritance etc. are also applied. However, other civil laws like the law of contract etc. are hardly applied. Some countries also try to apply laws pertaining to what is known as 'Islamic Banking' though there are many problems in this sphere due to universally accepted practice of interest banking. But rulers in the Islamic State try to enforce *hudud* laws.

As pointed out above the Islamic State is a post-colonial construct. The medieval ruling establishments also did not describe themselves as such. Only the Turkish ruler styled himself as the 'caliph' or *Khalifah*. Others described themselves as 'sultans' as sultan in Arabic means one who controls or one who has hegemony. The Umayyads and the Abbasids – the rulers of first two dynasties of early Islamic period – had styled themselves as Khalifah. But the succeeding rulers to these two dynasties often described themselves as 'sultans'. However, the only Shi`ah Ismaili Fatimid rulers of the early classical period of Islam called themselves as imams according to the Shi`ah doctrine of *imamah*.

It is also important to note that none of these medieval states were nation state as nation state themselves are modern day product. Peoples of different religions, cultures and languages lived in these 'sultanates'. Though Islam was the religion of overwhelming majority of the peoples the Islamic laws applied to them but they were not described as 'Islamic States'.

The post-colonial states in Muslim countries, be they in the Middle East, or West or North Africa or in South and South East Asia, could not describe themselves as kihlafah or *imamah* anymore. The world had changed so drastically ever since that this was not possible nor could any ruler in the Muslim country could claim the exalted status of a Khalifah or an Imam. Among all Shi'ah sects like the Ithna Asharis and Isma'ilis (the Musta'lian sect) the Imam is supposedly in seclusion (though Agakhanis and Zaidis earlier did believe in imam very much in the midst of their followers). Earlier the Zaidi Imam ruled the Yemen but has since been overthrown after a long drawn civil war during the seventies of the last century.

But after colonial humiliation, the Muslim countries wanted to retrieve not only political sovereignty but also religious identity as both were denied to them during the colonial rule. They got political sovereignty through democratic or armed struggle but tried to re-establish religious sovereignty through proclamation of 'Islamic State'. That gave them not only sense of pride but also political legitimisation in the eyes of Muslim masses.

However, the situation differed from countries to countries. For some it was age old historical tradition which was interrupted during colonial rule but for others it was a new invention. In newly created Muslim countries like Pakistan and Bangla Desh it was not the popular will, or historical tradition but creation of Islamic State was an act of military rulers to legitimise their rule. The South Asia never had the tradition of enforcing *hudud* laws and it was long after partition that the military ruler Zia-ul-Haq enforced *hudud* laws in eighties of last century.

In Bangla Desh too it was General Irshad, a military ruler who declared Bangla Desh an Islamic State for purposes of establishing his political hegemony. Bangla Desh had won its liberation from Pakistan through people's struggle and had no such historical tradition of being an Islamic State too. Neither in case of Pakistan nor in case of Bangla Desh there was any popular demand for establishing Islamic State. Nor was there any historical tradition as in countries like Egypt or Saudi Arabia.

Thus there is fundamental difference between the historically existing Muslim states with their own tradition of Islamic laws and those countries which, in post-colonial period, tried to create an 'Islamic State' under certain political compulsions. Here the case of Malaysia is quite unique.

Malaysia is a multi-religious and multi-ethnic country, which came under the British colonial rule. Also, there are several states ruled by kings and sultans, which form a federal structure. The Malay Muslims are in majority. Malays are also the sons of soil – *Bumi Putras*. Under democracy in the post-colonial period, they became conscious of their rights. The Malays were mostly of rural origin, much less educated and much less privileged. All Malays are also Muslims. Thus the Malay movement or the *Bumi Putra* movement put pressure on the rulers to make Islam a privileged religion in Malaysia.

Islam became a state religion but due to substantial presence of non-Muslim minorities like the Chinese it was not possible to enforce *hudud* laws. But other states in Malaysia like Kalantan are enforcing *hudud* laws. This worries many liberal and modern Muslims. Also, ulama and orthodox Muslims feel encouraged to practice polygamy and accord women traditional position in society.

Since all 'Islamic States' try to enforce *hudud* laws, it is important to throw some light on these laws and their position in Islam. It is very important to understand that Islam is basically a religion, a spiritual movement for self-control, for moral life and for purification of self. Its essence also lies in asserting values like equality, human dignity, justice, peace, freedom of conscience, compassion, benevolence, truth, wisdom and sensitivity to others suffering. These are the fines human values.

The tribal chiefs in Mecca in pre-Islamic period did practice some kind of morality known as *muru'ah* (though difficult to translate in English it roughly meant manly qualities). *Muru'ah*, which was widely held concept, included, among other things, hospitality, bravery, tribal solidarity, generosity and independence. These were the highest virtues for the Arabs in pre-Islamic days.

However, they hardly exercised self-control, had no sense of universal morality and spiritual values. Tribal solidarity was highest form of virtue. Their universe did not transcend tribal boundaries. Their values meant nothing outside these boundaries. Islam, on the other hand, was a universal religion, a universal code of conduct. It knew no such narrow limits. It transcended all boundaries – tribal, ethnic, racial and national. It also gave a notion of higher morality, much higher than embraced by the concept of *muru'ah*. We have already indicated the values stressed by Islam above. Islam laid great emphasis on equality and justice on one hand, and human dignity and freedom of conscience, on the other. These values effectively countered the concept of narrow tribalism. But to concretise these values in practice was very difficult and complicated task. So many factors, particularly pertaining to tribal and other existing practices mattered and could not be easily ignored. The Prophet of Islam (PBUH) was not only a preacher but also a great role model of Islamic teachings for his followers. He was often faced with complicated questions of Islamic teachings on one hand, and of existing practices, on the other. Also, he operated in environs where no state institutions for execution of laws existed. It was basically a tribal society wherein he had to apply higher Islamic morality.

Islam's basic objective was to produce a new human being, fashioned by higher values stressed by the Qur'an. The Prophet's main objective was to transform this world entirely. As a supreme teacher and a source of law (the Qur'an describes him as sirajan *munirah* i.e. a lighted lamp showing light) Prophet did two things: he blended certain tribal or other existing practices with higher Qur'anic morality so that his guidance could become useful for the immediate society he was living in.

Secondly, he also showed, through the Qur'anic revelations, the body of higher and transcendent morality. It is this morality and these values which have permanence and all our actions should be guided by this higher morality. The punishments prescribed by the Qur'an are not the essence of its teachings. Its essence lay in its higher morality. The Prophet gave enough indications of this through his *Sunnah* also.

The Holy Prophet very well indicated that compassion is far more superior to the punishment. When one person came to him and said that I was sick and a lady came to see me and I could not resist the temptation and did what is strictly forbidden (i.e. had sexual intercourse with the lady). Please punish me. He was quite weak due to his illness and could not have borne the 100 blows. The Prophet took mercy on him specially because he had confessed to his crime and he took 100 branches of palm date tree and gave him one gentle blow (thus fulfilling the need of the Qur'anic punishment of 100 lashes). This show of compassion had much greater impact on him than the100 blows.

There is another equally important story in the *hadith* literature. A child labour that was underpaid by his employer stole fruit from the employer's garden and ate. He was caught in the act and was brought to the Prophet by the employer demanding punishment of cutting off his hand. The Prophet made thorough inquiry and came to conclusion that the child was underpaid and suffered pangs of hunger, which led him to steal fruit.

Instead of punishing the child he admonished the employer for underpayment and made it obligatory to him to educate the child and provide proper food to him until he grows up. There are many such examples, which make it clear that punishment per se is not the final objective but the reformation of the offender.

There were certain tribal practices and traditions, which could not be ignored altogether by the Prophet (PBUH) if he were to successfully transform that society morally and spiritually. Also, mere acceptance of Islam by the Arabs did not mean they would automatically or easily leave behind all their acts of omission and commission. Certain acts of crime were rampant – murder, theft, rape and robbery. The society had to be cleaned of these crimes and for that the Prophet used certain institutions of tribal practices like cutting of hands for theft or stoning to death for adultery (there is no such punishment for adultery in the Qur'an at all.

Unfortunately these days enforcing these punishments have become very fundamental to any Muslim country declaring itself to be an Islamic state as if it is main criteria of being an Islamic country. In fact equality and justice are far more important criteria for the purpose. Equality of all human beings, protection of human dignity and ensuring socio-economic justice should be much more fundamental to setting up a state on the principles of Islam. But unfortunately hardly anyone pays any attention to such fundamental teachings of Islam and rulers generally rush to the press to announce that henceforth cutting off of hands for theft and stoning to death for adultery will be enforced.

Punishment of stoning to death for adultery has not been prescribed in the holy Qur'an at all. The Prophet is reported to have prescribed this punishment in some cases but there is debate whether he did so before revelation of the verse of 100 lashes for *zina* (rape, fornication and adultery) or after that. There is no conclusive proof that he enforced any such punishment after the revelation of the verse 24:2

In fact stoning to death was prescribed by the Jewish law and the Prophet (PBUH) enforced it in case of a Jew and a Jewess in one case (see Bukhari 23:61), and others apparently occurred before the revelation of the *Surah Nur* (i.e. chapter 24). Also, stoning to death is in contradiction to the verse 4:25 wherein punishment for adultery is half for the slave-girls. Stoning to death cannot be made half whereas 100 lashes, as prescribed in 24:2 can be reduced to 50 in case of slave-girls.

It is unfortunate that in many Muslim countries this law (of stoning to death) is being used more against women than men. This punishment can be enforced only either through self-confession or by producing four witnesses. Since no one ever commits adultery in presence of four witnesses, man goes scot free and woman gets punished as in her case her pregnancy becomes proof. However, no one inquires whether she submitted herself willingly to man's lust or she was raped.

In Pakistan a blind girl was raped by her uncle and she became pregnant and was sentenced to death. In case of her uncle it could not be proved by producing four witnesses. In Nigeria too a woman has been sentenced to death similarly and it has become international issue. This totally discriminatory application of law (about whose authenticity also there is doubt) brings bad name to Islam. If Allah desired to prescribe any such punishment He would have prescribed it clearly in the Qur'an. It is not true that the verse on stoning to death was revealed and that it was written on a leaf which was eaten away by a goat. Such statement would enable non-Muslims to raise many questions about the correctness of the Qur'an. When Allah Himself says 'We are protectors of the Qur'an", how a goat can eat away one of its verses.

In fact any law should not be understood mechanically. It is also important to understand the philosophy of law, causes of its genesis and intention behind enforcing it. Any law applied mechanically can result in grave injustice.

The philosophy of law is to establish a crime-free society by framing laws which will combine elements of punishment and reformation. Punishment can take various forms: by imposing physical pain or through physical confinement. Similarly reforming the criminal can also take various forms – through persuasion, making him undergo certain training or making him see the gravity of his offence, which causes pain to others. Or, one can combine elements of all this along with physical confinement. It will depend on gravity of the offence and individual criminal and extent of his/her crimes. It is for this reason that laws generally provide minimum and maximum punishments. The judge also often takes personal circumstances into account before prescribing the punishment.

Two of the Prophet's instances given above i.e. a child stealing fruit and a sick man submitting to sexual temptation and confessing to the Prophet clearly prove the wisdom with which the Prophet dealt with these cases.

The Prophet did not order cutting off hands of the child who was rather compelled to steal. Our Qadis impose these sentences without exercising such discretion and going into circumstances of the crime.

We should not mechanically imitate the Holy Prophet's reported sayings or doings without understanding the reasons for which he did something. We also have to take the period, tribal practices, geographical circumstances and available institutions. As long as the purpose of the preventing crime is met the nature of punishment does not matter. Prevention of crime is more fundamental than the nature of punishment. In the enforcement of law in Islamic countries punishment becomes more fundamental than prevention of crime. It is not kept in mind what is the purpose of law, what are the circumstances in which a crime was committed and whether it deserves minimum or maximum punishment.

Today more Muslims live in minority situation in non-Muslim countries than in Muslim countries. They commit all sorts of crimes in non-Muslim countries. They cannot be given *hudud* punishments. They are dealt with according to the law of the country they live in. That does not mean ends of justice cannot be met in their case. In India very large number of Muslims live, larger than in many Muslim countries. The British rulers had imposed their own secular criminal code in 19th century itself and the 'ulama had accepted it without any protest. In fact a very prominent *'alim* even translated it into Urdu. Since then Indian Criminal Procedure Code is applicable to Muslims as well as non-Muslims in India, all those Muslim who commit crime are punished according to this code.

The Muslim countries should re-think these laws and modify criminal laws wherever necessary so as to ensure the ends of justice are met and crime does not flourish. Even laws of contract and other civil laws prescribed by Shari'ah have already been given up long ago without causing any problem. Our 'ulama should be given thorough training in modern legal system also along with training in Islamic laws. This will enable them to work out a creative synthesis between Islam laws and modern laws within framework of Islamic shari'ah.

Unfortunately our 'ulama' do not undergo any such training and are trained only in Islamic jurisprudence, its methods and its philosophy evolved by early Muslim jurists. Earlier our Qadis are trained in modern legal philosophy better it is. It will be a great service to the Islamic world.

11
Religion and Economic Justice

It is usually thought that religion is on the side of establishment and vested interests – economic as well as political and it can never become a resource for justice. It is weapon in the hands of vested interests rather than weaker sections of the society. It is rather simplistic statement though it has some historical truth in it. Religion has been misused by not only the rulers but also by the priesthood. Every religious tradition has history of siding with the powerful ruling establishments.

The religious leaders and priests, though pose themselves as pious or religious persons have all the weakness of flesh. They sell religion for their own benefits or side with ruling establishments in their anti-poor policies. No religion has been an exception in this respect. Even Christianity and Islam which stand by weaker sections of society, if we go by the scriptural text of these religions, have no different history. Both the Christian priesthood and Islamic 'Ulama' often sided with oppressive and exploitative ruling establishments. This has led to this simplistic belief that religion *per se* shares the blame.

The priesthood in every religious tradition had had, as pointed out above, its own weakness for power and pelf. They often use religion as a legitimising cover to fulfil their personal ambitions. There is no dearth of such priests even in our own time, and in all religious traditions. Most of the religions began as protest movements against oppression and exploitation but were soon hijacked by vested interests in one way or the other. This is the history of political revolutions also. Even French and Russian revolutions succumbed to hegemonic or exploitative forces though their ideals inspire many even today. These ideals can help fight forces of exploitation even today.

Religion and its socio-economic role should also be assessed in the light of complex social, economic and political forces working in the society. An attempt should be made to study religion and religious ideals through scriptural injunctions and how they were interpreted and practised in the given socio-economic and political conditions. Also the role of priesthood has to be objectively judged whether it allows religion to be hijacked by vested interests or refuses to compromise.

The Biblical pronouncement that meek shall inherit the earth, is an indicator in this direction. Judaism too, lays great stress on justice and Islam of course treats equality and justice as fundamental value. In fact the prophets of these religious traditions belonged to weaker sections of society and they had to wage relentless struggle to liberate their people from the clutches of powerful vested interests both political and economic. These prophets were severely persecuted but they stood their grounds. During their lifetime religion indeed was an option for the poor and oppressed.

Let us examine the central teachings of some of the great religions of the world. Buddhism lays so much stress on compassion and middle path. It also makes its followers sensitive to suffering called *dukkha*. An engaged Buddhist intellectual Kuliyapitiye Prananda, laying stress on this aspect of Buddhist teaching succinctly puts it thus: "avoid improper investment; avoid improper treatment and avoid improper consumption."

These are very religious attitudes. A truly religious

person, will neither invest in improper way leading to exploiting the people nor will ever indulge in over or improper consumption. Many religious leaders lead life of great ostentation and their source of earning depends either on dependence on powerful vested interests and justifying their oppressive ways or on extorting money from their own followers in the name of religion. They, in order to perpetuate their power spread superstitions in the name of religion and induce in them fear of hell, if they do not obey their injunctions. This is, to say the least, most irreligious behaviour. Such behaviour of the priesthood should not be equated with religious teachings.

Christianity was also a great liberative force in its early history until it was adopted by the Roman ruling establishment. Christianity always laid stress on working for the poor. The Christ's companions were all from amongst the poor and he gave good news to them of their liberation. The liberation theologians of Latin America maintain that 'Kingdom of God' should be established here on earth – a Kingdom, which would liberate the poor.

Enrique Dussel, a liberation theologian of Latin America believes in interpreting the Bible in a way that will establish justice for the oppressed. He, in his essay on "Domination – Liberation" says, "Biblical symbolism shows us through the prophetic tradition an argument or line of thought which we shall here set out briefly. In the first place "Cain rose up against his brother Abel, and killed him" (Gen.4.8) and Jesus adds the comment "innocent Abel" (Mt. 23.25). To say "no" to my neighbour is the only possible sin, it is the "sin of the world" or the fundamental sin. The same "no" to my neighbour is said by the priest and the levite in the parable of the Samaritan (LK 10.31-2). Augustine, in the political interpretation of original sin, says clearly that "Cain founded a city, while Abel the wanderer did not". Historically and actually since the fifteenth century has taken the form of a "no" on the part of the North Atlantic centre to the

Indian, the African, the Asian and to the worker, the peasant and the outcast. It has been a 'no' to the woman in patriarchal families, and a "no" to the child in the oppressor's educational system."

In the Jewish tradition delivery of Israel from bondage of Egyptian Pharaoh is an act of liberation. This liberation of children of Israel was led by Moses and it has pride of place in the Jewish history. At the time of the Passover Feast, which the Jews celebrate, the following is recounted so that succeeding generation of Jews may recognise and acknowledge the God who saved them from oppression:

> A wandering Aramean was my father; and he went down into Egypt and sojourned there, few in number; and the Egyptians treated us harshly, and afflicted us, and laid upon us hard bondage. Then we cited to the Lord our God of our fathers, and the Lord heard our voice and saw our affliction, our toil, and our oppression; and the Lord brought us out of Egypt with a mighty hand and an outstretched arm, with great terror, with signs and wonders; and he brought us into this place and gave us this land, a land flowing with milk and honey. (Exodus 26/5-9).

In Islam too, as pointed out before, there is great emphasis on justice both social and economic. The Qur'anic text is full of such verses which exhort believers and non-believers to avoid concentration of wealth. Islam was basically the religion of justice and equality. It wants to do away with all forms of oppression and establish a just society right on this earth. Islam came into existence in Mecca, which was city of international finance in those days as all trade caravans used to pass through Mecca and all transaction took place there.

There was great deal of concentration of wealth in few hands in Mecca and the poor were neglected and exploited. Thus there was a great economic malaise in Mecca and all tribal norms were neglected. Even the near relatives were not taken care of. The Prophet of Islam was greatly disturbed by these conditions. He was greatly disposed towards a just society and no wonder Islam exhorted the Meccan rich not to exploit the poor and distribute wealth. It was distribution of wealth which could lead to establishment of just society. Islam never favoured concentration of wealth in few hands. There are several verses in the Qur'an to this effect.

Thus in an early Meccan *surah* (chapter 104) the Qur'an says: "Woe to every slanderer, defamer. Who amasses wealth and counts it. He thinks that his wealth will make him abide. Nay, he will certainly be hurled into the crushing disaster. And what will make thee realise what the crushing disaster is? It is the Fire kindled by Allah. Which rises over hearts...."

From the verses above it will be seen there is strong denunciation of accumulation of wealth as this accumulation in few hands in Mecca was causing great suffering to the poor and needy in that town. It was indeed for this exhortation for distributive justice that the rich and powerful leaders of Mecca became so hostile to the Prophet of Islam. Some of the scholars of Islam from Egypt have maintained that the hostility of the Meccan kafirs was not so much because of doctrine of *tawhid* (unity of God) as for uncompromising attack of the Qur'an on concentration of wealth. If the Prophet had ceased attacking riches of Meccan tribal leaders they would have accepted Islam in all probability. But that was not to be. The Prophet refused to compromise on that count.

Again in chapter 107 it is said in the Qur'an, "Hast thou seen him who belies religion? That is the one who is rough to the orphan, And urges not the feeding of the needy, so woe to the praying ones, who are unmindful of their prayer! Who do (good) to be seen, and refrain from acts of kindness."

This chapter is quite self-explanatory. The Qur'an says that those who do not take care of orphans and needy are in fact those who belie religion. Real religion is to be compassionate to the suffering of the needy and to help them. Those who pray and neglect the needy and poor are in fact praying to show off. Their prayer is not real prayer. The Prophet (PBUH) is reported to have said that feeding a hungry widow is more meritorious than praying whole night. The Prophet passionately believed in economic justice. Whenever he received some food he would invite others who were hungry to partake of that food. He always distributed the *zakat* amount received from well off Muslims equally among his followers. He never favoured even his own daughter Fatima in this respect. She was in great need of a servant as she had to grind grains herself and her hands had developed blisters but Prophet strictly refused to oblige her. There were more needy than her and they had to be taken care of. These were the exacting standards of the Prophet (PBUH) as far as distributive justice was concerned.

Some people came to the Prophet and asked him what to spend in the way of Allah, the Allah required the Prophet to say that spend what is surplus after meeting your essential needs (2:219). A philosopher-poet from India Muhammad Iqbal even saw in such verses the real alternative to communism. In a just society one should not have more than what is needed for ones basic needs. The surplus left thereafter should be given away to those whose basic needs are not fulfilled.

The concept of basic needs of course might change from time to time and in each epoch there can be consensus about common minimum needs. The state can also determine the level of common minimum needs. In any case there should not be conspicuous consumption when many others are dying of hunger. Islam totally disapproves of conspicuous consumption.

Islam prohibits man from wearing gold ornament

(except a gold ring in one finger) and eat and drink from golden or silver vessels and to wear silken clothes. The early Muslims followed this strictly. Even the early Caliphs used to wear patched clothes though they were rulers of great empire. They led exemplary simple life like the Prophet. It was during the Umayyad period that ruling classes began to lead life of utter luxury and built palaces for themselves in flagrant violations of Islamic teachings. The Abbasids even surpassed the Umayyads in their life style.

It was during these times that rituals became more important than the Islamic values of equality, justice and alleviation of poverty and working for upliftment of weaker sections of society. Islam does not approve of tyrant and exploiting rulers. The Holy Prophet is reported to have said that real jihad is to speak truth in the face of a tyrant. His companions like Abu Dhar Ghifari had this quality.

However, once Umayyad rulers like Yazid renounced all pretensions of following Islam and began to indulge in all pre-Islamic practices based on conspicuous consumption and ridiculed Islamic teachings the real spirit of Islamic revolution was lost. Then the 'Ulama who wanted to be on the right side of these rulers gave a *fatwa* that any ruler who enforces Islamic prayer (*salah*) must be obeyed even if he happens to be a tyrant and exploiter. This was total negation of true Islamic spirit of early period. Thus empire builders hijacked religion for their own purposes. Also, there were some 'ulama who refused to compromise and had to face severe persecution at the hands of rulers.

It is interesting to note that Imam Ghazzali, a great Islamic thinker and a sufi-cum-philosopher maintained that it is prohibited (*haram*) to look at the face of a tyrant ruler and if it be necessary to talk to him one should turn ones face in other direction and talk to him. Ghazzali wrote this during the last days of the Abbasid rule when the Abbasid caliphs had become very weak and Turkish dynasties ruled as sultans using them as mere symbols. These sultans hardly ever cared for Islamic norms. Their only interest was in political power.

The Qur'an requires wealth not to be hoarded; but spent on the poor and needy. In verse 9:34 the Qur'an says, "And those who hoard up gold and silver (dinars and dirhams, which was currency of those days) and spend it not in Allah's way – announce to them a painful chastisement."

It is quite clear from this verse that the Qur'an wanted social and economic justice to be promoted and opposed injustices resulting in turmoil and violence. This is possible only when all sections of society can fulfil their economic needs. But if wealth is concentrated in a few hands this will not be possible and, the rich would spend their wealth on ostentation.

As pointed out Islam discourages life of ostentation. And it was on the basis of such Qur'anic verses that the Holy Prophet even prohibited men to wear silken clothes and to eat and drink from golden or silver vessels and to wear gold ornaments. These were the signs of ostentation. Islam cannot at all brook situation in which while the rich indulge in ostentation, the poor and needy starve in the society which cause imbalances and disturbances. The Prophet's closest companion Abu Dharr used to recite the verse 9:34 quoted above and exhort the Muslims who began to indulge in luxurious living. He would not even shake hands with those who led the life of ostentation. He would demand that all Muslims should lead life of simplicity as the Prophet did.

In the changed environment persons like Abu Dhar found no support for his campaign. He was looked upon as a nuisance by the newly emerging rich. He was exiled to the desert of Rabza where he died a lonely death. His wife did not have even money for buying shroud for him. He was buried in his clothes he was wearing at the time of his death. He paid a heavy price for his Islamic idealism.

It is interesting to note that the Qur'an maintains that the whole social dynamics is determined by struggle between what it calls istid'af and *istikbar* i.e. struggle between the weak and those who have arrogance of power and that Allah is on the side of the weak. Thus we find in the Qur'an, "And We desired to bestow a favour upon those who were deemed weak in the land, and to make them the leaders, and to make them the heirs." (28:5). It is quite an important contribution of the Qur'an to humanity at a time when there was no concept of social justice and the weak and poor were looked down upon as of no consequence and having no rights.

Thus the message of the Qur'an, is clear. It is on the side of the weak and Allah's favour will be for them. There cannot be any compromise on this. According to the Qur'an this struggle will never cease until the weak (*mustad'ifin*) are empowered and since allah is on their side they will triumph one day. Hope and faith are most important weapons of the weaker sections of society and they should not give up these weapons. No struggle can be carried out without these weapons. The Qur'an clearly says "do not despair".

Since the Qur'an wants to bring about just distribution of wealth it gave the concept of the institution of *zakah* a word which means purification. Thus it is only through distribution that social wealth can be purified. And it is only purified wealth, which can bring happiness to all on earth. The Prophet of Islam himself was a role model in this respect. He led starkly simple life and distributed whatever came to the state treasury among the poor and needy. He also instituted the concept of *fitrah* i.e. to spare something for the poor and needy on the occasion of Eid so that the poor also could share the happiness. Giving fitrah is *the sunnah of the Prophet.* Thus Eid cannot be celebrated by the rich without sharing its joys with the poor.

Giving Zakah also is so important that every verse in Qur'an about *salah* i.e. prayer mentions *zakah.* Thus there cannot be real prayer without giving *zakah* on one's earnings. The poor tax is a must for every Muslim. Zakah thus has central importance in Islamic society. It is Islamic doctrine that no one should starve in a truly Islamic society.

The 2nd caliph Umar used to say I will have to account to Allah on the day of judgement even if a dog dies of hunger in my regime. Ali, the son-in-law and spiritual heir of the Prophet and heir to his knowledge also led, like the Prophet, starkly simple life and observed rigorous justice in distribution of wealth from state treasury.

Islam also stresses dignity of labour and forbids all forms of unearned income and stresses the concept of what is known in shari'ah literature as *kasb-i-halal* i.e. legitimately earned income. It prohibits buying food grains unriped in the field and unripe fruit on trees as it amounts to exploiting the peasant. It prohibits all forms of speculation as it often leads to making easy money. There should not be any place for stock exchange operations in Islam as it is purely speculative. Islam also prohibits *mukhabirah* i.e. share cropping as it amounts to unearned income and the Prophet wanted land to be possessed only by actual tillers. No one should retain land if he cannot till it.

Ribah (which means not only usury) but all forms of unearned income has been strictly prohibited by Islam. *Ribah* actually means unjust growth and not only interest. Unfortunately it is used only for usury or interest and not all forms of unjust and unearned growth.

Thus it will be seen that all religions in general, and Abrahamic religions, in particular, lay great stress on economic justice and are an option for the poor. It is in course of history that most of these religions were hijacked by vested interests and made them an integral part of ruling establishments. Thus religions were seen to be on the side of the rich and powerful. It seriously violated the spirit of religion. The capitalist, consumerist society of today has totally disowned religion. A religion, which stresses justice and compassion for suffering can only correct the wrongs of this society.

12
Islam, Muslims and Non-Muslim Countries

As it is well known majority of Muslims in the world live as minorities in non-Muslim countries and hence number of problems arise which need to be tackled. There is large number of Muslims in Europe and North America besides in number of Latin American countries. Certain problems have been aggravated after 9/11 attacks on twin towers in New York.

Number of problems are arising most important of which is Muslims' loyalty to the country they live in. Often it is maintained that they are not loyal to the country of their residence and show their loyalty to some other Muslim country especially where their holy places are situated. In case of Indian Muslims it is alleged that Indian Muslims are loyal to Pakistan. And their loyalty to India is doubted by communal forces in India. This has caused many a riot in post-independence period.

It is maintained that it is teaching of Islam that one should not be loyal to the country of residence if it is non-Muslim country. It is far from true. The Holy Prophet (PBUH) is reported to have said that love of one's country is part of faith (iman). There is nothing in the Qur'an or in hadith literature, which urges Muslims not to be loyal to ones own country. It is quite incorrect and un-Islamic to maintain such an attitude.

Writer's like V.S.Naipaul have also maintained that

those who convert to Islam renounce their pre-conversion culture and adopt Islamic culture. Mr. Naipaul has neither the knowledge of ground reality nor that of Islamic history. Each Muslim community has its own culture, which is basically native culture, culture of the soil. It is flying in the face of facts to say that all Muslims in the world have same culture called 'Islamic culture'. The anthropologists know it very well that no culture from any other country can ever be transplanted wholesale to another country.

And, no non-Arab Muslim country has ever adopted Arab culture, however, Islamic they might be. One has to differentiate between Islam and Arab culture. A culture can never be based solely on religion. History, geography, language, local customs and traditions all play their role in evolution of a culture. Religion, at best, could be, one among these factors. Often, Muslims in the same country like India have several regional cultures like North Indian Muslim culture, Tamil culture, Kashmiri culture, Kerala culture and so on. Thus in the same country Muslim community is far from being homogenous.

Whole of Iran converted to Islam over a few centuries but Iranian culture always maintained their distinctive features. They never compromised over it. Not only that they were often accused of being intensely loyal to their pre-Islamic beliefs like Zoroastrian dualism (thanaviyyat). They were even persecuted by Abbasid rulers for sticking to these beliefs.

This is true of Muslims all over the world. They do not give up their native culture and cultural traditions. Even the personal names never become wholly Islamic. The names of Indonesian Muslims, Malaysian Muslims, Thai Muslims are quite distinctive and not always Islamic. Mr. Naipaul is sadly mistaken if he believes otherwise. Even customs and traditions are quite different and have much in common with the native practices. In fact if anthropological surveys are conducted on what is called life cycle rituals between Muslim and non-Muslim communities of a country or a region of a country it will be found very much similar with minor differences.

Even in Shari'ah law there is provision for what is called *'aadaat* (customs). It is permitted to retain these customs as popular practices. In fact what is known as shari'ah law has incorporated many Arab *'aadaat*. Every Muslim community in every region practices such local *'aadaat* which are quite distinctive. Thus neither Muslims all over the world imitate Arab culture nor show disloyalty to their own country of residence and loyalty to any Arab country. Such allegations are made out of political interests rathe than on the basis of reality.

Well, Muslims may desire to go for *haj* to Mecca and Madina (in Saudi Arabia) once in life as a religious duty but it does not, in any way, translate into political loyalty to that nation. It is sheer canard to maintain that. Also, it is a political canard to maintain that Indian Muslims are loyal to Pakistan. Some Indian Muslims – particularly from North India – may have some sympathies with Pakistan due to cultural and blood ties but it has nothing to do with political loyalty to that country.

Pakistan is again is very diverse country culturally and linguistically. The East Pakistan could not stay with West Pakistan, as Bengali language and culture were very different from the Punjabi and Urdu culture. Thus two-nation theory also collapsed as language and culture proved to be more important than religion. In remaining Pakistan too, there is immense diversity and non-Punjabi Muslims like Sindhi, Baluchi, Pathan and Urdu speaking Muslims have very different cultural traditions. All these people are immersed in their respective cultural traditions.

Muslims in the Globalised World

In our globalised world new sets of problems are arising. Today a large number of Muslims are migrating mainly to the west i.e. to European and North American countries for better economic prospects. There is large number of Turkish Muslims in Germany or Muslims of Pakistani origin in U.K. One also finds quite a few Muslims in countries like Norway, Holland, France and several other European countries. In North America, particularly in the USA there are Muslims practically from every Muslim country be it Arab or non-Arab.

These migrant Muslims, like other non-Muslim migrants, retain their culture and language though it begins to diminish with coming generations. The first generation guards it jealously. America has also given up its earlier melting pot model of identity and has adopted mosaic model instead. Thus Arab Muslims in America are now referred to as 'Arab Americans' or Pakistani and Indian Muslims as 'Pakistani Americans' or 'Indian Americans' and so on. It is very good attempt to preserve and promote democratic pluralism. While in India we see growing intolerance and national chauvinism western countries, particularly North America (which includes Canada) is showing growing tolerance for democratic pluralism.

However, the events of 9/11 have created some strains and new questions are arising. Islam is coming increasingly under cloud. Its teachings are being critically examined. The Qur'an is being increasingly studied by Americans and they are raising questions about its teachings. Today the Qur'an is being read much more widely than ever before. However, reading the Qur'an literally or in translation creates its own problems. To understand the Qur'an in its proper spirit one should be thoroughly acquainted with its historical context. If one does not have this background many verses are likely to be severely misunderstood. For example, there are verses about unbeliever (*kafirs*), Christians and Jews which, if not seen in the context in which they were revealed, they are likely to be misunderstood.

There are verses in the Qur'an which say Christians

and Jews are friends of Muslims and there are verses which say they are not friends of Muslims and they cannot be trusted. All this leads to confusion or, if quoted selectively, can be misconstrued as Muslims being hostile to other communities. These verses, therefore, should be seen not only in the background of events but also in the context of overall teachings of Qur'an.

The over all teachings of the Qur'an is of tolerance of other faiths and acceptance of basic truth in all religions. The basic premise of the Qur'an is that Allah has sent His guides (*haad*) for every people and every nation (13:7) with the same truth. Therefore, it is duty of Muslims to accept all the prophets and show them eoual respect (2:136) In fact, according to the Qur'an, it is duty of all Muslims to show equal respect to all the prophets sent by Allah. Qur'an mentions all Biblical prophets among them but many sufis and theologians have added even non-biblical religious personalities including from India to this list.

Thus tolerance of all religions is a must for Muslims. Qur'an also maintains that there are different ways of worshipping Allah and one should not quarrel about them (2:148). And even if some people worship other than Allah, one should not abuse others Gods (6:109). Thus Qur'an does not teach conflict with other religions but tolerance and harmonious living and mutual respect for each other. Today we promote pluralism but Qur'an required Muslims to accept pluralism as Allah's Will. Allah has given each nation a law and a way and this pluralism is the test for us (for living in peace and harmony) (5:48)

Today freedom of religion and free speech is among the basic values of our society. When Islam appeared on the scene in 7th century A.D. these values simply did not exist. Intolerance and fanaticism were widely prevalent. But the Qur'an promoted respect for all religions and acceptance of basic truth of all religions. It also taught freedom of conscience and laid stress on it (2:256). Of course it is about no compulsion in religion but it applies to all matters of conscience. Religion is an integral part of ones conscience and hence when there is no compulsion in matter of religion there cannot be compulsion in any other matter and according to the Qur'an human beings have full freedom of conscience.

Islam is thus most modern religion. It guarantees religious freedom on three levels: 1) one can follow any religion one likes or no religion at all; 2) one can worship any god one likes and 3) one can worship in any way likes. Islam has its own beliefs and its own way of worship but others cannot be compelled to adopt them.

Also, the Qur'an clearly says that there are different laws and different ways for different communities to follow. The Qur'an says, " For everyone of you We appointed a law and a way. (5:48) Thus the law and the way depends on the genius and requirements of the community. Many Muslim 'ulama (theologians) also maintain, on the basis of such verses that *din* (basic religion) is one and laws (shari`ahs) differ from people to people and community to community.

There is thus no question of coercion in matters of religion. Everyone should be free to follow any religion or no religion at all. Muslims should respect others freedom according to their scripture. In other words Muslims should co-exist with others in peace and harmony. They should respect laws and ways of other communities. If there are any problems they should be solved through dialogue

Muslims have been exhorted by the Qur'an to "argue not with the People of the Book except by what is best ...(29:46). The definition of the People of the Book should also not be restrictive but inclusive. In the past Muslim `ulama when confronted with other communities, sought to include them among the People of the Book. The modern constitutional laws should also be respected as these constitutions are based on certain values like justice, freedom of conscience, human dignity, freedom of religion and rights of individual.

Thus where Muslims are in minority and living in non-Muslim majority countries they should respect the constitutional provisions. The right to freedom of religion is very valuable right and it should be used as creatively as possible. The Muslims in many non-Muslim countries like India, America, Canada and European countries do live in peace and harmony with their non-Muslim co-citizens.

Another important provision in the Qur'an which is obligatory on Muslims is practicing justice (*'adl*). A Muslim cannot be unjust, if he is true Muslim. An unjust Muslim is a contradiction in terms. In the Qur'an justice is integrally connected to the concept of piety (5:8). There are several injunctions in the Qur'an to stand by justice. The Qur'an says "O you who believe, be upright for Allah, bearers of witness with justice; and let not hatred of a people incite you not to act equitably. Be just; that is nearest to observance of piety. (5:8). Also in 4:58 the Qur'an says, "..and that when you judge between people, you judge with justice."

Thus justice is very fundamental to Islam. Even hatred and hostility with people should not make any Muslim act with injustice towards them and he should always judge between people justly. Again it is most modern value which the Qur'an so much emphasized hundreds of years ago. Justice is emphasized by all modern constitutions in democracies. Thus Muslims should feel quite comfortable in modern constitutional democracies. A Muslim should not approve of any undemocratic regime based on coercive dictatorship. Coercive dictatorship flouts, all norms of justice most flagrantly. Thus, if justice is such fundamental value, a Muslim should not tolerate dictatorship in any form. He should wage peaceful struggle against it and for ushering in democracy.

Democracy is so essential for an Islamic set up as without it one can neither realize freedom of conscience nor have a just dispensation. As pointed out freedom of conscience and justice are most fundamental to Islam, democracy also becomes essential, as these values cannot be realized without democracy. Respect for human dignity is also an essential teaching of Qur'an (see 12:70). Human dignity cannot be respected in a non-democratic system.

It is also to be noted that justice cannot be achieved through violence or feeling of revenge. Such an attitude begets more violence. It is totally wrong to think that one can achieve justice through violent or terrorist means. On the other hand, it begets more violence. It is for this reason that Qur'an's emphasis is on peace, not on violence, as many people think. Jihad is nothing but utmost efforts to realize justice peacefully.

In non-democratic set up violence becomes the rule and one has to use violence to ward off violent attacks. Islam permitted violence in defense in non-democratic tribal society where war was rule rather than exception. Peace was exception in that society. The concept of *qisas* (retaliation) is not a norm; it is only permitted in the given society. The norm is forgiving (*ghafr*), for Allah's name is *Ghafur al-Rahim* i.e. (Forgiver, Compassionate).

Thus retaliation was permitted in a society, which was non-democratic and violent and for a democratic society one should not practice revenge and retaliation but forbearance and forgiveness. These are high moral qualities. In a democratic society jihad takes the form of only peaceful democratic struggle for justice. The understanding of jihad in early Islamic society cannot, and should not be binding on today's generation of Muslims. Today Muslims have right to attempt *ijtihad* (reinterpretation) of jihad as democratic struggle for justice. Jihad can be permitted only for realization of justice and in modern democracy it can take only democratic form.

It should be remembered that values *per se* are any time more important than what form realization of these values take in a given society. If justice could be realized in medieval society through war it can be realized today through peaceful democratic manner. What is ultimately important is justice, not war or *jihad*. The forms of struggle would be decided according to the given situation. But often, on account of dogmatism and narrow mindset form struggle takes becomes more important than the reason for that struggle. Thus in Muslim mind jihad has become more important than the reason for waging it. We have to reverse this and make people understand that it is justice, which is important, not jihad (as war), which was the possible form in those days.

We have also to bear in mind that in democracy all people live under rule of law and the struggle for justice has to be collective, Muslims and non-Muslims together. It should be a common project. The Qur'an expresses this by using the word *naas* (people). All people in a democracy should ensure justice through democratic struggles. However, it is obligatory for believers – Muslims – to struggle for justice, even others do not join in. It is obligatory for Muslims to ensure justice not only for themselves but for people as a whole, even for their enemies. This is not only desirable but obligatory.

Thus any act that leads to gross injustice in the society, much less an act of terror, must be fought against. One cannot condone violence by one section of society against another section, be it on grounds of religion, or any ground. It runs against the spirit of qur'an.

It is duty of Muslims living in any non-Muslim country to fight for justice not only within the country but also against external forces. If anyone commits aggression against the country (Muslim or non-Muslim) it is patriotic duty of Muslims to defend the country against external aggression. The Prophet of Islam has set an example in this respect through what is known as *Mithaq-I-Madina* i.e. covenant of Medina. When the

Prophet migrated from Mecca to Madina he drew up a covenant with the people of Medina irrespective of their religion – Jews of various tribes, Muslims of various tribes and non-believers (pagans) of various tribes to form a community, which he called *ummah wahidah* (one community) and made it obligatory for all the signatory to the covenant to defend Medina together, if attacked by outsiders.

It should be noted that in this covenant religion was no condition for forming an *ummah wahidah* (one community) and defense of the city was duty of all. It should be noted that at the time of drawing up the covenant Muslims were in minority in Medinah. Thus wherever Muslims are in minority it is their duty to defend their country along with other non-Muslims.

And wherever Muslims are in majority it is obligatory for them to ensure full justice to religious minorities. Justice is more fundamental than any ones religion. Non-Muslim minorities should not only be free to follow their religion and protect their identities but also should be entitled to equal political rights. One must distinguish between religious community and political community. As religious communities they may have their distinctive practices but as political community they should have same rights and this is what the Prophet (PBUH) meant by calling the Medinese community, which included Jews, Muslims and pagans as *ummah wahidah*.

In modern democratic polity Muslims should enjoy equal rights if in minority and by same logic non-Muslims should enjoy equal political rights, if Muslims are in majority. This is what justice demands. As pointed out at the outset majority of Muslims lives as minority in various countries and is enjoying equal political rights. They should also reciprocate in the same spirit.

13
Armed Fight is Not Jihad

These days the American scholars and academics are having repeated discussions on the meaning and significance of jihad in Islamic tradition. There are those scholars who are genuinely interested in understanding the meaning and significance of jihad and those who, with agendas of their own, want to either deliberately distort meaning of jihad or select Islamic sources selectively to prove their pre-conceived meaning. Some of them do it with malicious intention, no with academic objectivity. This trend has existed for centuries but has again been accentuated in post 9/11 of 2001.

We have before us an article "Jihad and the Professors" written by Daniel Pipes and published in *Commentary* of November 2002. The author is bent upon proving that jihad in Islam is nothing but an "armed warfare" against non-Muslims. Nothing else could be admissible. No amount of different meanings given by respectable academics is admissible. It is explained away as an attempt "to advance their agenda within Western, non-Muslim environments". Mr. Pipes has no regard for conscientious opinion of many Muslim scholars and even some Muslim clerics. For him jihad is only armed conflict with no-Muslims. In fact Pipes even says that it is not even defensive war but offensive and aggressive warfare against non-Muslims.

In the beginning of his above article he quotes opinions of many Muslim and other sympathetic non-

Muslim scholars but only to refute them. For example, David Little, a Harvard professor of religion and international affairs, had stated after the attacks of September 11, 2001 that jihad "is not a license to kill," while to David Mitten, a professor of classical art ad archaeology as well as faculty adviser to the Harvard Islamic Society, "true jihad is the constant struggle of Muslims to conquer their inner base instincts, to follow the path of God, and to do good in society." He also quotes Iranian professor Roy Mottahedeh saying " a majority of learned Muslim thinkers, drawing on impeccable scholarship, insists that jihad must be understood as a struggle without arms."

Mr. Pipes also tells us that he surveyed more than two dozen experts and only four of them admitted that jihad has any military component whatsoever and even they, Pipes says, "with but a single exception, insist that this component is purely defensive in nature. Vaslerie Hoffman of the University of Illinois is unique in saying that, "no Muslim she knew would have endorsed such terrorism [as the attacks of September 11], as it goes against Islamic rules of engagement." Then she comments "No other scholar would go so far as even this implicit hit that jihad includes an offensive component."

He also quotes John Esposito of Georgetown, perhaps the most visible scholar of Islam, holds that "in the struggle to be a good Muslim, there may be times where one will be called upon to defend one's faith and community. Then [jihad] can take on the meaning of armed struggle." He quotes another specialist holding this view is Abdullahi Ahmed An-Na'im of Emory, who explains that "War is forbidden by the *shari`ah* [Islamic law] except in two cases: self defense, and the propagation of Islamic faith." And Pipes also quotes Blake Burleson of Baylore to the effect that "in Islam, an act of aggression like September 11 'would not be considered a holy war'.

He surveyed more scholars as to their opinion of jihad. Many of them, a large contingent indeed, deny that jihad has any military meaning whatsoever. For Joe Elder, a professor of sociology at the University of Wisconsin, the idea that jihad means holy war is "a gross misinterpretation." Rather, Elder says, jihad is a "religious struggle, which more closely reflects the inner, personal struggles of the religion." Another scholar Dell De Chant, a professor of world religions at the University of South Florida, jihad as usually understood means "a struggle to be true to the will of God and not holy war."

Daniel Pipes quotes opinions of many more academics all of whom maintain that jihad is internal struggle to be a good Muslim and not a military offensive of any kind. The Qur'an hardly uses the word jihad for war or for fighting with arms. It mostly means striving in the way of Allah and striving hard. For example the verse 2:218 says, "Those who believed and those who fled (their houses) and strove hard (*jahadu*) in Allah's way- these surely hope for the mercy of Allah." Similarly in 29:6 Qur'an says, " And whoever strives hard(*jahada*), strives for himself. Surely Allah is Self sufficient, above (need of) (His) creatures."

In the Qur'an jihad has always been used in the sense of 'making efforts' or 'striving hard', not making war. Jihad in the sense of war, is a post-Qur'anic usage. This itself is an interesting area of research as to when and how the word jihad came to be used in the sense of war. In Arabic language jihad does not mean war. For war there are other words like *harb* or *qitaal*. The Qur'an also uses these words for war. Thus we find the use of the word harb in the sense of war in verses like 9:107, 5:33, 2:279, 5:64, 8:57 and 47:4. In all these verses the word harb and its derivatives have been used for war.

And the word qital has been used in Qur'an in 167 verses. If we consult Arabic lexicon we will find that the words *jahada* and *jaahada* signify that a person strove, laboured or toiled; exerted himself or his power, or efforts, or endeavors, or ability; employed himself vigorously, diligently, studiously, sedulously, earnestly, or with energy; was diligent or studious, took pains or extraordinary apins. These meanings are derived from well-known lexicons like *Lisan al-Arab*, Qamoos of Firozabadi and Lane's Arabic English lexicon etc. This is the classical usage of the word and also its usage in the Qur'an.

However, Daniel Pipes is not at all convinced of this meaning of jihad despite array of opinions of eminent scholars and Islamic thinkers. Mr. Pipes, maintains that jihad means nothing but war irrespective of what was its original usage and what is its usage in the Qur'an. He does not even refer to the Qur'anic usage of the word. He quotes only from the post-Qur'anic sources to substantiate his case.

Thus Pipes says, "In pre-modern times, jihad meant mainly one thing among Sunni Muslims, then as now the Islamic majority. It meant the legal, compulsory, communal effort to expand the territories ruled by Muslims (known in Arabic as *dar al-Islam*) at the expense of territories ruled by non-Muslims (*dar al-harb*). In this prevailing conception, the purpose of jihad is political, not religious. It aims not so much to spread the Islamic faith as to extend sovereign Muslim power (though the former has often followed the latter.) the goal is boldly offensive and its ultimate intent is nothing less than to achieve Muslim dominion over the entire world."

If Pipes had carefully studies the Islamic history he would have known that Muslims, right from earliest times never used war (not jihad in any case) for spreading faith. Faith can never be spread with the help of sword or gun. It is only political sovereignty, which can be imposed through sword. But as far as Qur'an is concerned it does not permit war or aggression for any purpose, not even for spreading political sovereignty, much less for spreading the faith. There is not a single verse in the Qur'an for using arms for any purpose except for defensive purpose. And even while defending, the Qur'an advises Muslims not to transcend certain limit.

The verse 2:190 is quite categorical about it. "And fight (*qaatilu*) in the way of Allah those who fight against you *but be not aggressive. Surely Allah loves not the aggressors*" (emphasis supplied). Thus both things are clear here. You fight only those who fight you and do not be aggressors as Allah does not love aggressors. Those who accuse Islam of being a religion of aggressors and fighters do so either out of ignorance of the text of the Qur'an or do so maliciously.

There are several verses in the Qur'an about war and fighting but if read in proper context in which these verses were revealed, it becomes quite clear that they were all revealed in the background of aggression by the unbelievers of Mecca. It should also be noted that the unbelievers of Mecca, called kafirs or *kuffar* (Arabic plural) were not fighting against the Prophet of Islam and has followers just because the Prophet was attacking idol worship. The motives of conflict with Muslims were very complex. And the Prophet's objective was also not simply to oppose idol worshipping. That was not the only evil prevailing in the Arab society of his time.

It is very important to understand all this for developing proper perspective on Islam and its teachings. Such oversimplified approach that the conflict was mainly on the question of idol worshipping, distorts the issue and gives rise to the belief that Islam urged Muslims to do away with idol worshipping even with the help of sword.

The Qur'an considers religious beliefs a matter of conscience and there can be no compulsion in matter of religion as the Qur'an puts it in 2:256 (*la ikrah fi' al-din*). Every one can believe and worship God the way one wants (2:148). Where is then the question of spreading the faith with sword?

In fact the Qur'an was preaching a new way of life which was not acceptable to the kafirs of Mecca. In Meccan society of the Prophet's time there was no respect for morality and there was widespread corruption, moral corruption above all and total neglect of weaker sections of society. There was concept of tribal morality but in urban areas like Mecca a new society was emerging and new moral code was absolutely necessary. Also, the tribal code, even if followed meticulously, was far from enough for the new society emerging in Mecca.

The Qur'an gave a universal code of morality with emphasis on equality, justice, truth, non-violence (yes, there is great deal of emphasis on non-violence as a value in Islamic ethic), compassion and human dignity. These values, as can be seen, are quite universal and transcend narrow tribal limits. The pagan Arabs and their leaders rejected this universal morality, as they were too proud of their tribal code. Any one not belonging to their tribe could be fought against and considered inferior. And all non-Arabs were inferior to Arabs. There was no concept of human dignity.

The Meccan chapters of the Qur'an lay great emphasis on social justice and taking care of the weak. The powerful merchants of Mecca who had become international traders were neglecting even tribal morality, let alone accepting universal morality of the Qur'an. According to the tribal morality of Arabia the tribal chiefs should take care of orphans, widows and the poor. Even they were being totally neglected. The Meccan chapters of the Qur'an exhort them to take care of these weaker sections of society.

Also, the tribal chiefs of Mecca looked down upon the poor, the slaves and women. All those who were from lower strata of society had no worth for them. They looked down upon the Prophet as he was a poor orphan, too low in their esteem and now this poor orphan was claiming to be prophet and exhorting them how to behave. And, he was also exhorting them not to accumulate wealth (something they were very much after) and spend it for welfare of weaker sections of society in the name of Allah.

The tribal chiefs referred to as *kuffar* by the Qur'an were vehemently opposed to the Prophet for these reasons and not merely because the Prophet exhorted them not to worship idols. They could have gladly accepted worshipping one God if the Prophet had not insisted on giving up accumulation of wealth and living life of luxury these *kuffar* would have gladly accepted Islam. What they did not like was that the Prophet gave equal respect to slaves and treated them as dignified human being as per the Qur'anic injunction in 17:70 (We have given dignity to all children of Adam).

Thus this new morality of Islam wanted to create a new human person what is called in the Qur'anic terminology a *mu'min* – a believer, a faithful – a believer in and faithful to the Qur'anic values and morality. The leaders of Mecca were not prepared to give up life of luxury, life of ease and comfort and were too proud to accept equality of all human beings, of poor and rich, of slave and free beings, of man and women.

And the Prophet was not prepared to make any compromises on these issues. And all tribes had their own gods and goddesses and their identities were tied up with them. This led to social fragmentation and tribal wars. Islam wanted to end this by preaching unity of God and consequently unity of all human beings. While the Prophet would not compromise on this the kuffar would not accept this and hence the conflict between Muslims and them.

We should also bear in mind that in pre-Islamic society there was great deal of violence and it is this violence which continued when the Prophet began to preach. Some people who do not know the history of pre-Islamic Arabia or are prejudiced against Islam see violence as product of Islam. Nothing could be farther than truth.

The Prophet's (PBUH) mission was to establish a just and peaceful society. And the tribal chiefs of Mecca were a powerful obstacle in his project. Without justice it was not possible to have peace. When the Prophet talked of justice the powerful merchants of Mecca began to inflict violence on him and his followers. All weaker sections of society had rallied round the Prophet, the poor, the slaves, the women and the youth. The Prophet's clearest choice was justice and peace.

When the Prophet migrated to Madina due to severe persecution of his followers and to avoid violence and bloodshed the powerful of the Mecca pursued him to Madina and wars followed. The Prophet tried to win over the Jews by entering into a covenant with them and pagan Arabs (*mithaq-e-Madina*) to have peace in Madina the *kuffar* of Mecca secretly negotiated with the Jews and struck a deal with them. The wars followed and Jews broke the covenant of security and peace with the Prophet and tried to help the *kuffar* of Mecca. They even tried to eliminate the Prophet. Who is then to be blamed for violence that followed?

The Qur'an showed highest respect for the Jewish religion and even prayed in the direction of the Bait al-Maqdis which was a Jewish sacred place. What more the Prophet could have done to have peace. But it was his enemies who did not want peace in the society, the vested interests who thrive on exploitation and denial of justice always resort to violence.

In view of so much violence in the society the Qur'an also had to permit defensive violence. It is a fact of human history that justice could never be established in any society without fight against the powerful vested interests. Even America could not establish a democratic society without a fierce civil war. Freeing slaves was not an easy task. There was so much turmoil in American society even for conceding equal rights to blacks. The whites are not ready to concede equality to blacks even today in practice, though in theory American Constitution accords equality to them.

How difficult it must have been for the Prophet to establish peace in a violent Arab society where various kinds of interests were clashing, one can imagine. The Qur'an had to emphasize two different dimensions of peace – the external and internal. The external had to be met by defensive resistance, a comparatively easier project. But more difficult was to resist and control inner self and to transform ones inner self – a true jihad. If one cannot transform inner-self the external peace, even if established, cannot last longer. That is why in one of the Prophet's hadith we find that greater jihad (*jihad-i-akbar*) is to control ones inner-self.

It is just not true that Qur'an urges Muslims to fight aggressively against people of other faiths to spread Islam. This goes against the very spirit of Islam and its doctrine of freedom of conscience. It is important to note that Qur'an again and again repeats four words which also represent its value-system - *'adl, ihsan, rahmah* and *hikmah* (justice, benevolence, compassion and wisdom). Thus the Qur'an wants to establish a just society for benevolence of human beings with compassion and wisdom. Violence has no place in ushering in such a society.

Mr. Daniel Pipes asserts that jihad was always used to expand Islamic territories what he calls *dar al-Islam* and to extend control over non-Muslim territories or over dar al-harb. And this was considered jihad. He also asserts, but gives no citation or proof that the Prophet fought 78 wars of which only one was defensive. The burden of proof of course lies on Mr. Pipes. All Islamic scholars and classical theologians are unanimous that the Prophet never aggressed against others. He was forced to fight the battles. Even while conquering Mecca (in fact conquering is a wrong word, he just peacefully entered Mecca) he did not shed blood. He pardoned all his enemies. He pardoned even Hindah who had taken out liver from the body of Hamzah, Prophet's uncle who was great soldier of Islam, and chewed it. That was in keeping with the Qur'anic morality – to suppress ones anger and not to thirst for revenge.

To fight wars of aggression as Pipes alleges, is strictly forbidden by the Qur'an. And the prophet never violated the injunctions of the Qur'an. But it cannot be said of other Muslims. It is not my case that Muslim rulers did not aggress against other non-Muslim rulers. That might have even claimed it to be jihad to legitimize their wars of aggression. But any ones claim cannot make it jihad.

It is also important to note that the word jihad in the sense of armed fight is post-Qur'anic usage. Jihad, as already pointed out earlier, has not been used in this sense in the Qur'an. There may be this kind of usage however, in hadith literature but let us remember that *ahadith* contained in the six authentic collections (*Sihah Sittah*) were compiled centuries after the demise of the Holy Prophet. We know that meanings of words do undergo transformation with passage of time and they acquire new usage and new meaning.

Also, it is highly necessary to ascertain what scripture prescribes and how its followers behave. And also, one should not hold entire community guilty for what some members of the community do. The Christians also have not practiced what is prescribed by the Bible. Many Christian rulers have indulged in bloodshed on large scale but for this neither Christianity nor all Christians can be blamed.

It is not true that Muslims in modern times, as Pipes writes, are indulging in apologia for jihad. In earliest times in history of Islam there were Muslims who did not agree with those rulers who invoked jihad for their territorial aggrandizement. The Sufis, for example, never supported wars. They were peace lovers and were devoted to love of God and practiced it with great intensity. Most of the Muslims in our own times are opposing what happened on 9/11 with all sincerity. They are not doing so only to live in America as Daniel Pipes assumes unjustly.

14
American Aggression Against Iraq – Who is Terrorist ?

(I)

The aggression against Iraq by President Bush of America and Prime Minister Blair of the U.K. has attracted worldwide condemnation and rightly so. The forces of these two countries are ruthlessly bombarding Iraq. Even market places and civilian buildings have not been spared – probably deliberately targeted. Hundreds of civilians have been killed in last two weeks. More they (USA and U.K.) get frustrated more ruthlessly they bomb particularly Baghdad. And ironically now it is Bush and Blaire who are villains and President Saddam Hussain who is a hero.

This raises one question – who is greater terrorist – Osama bin Laden or Bush and Blaire? When the New York twin towers were attacked on 9/11 the world media raised hell and condemned not only bin Laden (which would have been justified) but Islam itself and equated Islam with terrorism. There were host of articles in leading news papers and magazines round the world condemning Islam as responsible for terrorism and that Islam is a violent religion which urges upon its followers to wage jihad.

Now that President Bush is committing all these crimes against humanity in the name of 'liberating Iraq' who shall we blame for it? Osama bin Laden was of course an individual, a head of al-Qaida, an organisation floated by Osama himself, and not elected by any people or Muslims of the world or any country, for that matter. Even then American media wrote as if all Muslims were responsible for the crime committed by Osama.

Can the crimes against humanity being committed by Bush – an elected representative of USA - on the people of Iraq be blamed on Christianity since he invokes Christianity, like Osama who invoked Islam for the crime he committed against three thousand or so people working in those towers. Bush is also invoking Christianity but organising Christian prayers in White House or conducting the Bible study circles and invoking God time and again?

No, clear no. Christianity or Christians are in no way responsible for what Bush is doing. Like Osama, Bush himself alone is responsible for his crimes. His greed for oil makes him shed pints of human blood. And, let us make no mistake, it is not oil alone. He is being backed in his crimes by scores of American multi-nationals, apart from Israel, are also backing this aggression against the innocent people of Iraq. The military-industrial complex is well known for its greed for money and this formidable combination in the USA keeps war machinery going in one part of the third world or the other so that it can make tons of money. The Zionists of Israel also are powerful block urging American ruling establishment to destroy the Arab countries around them so that it can fulfill its expansionist dreams.

It is well known that whenever vested interests want to grab power or someone elses wealth or property they invoke God on their side and create religious sanctions to legitimise their misdeeds. Laden and Bush-Blaire are no different in this respect. If one examines the terminology being used by Bush-Blaire it makes things abundantly clear.

Bush makes it out as if he is doing all this to 'liberate' Iraq from a dictator. Mr. Blaire also recently said when confronted by some for killing innocent civilians said that one had to pay this price for ridding this world of dictators. If such wars are not fought, the world, according to Bush and Blair will be full of dictators. What an excuse for war. As if America has not supported dictators in Asia, Africa and Latin America all these years.

These dictators have committed worst crimes against their people with full support of American ruling establishment for years during cold war. Mr. Blaire is also fully aware of all this. And yet today America wants to project itself as champion of Iraq's liberation by getting it rid of Saddam Husain.

America has been demanding for years now that Iraq be disarmed and weapons of mass destruction (WMD) be destroyed. Now this war of aggression has clearly shown who possesses weapons of mass destruction Iraq or America? America is the only nation in possession of huge piles of WMD, no one else. It can destroy the world several times over. It has used these weapons in several countries in killing innocent people. In Hiroshima-Nagasaki it killed hundreds of thousands of people, in Vietnam it killed unarmed peasants working in their fields. For what? To destroy communism.

What kind of liberty it wants – liberty for people or liberty for American ruling establishment to loot and exploit poorer nations? However, though American ruling establishments have been using rhetoric of freedom only to establish their hegemony all over the world. To retain this hegemony it can destroy all those who come in its way. As far as America is concerned the words like freedom, liberty, human rights and so on are nothing but empty rhetoric. Any person of common sense knows this.

As for WMD America has been insisting on this for last 13 years. Who does not know that America had supplied technology to Iraq to manufacture poisonous gases so that these weapons could be used against Iran to destroy Khomeini's revolution. It was American ruling establishment, which wanted to use Iraq to destroy Islamic revolution in Iran. It is for this reason that Bush is so sure that Iraq posses WMD. USA itself had supplied this technology for its own selfish ends.

Iraq did try to develop nuclear capability for manufacturing weapons. But much before it could do so Israel destroyed Iraq's nuclear plant through air raid. It was also an act of great aggression but USA allowed it and it allowed it with impunity. Unfortunately no other country condemned it, not even the Arab countries.

In the Arab countries all monarchs and Sheikhs who suppress democracy in these countries have been friends of American rulers as they serve American interests in a most servile way. America has launched its war of aggression from Kuwait and without support from Kuwait and without use of Kuwait territory it could not have launched this aggression against Iraq. Who is ruling over Iraq? Is the Sheikh of Kuwait not a dictator? Why then America so keen to support the ruling Sheikh in Kuwait? It is greatly handicapped since Turkey's Parliament did not allow USA to land its army in Turkey and launch invasion against Iraq from Turkey. Now Powel is on the visit to Turkey to persuade its rulers to allow American army to invade Northern Iraq.

Thus most of the Islamic countries do not have democracy today thanks to US support for dictators in Islamic countries. And in Iraq they want to establish 'democracy' and want to 'liberate' people of Iraq. US did not have time to study the social and political history of Iraq. People of Iraq may or may not like Saddam but they do love their country, their nation. They will not allow outside aggressors to 'liberate' them.

It is heartening to note that unlike the cold war era people cannot be easily deceived now by deceptive rhetoric. The US and U.K. ruling establishments can no longer deceive people of their own countries by this deceptive rhetoric of 'democratic values' and 'liberating' people of 'corrupt and ruthless dictatorship'. People today can easily understand the real intent of aggressors and their naked interests. In fact the American aggression against Iraq is any time worse than 19th century colonial invasions of European countries.

Earlier the Christian church used to remain silent as USA often used anti-Communist rhetoric to invade other countries. This time in the absence of any communist power USA cannot deceive Christian Church to justify its aggression against Iraq. The Churches, both Catholic and Protestant, did not buy American position and have protested, in most cases, vehemently, against war against Iraq. The Pope appealed to his followers throughout world to fast on a particular day to protest aggression against Iraq. The World Council of Churches has also issued a strongly worded statement against the USA for its war against Iraq. Many Catholics in Latin America are also strongly condemning the US for launching aggression against Iraq. Some activists of these churches even tried to appeal for forming human shield in Iraq against American bombing.

Such an act of solidarity by the Christian Churches is a matter of great significance and must be enthusiastically welcome by all concerned. Bush's Christian rhetoric thus cannot deceive anyone. God is being invoked by Bush (the American soldiers have been asked to pray every day and even send their prayers to White House as if they are fighting a 'just' war and God is on their side. God cannot be on the side of those who kill innocent civilians who have nothing to do with either Bush' vested interests or Saddam's political designs. These innocent people want to live in peace.

Christ is considered the prince of peace and he cannot be on the side of aggressors who kill innocent people ruthlessly even though they may take his name thousand times. Christ always talked of peace and was always on the side of the oppressed. According to the Bible the meek shall inherit the earth. The Qur'am also says the same thing in 28:5. Thus the Church is on the side of the poor and weak and so is the Qur'an. It is only the vested interests and the powerful are on the side of Bush and Blaire, none else.

We also have to reflect deeply about the way our democracies are functioning. Democracy tends to become pocket borough of the rich and the powerful. They can maneuver it quite successfully. The people of America, at least a large number of them, are against the war in Iraq. There have been huge demonstrations against war in New York, Washington and Los Angeles and so many other cities of America. Similarly there were massive protests against war in London and other cities of U.K. and yet the rulers in USA and UK went ahead with war dismissing these protests with contempt. Not only this these powerful individuals manipulate media and propagate lies and half -truths to legitimise their aggression against another country.

It is ironical that these very people criticise those countries, which lack democracy. America has declared war ostensibly to eliminate the dictator Saddam and gift people of Iraq 'democracy' so that they can enjoy 'freedom'. And Bush is even prepared to kill hundreds of innocent citizens of Iraq so that the people of Iraq can enjoy 'freedom and democracy'. It is also a matter to be reflected upon that due to such aggressive invasion against other countries the quality of democracy in USA is being eroded.

Dissent is no more tolerated by the Bush administration. While Bush is keen to gift freedom to the people of Iraq, he is unhesitatingly suppressing freedom at home. The police is pouncing upon the demonstrators against war and those journalists who do not agree with the analysis of war situation in Iraq are loosing their emplcyment. The case of Mr. Peter Arnett, a veteran war reporter with the NBC T.V. has received enough attention worldwide. Since Mr. Arnett appeared on Baghdad T.V. and gave opinion that the war is not going as planned by the USA and its allies, lost his job.

It clearly indicates that democratic freedoms are under attack in USA. It has never happened before. After the terrorist attack on twin towers in New York democratic values have come under serious challenge. Of course it is for the people of America to struggle against such violations of democracy in their own country. They should not, under any circumstances allow McCarthian era to return.

It is difficult to predict the outcome of war in Iraq at this stage. America has terrible superiority of arms over Iraq. Iraq has been virtually disarmed over last one decade. A few weeks before war it was compelled to destroy its Samoud missiles having more than 150 kms range. It is virtually fighting against most powerful allies armed to teeth without arms. It now possesses only some outdated small arms.

It is irony of the situation that the country which possess most dreadful arms of mass destruction is considered 'champion of world freedom' and Iraq which hardly possessed any arms was being pressurised by the whole world to disarm and disclose all its weapons of mass destruction. In the region if any country possesses WMD it is Israel. Israel possesses all sorts of weapons including nuclear weapons. But since it is faithful ally of USA and guards its interests in the region, it is no threat to world security. According to American rule, those who threaten American interests are 'threat' to world security.

Everyone knows the world has totally skewed structure and everyone bows before power and minds his interests. Principles and values are only to be invoked by the weak. The powerful has to dismiss such a discourse. America also uses human rights rhetoric when it comes to third world countries. But there too, if the regime is US friendly ths discourse can be dispensed with.

(II)

We would now like to turn our attention to the role of Islamic countries in this whole affair. There too Islamic rhetoric is used by vested interests to protect themselves. This Islamic rhetoric is, of course, meant for Muslim masses. The most obvious rhetoric used is of 'ummah'. Muslim ummah is supposed to be united like rock and stand up to all crises. However, such unity of ummah is never to be seen from earliest part of Islamic history. Muslim ummah split into various interest or sectarian groups with few years of Holy Prophet's death.

Such unity is no where to be seen since that early period. Today the ummah is as much divided with no signs of ever taking a united stand on any issue. On aggression against Iraq too Muslim countries are deeply divided. Unfortunately Kuwaiti rulers are more than eager to provide all facilities to the US and its allies to launch aggression from its territory. The Allied troops were first massed in Kuwait and all the provisions for the troops are also being supplied from there. Thus Kuwait is the lifeline for the Allied forces for their war against Iraq.

Saudi Arabia, Jordan and Egypt also are amongst the supporters of the USA in the region. Though they are not actively helping the US they are all silent spectators. They are not even protesting, as it will harm their interests. Pakistan has also been cowed down and its military rulers are cooperating with the US. They are afraid of earning wrath of US masters. Syria is of course protesting and will invite wrath of America.

Of course the Muslim masses in these countries are seething with rage and are eager to help Iraq. In some countries like Pakistan Muslims are staging massive demonstrations under the leadership of Ulama. However, it is possible to demonstrate in Pakistan but people in other countries are not that lucky. In Saudi Arabia for example, though there is no less anger against America but they cannot even demonstrate and vent their spleen. The accumulated anger can have disastrous consequences.

It is also important to note that such acts of imperialist aggression that lead to terrorism in the Muslim world. There are two things, which are mainly responsible for promoting terrorism: acts of aggression against Muslim countries and suppression of democratic freedoms with the help of authoritarian rulers ready to align with the US.

Unfortunately Osama bin Laden's acts of terrorism thus find justification in the eyes of Muslims due to such acts of aggression on the part of US. Many people including Hasni Mubarak, President of Egypt are now suggesting that there will be many more Osamas now in the Islamic world. This will in turn be blamed on Islam and 'clash of civilisation' theory will find even more acceptability in the western world.

The technological progress has enabled nations like the USA, which want to dominate the world, to develop weapons of mass destruction and kill hundreds of thousands of people across the world. There is nothing to be proud of to be in 21st century. Even Chengez Khans of the medieval world could not have killed as many people as countries like USA are killing in wars today. In the two world wars in 20th century millions of people were killed because of this killer technology. We should feel ashamed that despite so much progress of science we have not been able to suppress our desire to rule or dominate over others at any cost. We have hardly succeeded in refining our aggressive instinct.

It is here that we need value based approach to our problems. Science without human values can be an unmitigated desire. From Hitler's Germany to Hiroshima to Vietnam to Iraq it has been long history of this unmitigated disaster. Unfortunately most of these people were killed in the name of saving democracy and freedom.

All religions of the world can be great boon for humanity if their leaders do not ally with vested interest as they have done in the past and stand by spiritual values like compassion and mitigating suffering. Like Buddhism and Christianity, Islam too, lays great emphasis on compassion and justice. The religious leaders across the world should come together to fight against mass killings by powerful nations of the world by invoking hollow words like freedom and democracy.

It is highly gratifying that religious leaders have given a call to protest against American designs in Iraq. Some of them even proposed human shield against ruthless American bombing. Unfortunately many Muslim religious leaders – though not all – are not showing, enough courage to give a call to resist American aggression in Iraq. Islam is a great religion, which inspires people to fight against injustice, though not necessarily violently. We must use the concept of non-violent struggle to fight against injustices all over the world. It is the only way to fight terrorism too.

If Muslim religious leaders take initiative to promote non-violent resistance against such acts of aggression by USA and its allies, it will be a great service to humanity. It will save hundreds of innocent lives in future. If there is no such non-violent resistance which needs tremendous courage, likes of Osama will rise again causing tremendous suffering to the people. We must impress on Muslims that taking innocent lives is an un-Islamic act (5:32). Also, a Muslim has to act with wisdom (Allah is Hakim) and has to suppress his/her anger (3:134). Suppressing anger, however, does not mean compromising with injustice but to elevate it to higher form and combining it with wisdom and using on-violent means so as to save human lives and minimise human suffering while fighting against injustices.

Let us hope our religious leaders would not issue fatwas resulting even in more human suffering and would give creative lead to struggle against injustices being inflicted on Muslim world by America in its arrogance of power. In the Qur'anic language America is resorting to istikbar and Allah brings downfall of all mustakbirin (arrogant rulers drunk with power) and this downfall can be hastened by human agents acting with wisdom.

15
Engaged Islam

Islam and Muslims are very much under attack today for various reasons, chief among them is attack on New York towers on 9/11/2001. Also, the Islamic world on the whole tends to take very conservative stands on number of issues and still implements laws formulated during medieval ages by eminent Islamic jurists presumably based on Qur'an and *sunnah* but introducing considerable changes in them through interpretations to suit their times. The laws pertaining to women are in great need for change, specially the way people like Taliban and Saudis implement them making Islam target of attack.

It seems the very spirit of Islam has been lost the way Muslims behave. The orthodox ʿulama insists, in Muslim majority states, to implement Shari`ah laws as they are and even insist on stoning adulterers to death. This is so from Indonesia to Algeria. There are very few Muslim states, which can be termed as liberal and democratic. Millions of Muslims are suffering as a result of this, particularly women. In countries like Kuwait women cannot vote, in countries like Saudi Arabia they cannot go out alone, Taliban did not allow them to go to schools and in most of the Muslim countries they have to wrap themselves into veil. In Saudi Arabia recently when a girls school caught fire, some girls tried to escape but were pushed back to burn alive simply because they had left their veil behind in a rush. Thus human life has no value and Islamic dress for women has.

These are such matters that Muslims have to reflect deeply about and engage themselves in the serious project of changing society so as to be more progressive in keeping with Islamic values. A Muslim is, above all, believer in these values. Islam had conceived of emergence of a new man – a *mu'min* – who firmly believed in Islamic values and engaged himself in changing the world in accordance with those values.

First, I would like to throw some light on these Islamic values. The most fundamental Islamic value is justice *'adl* and Allah's name is 'Aadil i.e. Just. Allah is Just. A Muslim cannot be a Muslim without being just himself or herself. He has to engage himself in promoting justice in the whole world.

Another important Qur'anic value is *ihsan* – benevolence, doing good to others and Allah's name is Muhsin i.e. Benevolent. Allah is benefactor of one and all without any distinction of caste, creed or colour. A Muslim also has to be benefactor of all Muslim or non-Muslim. The prophet has also said that a hand of a Mu'min should not do any harm to the other.

Another significant Islamic value is equality. All human beings are equal in as much as we share our humanity with each other. All children of Adam, according to the Qur'an (17:70) possess honour and dignity accorded by Allah. This is to be seen in conjunction with freedom of conscience (2:256). Once cannot think of human dignity without the concept of freedom of conscience. Thus equality, human dignity and freedom of conscience all are related with each other and cannot be compromised in any way. A society which is Islamic in substantial way must ensure all three to all human beings.

Yet another important value is compassion called in the Qur'an as *rahmah*. Allah is called Rahim, Compassionate. He is also referred to as Rahman which means almost the same i.e. compassionate though the

Muslim theologians make some fine distinctions between the two. *Rahman,* according to the theologians is Allah's attribute of Mercy for all whatever the caste, creed or nationality. Thus a Muslim must display compassion for all and should be extremely sensitive to others' suffering. A Muslim cannot be indifferent to suffering of others including animals.

A *mu'min* should also strive continuously for removing suffering from earth. It comes very close to Buddha's concept of *dukkha* and its removal from earth. A Muslim must dedicate himself to removal of suffering in all its forms from this earth. And any form of injustice causes suffering and hence establishment of justice is directly related to removal of suffering from earth. The Qur'an repeatedly condemns oppression and exploitation what it calls *zulm*. The word *zulm* is derivative of *z.l.m.* which has meaning of deviating (from right or just course) and *zulmat* in Arabic means darkness. Injustice leads to darkness.

Thus an engaged Muslim must devote himself to fighting *zulm* i.e. any form of injustice and oppression on earth. He should help all those who are victims of injustice. According to the Qur'an Moses actively helped the Israelites throw away the bondage of Pharaoh. He rid themselves of the oppression and exploitation and gave them sense of dignity and honour as free people.

In our own times we have various forms of oppression and exploitation be it capitalist exploitation, be it due to globalization or be it due to any other form of injustice between two individuals or between two nations or communities.

A real jihad for a Muslim is to fight against all forms of injustices and all forms of exploitation and make all forms of sacrifices to remove these injustices to establish real peace on earth. As long as there is any trace of injustice and exploitation on earth there will be violence in some form or the other and it is duty of a *mu'min* to wage struggle to remove all traces of injustice. An engaged Muslim has to be committed to peace on earth and without peace this earth will not be worth inhabiting for all human beings.

And peace can be established only through jihad against all forms of *zulm* on earth. Another important value is truth called *haq* by the Qur'an. Allah Himself is referred to as Haq in the Book. Thus an engaged Muslim has to fight for truth. Truth is God and thus god cannot be realised without realising truth in all its forms.

Truth, it is important to note, is much more than mere conformity with fact or empirical reality. Truth is nothing if not value-oriented. The given facts of life may not be conducive to promoting justice and peace. There may be *zulm* all around us. An committed Muslim cannot accept such a reality. His dedication to truth will inspire him to fight against such earth filled with exploitation and oppression. Being truthful means being just. Truth is not mere statement but praxis.

A Muslim who is engaged seriously with his religion and his conscience would never be at ease with himself if there is gender injustice in his society or country. Today gender injustice is widespread throughout the world. The Prophet of Islam both through revelation and through his own words and practices (*sunnah*) did all he could not only to improve the status of women in society but also to accord them equal status to her with that of men.

The medieval society robbed women once again of their high status and subjugated them to male domination. And this persists today throughout Islamic world. Thus an engaged Muslim would not rest in peace if such bondage of women persists throughout Islamic world today. The 'ulama are constantly demanding strengthening of medieval practices and trying to rob women of whatever rights they have won in recent times.

It is not only that. The modernity is so dominated by the unrestrained capitalist system that women have been reduced to a saleable commodity. If the conservative 'ulama demand confining her to four walls of home and putting all sorts of restrictions on her the modern capitalist system exploits her body to sale commodities. Her naked or semi-naked body is for sale everywhere to promote consumerism. Thus the modern capitalist system has cheated her of her sense of dignity.

Thus an engaged Muslim has to face double challenge – challenge of orthodox 'ulama on one hand, and that of modern capitalism and its utterly exploitative attitude towards women, on the other. Both are not acceptable. If the former is violation of Islamic spirit of justice the latter is total negation of her human dignity and is result of capitalist greed. To call it freedom is misnomer. There cannot be any freedom without dignity as pointed out before. Both compliment each other. How can she be free if she is reduced as a commodity and her body is used or selling consumable items.

In some Muslim countries women are still quite low on education. The Prophet has said that acquiring education is obligatory (*faridatun*) for both Muslim men and Muslim women. Thus an engaged Muslim has to wage a jihad against high rates of illiteracy among women in these Muslim societies. It is also to be mentioned here that in some Muslim countries like Indonesia and Malaysia the rate of literacy among women is quite high but in countries like Pakistan, Bangla Desh, India etc. where a very large number of Muslims reside the rate of literacy among women is quite low and this should engage Muslims of these countries to wage jihad against illiteracy.

Illiteracy be it among men or women is to be removed. The Qur'an describes ignorance (*jahl*) as darkness and *'ilm* (knowledge) as light (*nur*). And the first revelation to the Prophet of Islam (PBUH) began with the word *iqra'* i.e. recite or read which is synonymous with knowledge. Knowledge is a value and Allah is described in the Qur'an as 'Aalim i.e. the Knower.

Thus it is duty of Muslims to engage themselves with latest developments of knowledge in the world. Even the word for science in Arabic is *'ilm*. It is very comprehensive word embracing all forms of knowledge religious as well as secular. In fact an engaged Muslim should always be engaged in knowing what is created by Allah in this universe. The 'ulama (knowers, scientists) according to the Qur'an reflect on Allah's creation day and night. Thus in verse 3:190 the Qur'an says: "Those who remember Allah standing and sitting and (lying) on their sides, and reflect on the creation of the heavens and the earth: Our Lord, Thou has not created this in vain! Glory be to Thee! Save us from the chastisement of the Fire." And in verse 35:28 the Qur'an says that only who are possessed of knowledge really fear Allah.

From both these verses the importance of knowledge in Islamic civilisation is quite obvious. Islam greatly encouraged knowledge. In fact as in 3:190 a true believer reflects on creation of this universe day and night and sitting and standing and through reflection on His creation they affirm Glory of God. And an ignorant person cannot even fear Allah and cannot acknowledge His greatness.

Thus a committed Muslim will spend day and night on acquiring knowledge and spreading its light among all. Is it not very sad thing that the record of literacy in Islamic world is so poor compared to non-Muslim world? And when it comes to study of science it is even worse. The Islamic world has not created one great scientist who could have lasting impact on the world as a whole? Even the Noble Laureate Dr. Abdus Salam though hailed from Pakistan had worked all along in USA and did all his research in Physics there. It is an irony that in Islamic world Pakistan is considered most advanced in science and technology though compared to even India Pakistan is far behind in this race.

Many orthodox 'ulama even reject science and maintain that when the Qur'an talks of *'ilm* (knowledge) it talks of only knowledge of religion. Thus after florescence of knowledge during the Abbasid period in 2nd and third century Hijra (Islamic calendar) when science and philosophy registered great achievements there has been not much progress in these fields. Science and technology, even philosophy became stagnant. The sack of Baghdad in 1258 destroyed what had remained of it.

Ever since the Islamic world remained far behind in the fields of science and philosophy, even unfortunate as it is, in the field of Islamic knowledge (*'ulum-i-diniyyah*). Not much worthwhile contributions were made by the 'ulama in these fields. They began to stress only taqlid i.e. imitation, an new contribution was denounced as heresy. And there were not many heretics.

Only during colonial period one notices some intellectual stir under the influence of the west. Jamal al-Din Afghani and his disciple Muhammad Abduh who later became Grand Mufti of al-Azhar produced fresh thought and egged on Muslims to think afresh. In India Sir Syed Ahmad Khan founded MAO College on the patterns of Cambridge and Oxford Universities and induced Muslims to go for western secular knowledge. However, the Islamic world is far behind in the field of knowledge and still conservative 'ulama rule the roost particularly in oil rich countries like Saudi Arabia, Kuwait etc. In these countries it is so difficult to challenge even age-old traditions. The rulers are afraid and any intellectual dissent is suppressed with heavy hand.

A committed Muslim must take inspiration from the Qur'an and work for spread of all kinds of useful knowledge systems in the Islamic world. Unfortunately in Islamic madrasas and universities even today outdated sciences as developed during early Islamic period and Ptolmian Astronomy are taught and anything else is considered deviation from religious teachings.

Ours is the age of information and knowledge and knowledge is advancing at an exponential speed. Any country, which ignores the rapid advancement of knowledge, will be ignored by the world. The rulers in the Islamic world strictly control information as it is threatening to their authority which is based on the support of conservative 'ulama and the 'ulama in turn consider any change a threat to their own authority.

Thus commitment to knowledge is commitment to change and democratic freedoms. Unfortunately most of the people think that there is no democracy in the Islamic world because Islam is against democracy and supports authoritarianism and opposes any progress and change.

This is far from true. Islam has never approved of monarchy or authoritarianism. Monarchy developed in Islam under the influence of feudalism and under the influence of Roman and Sassanid empires, not because of Islamic teachings. In fact The Holy Prophet was not followed by any monarch but by a Khalifa elected by the Muslims (according to Sunni Muslims) or by Imamat (according to the Shi'ah Islam). Authoritarianism has no place at all in Islamic teachings.

In fact all early Islamic thinkers approved of rebellion if it was inspired by Islamic teachings against any ruler who was deviating from teachings of Islam. Most of the great Islamic thinkers and companions or companions of the companions of the Prophet (PBUH) strongly opposed the Umayyad rule because it deviated from the system of khilafah and usurped power undemocratically and converted into a synastic rule. An Islamic thinker of the eminence of Hasan Basri was opposed to the Umayyad rule.

Submission to authoritarian rule itself is un-Islamic. Right to open criticism is a sacred right, not because the western democracies approve it but in the earliest Islamic period the Prophet's successors accepted it. The Prophet himself never discouraged any of his followers to ask him questions even when they went against some of his practices. He always gave them satisfactory answer and never allowed, especially in secular matters, any mystique to develop around him. Similarly his successors like Abu Bakr, 'Umar and 'Ali were publicly criticised and they never took a position that Muslims had no right to question their conduct. There is a hadith that there is no obedience in sinful conduct (*ma'siyah*).

Thus freedom of conscience, as pointed out above, is a sacred freedom, which every Muslim should guard jealously and promote fearlessly. Thus a true Muslim should be strongly committed to democratic values and should refuse to accept any authoritarian regime be it in the field of religion or in the filed of politics. The culture of *taqlid* (blind imitation) can never be an Islamic culture. Freedom of information and freedom of action are sanctioned by The Qur'an and practice of the Prophet.

Similarly a true Muslim must be as much committed to the concept of human rights as this concept is very closely related to democratic rights. The greatest violation of human rights takes place in authoritarian regimes.

Not that there are no violations of human rights in democratic regimes. There can be serious violations of human rights in democracies as we so often observe in western democracies too. It is not sufficient to establish democracy; it is also necessary to be vigilant to the practice of democratic rights. A Muslim should engage himself/herself continuously to oversee implementation of human rights in his/her own society.

Any suppression of ones freedom be it physical or spiritual is against humanity and hence against Islam. In Islamic world today we see great violations of human rights. In fact the Islamic world should have been precursor in the field of democratic and human rights. But historically the Muslim world deviated from the Qur'anic teachings and, under the alien influence of medievalism, it discarded Qur'anic teachings and took to authoritarian culture and unfortunately maintained it throughout colonial period and now even during the twenty-first century.

It is true that western imperialism and now neo-imperialism is strengthening this authoritarian culture for its own political vested interests. It has made the situation extremely complex and one sees very few signs of change. The Western powers have very high stakes in maintaining this culture of authoritarianism in the Muslim world. The popular aspirations and democratic rights are being crushed by the authorities. It is much more so in case of women. They do not enjoy even right to vote in some countries like Kuwait in the name of Islam.

Thus those committed to democratic and human rights have to fight against very heavy odds but fight they must under inspiration from the Qur'anic culture of openness and freedom. This has long been lost through the ages. It needs to be revived. It would be real Islamic renaissance.

For this we need a strong force of committed Muslims equipped with Islamic values and modern knowledge. It has to wage jihad against medievalism and authoritarianism and obsolete knowledge systems. This jihad would be true jihad and it needs not only utmost efforts but also sacrifices. This jihad would be for peace, progress and change and has to be waged against selfish rulers. The Holy prophet is reported to have said that best form of jihad is speaking truth in front of a tyrant ruler. We need Muslims to wage this kind of jihad and it is only this quality of jihad, which would rid Muslim world of tyrants and authoritarian rulers who suppress all basic rights and deny democracy to people. It would greatly improve the quality of governance in the Muslim world and would help greatly in fighting terrorism of the frustrated youth. It would bring real glory to Islam and Islamic teachings.

16
On the Causes of Violence In Early Islamic Society

(PART - I)

There is great deal of misunderstanding about place of violence in Islam. It is generally thought that Islam teaches its believers to use violence against non-Muslims and thus it legitimises violence to promote itself. Nothing can be further from truth. Islam is far from being a violent religion. Its basic aim is to promote justice and peace and establish a just, non-exploitative and humane order. It denounces exploitation of one human being by the other and believes in equality of all human beings – believers or non-believers. It teaches human actions to be based on peace (*salam*), compassion(*rahmah*), benevolence(*ihsan*) and wisdom(*hikmah*).

Such a religion cannot preach violence against others, including kafirs. Before we proceed further it is important to note that the word kafir has also been much misunderstood and much misused by certain Muslim theologians. The Qur'an uses this word very carefully and in a definite sense. However, in Islamic history this word has been often used loosely, carelessly and for denouncing rivals among Muslims, more than against non-Muslims. Had it been used strictly in the sense in which it has been used in the Qur'an, much bloodshed and conflict could have been avoided.

Qur'an uses the word *kafir* for those Meccans who not only refused to believe in the message brought by the Holy Prophet but also turned hostile and used violence – both psychological and physical – against the Prophet (PBUH) and his followers. It was not only the question of worshipping idols that qualified them to be *kafirs* but their rejection of entire value system of Islam (i.e. values like justice, compassion, non-violence, peace, truth, equality and human dignity and sensitivity to others suffering).

As for idol worshipping was concerned the Qur'an, though against it, had allowed the kafirs to do so (see chapter 109) as a matter of freedom of conscience. Idol worship was not the only criteria for *kufr* (non-belief), it was rejection of these values to constitute a humane society. Not only this these powerful tribal chiefs and their supporters severely persecuted the Prophet for preaching unity of God, His creatures and bringing about a humane social order.

In Arabia and outside Arabia there were people who followed their respective religions (either religions of the books like Torah and Bible or their traditional religions) and did not accept Islam but Muslims never insisted on their accepting Islam, let alone persecute them for doing so. They were left to follow their religions. The Prophet (PBUH) himself allowed, for example Zoroastrians of Bahrain, to follow their religion and entered into a pact with them as people of the book (*ahl al-kitab*). Uthman, the third caliph after the Prophet, even accepted Berbers as *ahl al-kitab* though they had no revealed scripture and were following traditional religion.

It is also very interesting to note that the Qur'an, the revealed word of God, does not prescribe violence against the kafirs unless they use violence against Muslims. Thus we find in the Qur'an in verse 2:190 that "And fight in the way of Allah against those who fight against you but be not aggressive. Surely Allah loves not the aggressors." This verse makes three important points.

First, the fight must be only for Allah and not for personal reasons (revenge or aggrandisement); second, one should not initiate the fight but should fight only if attacked and three, one should not persist in fighting and become aggressor once the other party lays down weapons and sues for peace. Allah does not love aggressors.

If one keeps this in mind it becomes clear that the Qur'an, the main source of Islamic teachings, does not sanction violence but permits it for self-defence and in certain well defined circumstances and with rigorous conditions. It nowhere sanctions violence for spread of religion or any other religious purposes. It upholds the principle of freedom of conscience as propounded in the verse 2:256 and never deviates from it.

Thus commenting on verse 2:193 Maulana Muhammad Ali of Lahore comments as follows: "When persecution ceases, and men are not forced to accept or renounce a religion, being at liberty to profess any religion of the truth of which they are convinced, then there should be no more fighting. The words that follow make the sense quite clear. *If they desist* from persecution, the Muslims are at once to stop fighting against them, and hostilities are not to be continued against any except the aggressors." (Holy Qur'an, Lahore, 1973, pp- 82)

The Maulana further points out that "A comparison with 22:40 will show that this is the correct explanation. There the object of the Muslim fights is plainly set forth in the following words: 'And if Allah did not repel some people by others, cloisters and churches and synagogues and mosques in which Allah's name is much remembered would have been pulled down'. This shows clearly that the Muslims fought not only in defence of mosques, but also in that of churches and synagogues, and even of the cloisters of monks. The same object is stated here in the words *religion is for Allah*, so that there is no persecution on the score of religion, and everyone is at liberty to hold any belief which he likes. The verse, in fact, lays down the broad principles of religious freedom." (ibid)

Thus it is quite clear that Qur'an in no way permits violence for suppression of religious freedom; it is quite to the contrary. It permits violence even if others religious freedom is in danger. Freedom of religion and freedom of conscience should be defended and should not be allowed to be endangered. If it is in danger such a situation is referred to in verse 2:193 as *fitnah* (i.e. persecution). Persecution in every form should be ended and hen only a just and peaceful society could be established.

II

Often comparison is made with Buddhism or Christianity and it is concluded that while these religions are advocates of peace, Islam promotes violence. It is very mistaken view as violence or absence of it is ascribed to religion rather than to circumstances in which a religion comes into existence or spreads. Islam, if one goes by teachings alone, is as peaceful a religion, as Buddhism or Christianity. The violence is not borne of religious teachings but from circumstances. This is what is most important to understand. People often confuse violence present in a society for various reasons with violence produced by religious teachings.

Let us examine this further. The beginnings of Buddhism and Islam are very similar but circumstances are very different. Buddha was highly dissatisfied with conditions around him. He was greatly disturbed by the suffering of people around him. He left his house, his family in search of truth, in quest for solution. He spent number of years reflecting, brooding and meditating and came out with his eight-fold path and the values he considered most fundamental, values like compassion and sensitivity to suffering and ways to remove *dukkha* (suffering).

He began preaching his doctrines among the people and did not meet with strong resistance, nor was he persecuted by powerful vested interests. He was wandering monk and did not stay at one place. He did not confront any religious establishment or political power. He did have religious debates with those who upheld certain Vedic practices but faced no persecution. Thus his circumstances were very different from those of the Prophet. As Buddha did not face violence while preaching he did not refer to permissibility or otherwise of violence.

The Prophet of Islam too was greatly disturbed by what he saw around him in Mecca. There was malaise all around, suffering of weaker sections of society, slavery, maltreatment of women, absence of any higher spiritual goal and corrupt religious practices like superstitions and exploitation in the name of religion, *kahins* (priests) enriching themselves and worshipping idols as God and asking them to solve their problems.

Like Buddha the Prophet (PBUH) began reflecting deeply over this malaise in a cave of Hira, outside city of Mecca on a rugged mountain (now known as Mount of Light – *Jabal al-Nur*). He spent great deal of time reflecting and meditating and Truth was revealed to him. He came from Cave of Hira with revelation, which continued for next 23 years until he died. Now he was spiritually enriched man and a man with a message from Allah.

But unlike Buddha when he began to preach his message he met with stiff resistance from powerful tribal chiefs who took pride not only in their tribal and social status but were arrogant of their wealth which they had acquired from international trade. Their arrogance knew no bounds. They were all the more disturbed as the Prophet Mohammad, though belonged to the clan of Hashim, a branch of tribe of Quraysh, which enjoyed highest social status but was orphan and poor. How can an orphan from a poor family claim to be the Messenger of Allah and teach them spiritual values.

Not only their pride was hurt but they were greatly

disturbed since he sided with the poor and exploited sections of society and attacked accumulation of riches and warned them of dire consequences (chapter 104). He also talked of giving their slaves a dignified place in society. This was not acceptable to them at all. They considered it an attack on their social status and social hierarchy. He also opposed all their superstitions and laid emphasis on reason. This was totally unacceptable to the Arabs of Mecca. It went quite contrary to their customs, traditions and practices. Above all the Prophet's teachings challenged the vested interests of tribal leaders.

They failed to persuade the Prophet to stop preaching his religion. When he could not be dissuaded they began persecuting him and using violence against his followers. It is also important to note that violence was thought to be quite legitimate in pre-Islamic Arabia. There were long drawn wars between different tribes and violent retaliation was an accepted practice. Many tribes outside Mecca (Mecca was an urban area and had developed its own traditions) raided each other for their own sustenance. It was the only means for their sustenance. Thus the pre-Islamic Arab society was quite violent one and violence was thought to be quite legitimate instrument of settling scores. Neither there was any government nor any rule of law nor any legal corpus.

It was Islam which first gave concept of law and governance. In pre-Islamic period violence was the only instrument for having ones way. Thus the Prophet of Islam had to deal with this situation. Violence was in the air and no one could avoid violence. The concept of non-violence simply did not exist. As there was no ruler, no governmental authority only tribal customs could be invoked to settle disputed matters and tribal customs fully approved of violence.

The Prophet had very limited choices. He tried non-violent resistance while in Mecca but violence was so thick in the air that it did not have any impact on the tribal leaders and powerful vested interests. Unable to bear persecution he sent away some of his followers to Ethopia with whom Meccans had trade relations. The King of Ethopia was impressed by the teachings of new religion and its closeness to Christianity (The chapter 19 of the Qur'an on Mary was recited before him which greatly impressed him and he granted these Muslims refuge in his kingdom.

But those who remained in Mecca continued to be severely persecuted and a plot was hatched to assassinate the Prophet. On learning of this plot the Prophet migrated to Yathrib which was renamed Madinatun Nabi (city of the Prophet) but properly known as Madina. He had received good response from people of Madina many of whom converted to Islam and had promised him to help. For this reason the people of Madina were known as Ansar i.e. helpers.

III

In Madina too the Prophet could not rest in peace. Though he entered into a covenant with all tribal leaders of Mecca, Muslim, Jew as well as pagan giving them full freedom to follow their respective religions but to defend Madina, if attacked. The Jews however, quite apprehensive of the rising power of Muslims and began to secretly conspire with the tribal chiefs of Mecca to attack Madina. The Jews had established their leadership in Madina and had become quite influential and benefited from internecine wars of non-Jewish Arab tribes. Tired of Jewish moves to make them fight these Arab tribals had invited the Prophet to Madina to make peace between them. The Prophet brought peace and united them. This endeared the Prophet to the Arab tribals of Madina.

The Prophet, however, was quite apprehensive of the Meccan moves to attack Madina and he kept vigil and sent his men to keep watch on Meccan trade caravans.

The battle of Badr was the first battle fought between Muslims and Meccan unbelievers. Though there is lot of controversy as to who attacked first but if we go by the Qur'anic verse (2:190) the Muslims must have attacked only to defend themselves.

Thus the Meccan unbelievers were keen to humiliate the Prophet in Madina too so that he and his followers did not emerge as a force. They feared Islam on two counts. Firstly because its teachings were based on justice, compassion, taking care of weaker sections of society, giving women an honourable position, equality of all human beings including of slaves and non-Arabs and the Meccans disliked these teachings as they thought Arabs are superior to all other, particularly the Quraysh of Mecca and they were not ready to accept any other code of conduct except their own. Secondly, they thought if Muhammad (PBUH) succeeds they will loose their hegemony.

Thus the Meccan Arabs would not leave Prophet in peace. Prophet did his best to promote peaceful settlement as the peace of Hudaibiyah also shows very clearly. The Meccans would not let him perform Hajj and the Prophet did not want to use force although he had more than 10,000 followers with him. The Meccans would not even agree to an honourable settlement. The Prophet could have used force but did not do so and accepted peace even on humiliating terms. His own followers opposed peaceful settlement on such humiliating terms but the Prophet persisted and signed the peace pact. The Prophet wanted to make peace as a norm and violence an exception.

However, no individual, however morally powerful and influential, can control the given circumstances and placed in a situation the Prophet was placed in. The violence was there all around him and he had to survive in those given circumstances. Also, the Arabian peninsula was surrounded by powerful empires like Sassanid and Roman empires. Islam was feared by all those who saw real threat in its moral teachings, teachings of equality of all and discrimination against none. It was seen as empowering the weak, the oppressed and exploited.

Islamic teachings were highly subversive for the powerful establishments based on exploitation and oppression. It wanted to make the weaker sections of society the leaders and inheritors of earth (28:5) and Islam wanted to bring about this revolution in most peaceful manner. Islam did not approve of feudal ownership of land. The Prophet wanted land owned only by tillers. He made it obligatory for rich to pay zakat to meet the basic needs of the poor and needy. Such a concept was not acceptable for feudal lords and their hangers on. Also, on the other hand, the rich merchants of Mecca were not ready to spend their wealth for the poor and needy.

In Mecca, as pointed out before, there was no legal governing authority and hence no taxes. They were thus not ready to pay any tax to any authority. Islam demanded that and made that obligatory. Such a concept was totally alien to them. It is also proved by the war of *riddah* (i.e. war on those going back on Islam). After the death of the Holy Prophet some tribes refused to pay zakat and declared that if zakat were made obligatory on them, they would rather turn away from Islam. Abubakr, the first caliph, did not agree to this and a fierce war was fought between the Islamic government and the rivals refusing to pay zakat, the poor tax.

It is important to note that zakat was highly desirable tax for removing poverty from the society and was meant to bring about redistribution of wealth in society. It was to be spent on poor and the needy, the captives and those in debt, for wayfarers and in the way of Allah (see 9:60). Thus it is meant for all weaker sections of society. In early seventh century no government was levying such tax for the weaker sections of society and no one was prepared to accept such a thing.

Islam gives primary importance to justice and all governments of time were based on injustice and exploitation. Islam was also trying to change the existing power equations in society – power to impoverished and powerless. The powerful resisted this with all their might. Also, the powerless began to test power and organised themselves better to retain their power. And it is human psychology that when powerless becomes powerful they use violence with as much ferocity, or perhaps with greater ferocity. Thus changing power equations in a changing society develops its own dynamics in power struggle.

All this we witness in the early Islamic society in the post-prophetic phase i.e. after the death of the Prophet. Thus violence in early Islamic society was not due to the Qur'anic teachings but because of new power equations coming into existence in the early Islamic society. New vested interests began to develop in this new society and these powerful interests began to use violence to seize power.

In this power struggle more Muslims were killed by Muslims themselves than by non-Muslims. Even the Prophet's own grandson was not spared. He refused to accept authority of those who seized power in an unjust manner and was martyred in Karbala on 10th of Muharram along with his close relatives and friends. We will throw more light on this civil war among Muslims in early Islamic society in another paper.

What we intend to emphasise here is that the Prophet wanted to establish a just, peaceful and non-exploitative society in which all human beings, without distinction of low and high or of sex or of Arab and non-Arab could live in peace and harmony. However, vested interests both inside and outside the Islamic society did not allow it to happen and most organised and sustained efforts for the first time in history to bring about social and economic justice came to a tragic end.

In no society, as long as there are powerful vested interests, and no society is free of that, social transformation can be brought about peacefully. Vested interests sabotage all such efforts violently and peace remains only a dream. So it happened in Islamic society.

(PART - II)

I

In part one of this article we threw light on why there was so much violence when the Holy Prophet, who is described as the "Mercy of the World" (*Rahmat li al-'alamin*) was basically committed to peace. We have shown that Islam was the first and most systematic attempt to establish a just society in the history of humankind and thus violence was unavoidable. When you try to establish a just society you hurt the interests of powerful forces of exploitation and oppression and they use violence, if needed, with brutality and ferocity.

The Prophet had to face violence consistently from enemies of Islam who were out to sabotage establishment of a just society in Arabia. The *kuffar* (unbelievers) did not oppose the Prophet only because he attacked idol worship and preached *tawhid* i.e. unity of Allah but much more because he emphasised social justice. *'Adl* (justice) is a key word in the Qur'an along with ihsan (benevolence), *rahmah* (compassion) and *hikmah* (wisdom). These values are very important in Islamic ethics; in fact so important that these are also Allah's name in the Qur'an i.e. Allah is Just, Allah is Benevolent, Allah is Compassionate and Allah is Wise.

The Vested interests in Mecca wanted free hand to exploit their own people and wanted to keep themselves free of an moral or ethical obligations. As we know there was no state structure in Arabia of the Prophet's time and the tribal leaders were completely free to take their own decisions and enact them in their interests. If Islamic system was established they would have been subjected not only to moral and social obligations but also to a governmental system on the basis of laws enacted in keeping with the Islamic teachings.

But these tribal leaders did not want them to be subjected to any such obligations or laws and resisted attempts of the Prophet very violently. Since the Prophet had migrated to Madina, away from the clutches of the powerful tribal leaders but they did not leave him in peace in Madina either. They were afraid if the Prophet succeeds in establishing such a system in Madina it is bound to influence Meccan society as well. Thus Madina was attacked and the prophet had to fight against the Meccan forces.

The Prophet had entered into a covenant with various Jewish and other tribes in Madina giving them complete autonomy to follow their religion, customs and traditions and thus created a political community. The terms of this covenant were most liberal but the Jewish leaders resented the emerging community of Muslims based on religion of their own and though they signed the covenant, they looked for opportunities to wreck it, if possible, with the help of Meccan leaders. And they got the opportunity when the Meccan leaders attacked the prophet and his followers. The Jewish leaders did not fulfill their obligation to defend Madina along with Muslims as per the terms of the covenant.

The Jewish leaders secretly conspired against the Prophet and his followers. Thus conflict arose between the Muslims and the Jews, which could not be resolved peacefully. Thus Muslims and Jews fought and Jews ultimately lost out. Thus the conflict between the Jews and Muslims was not of religious nature. The Prophet had given them full freedom to follow their religion. But what they resented was ascendance of Muslims and taking control of situation. Thus violent conflict became unavoidable between Jews and Muslims of Madina.

II

The Islamic society in the period after the death of the Holy Prophet also had to face many challenges and could not remain peaceful as ideally desired. We would like to discuss in this paper the causes of violence in Islamic society after the death of the Prophet. An attempt will be made to analyse the situation that developed after the Prophet was no more.

We have to keep this in mind that the Islamic society then was continuously in throes of change and was, in fact, fast changing. It was most dynamic society. Violence erupted in that society both for external and internal reasons. No society can ever change peacefully as these changes also bring change in power equations among countries, tribes, castes and classes. The Arab society in Mecca in pre-Islamic period was in throes of change. Islam gave this change a definite direction, which was moral and ethical.

In pre-Islamic period it was urban society of Mecca which was mainly affected by socio-economic changes taking place but the Bedouin society was by and large unaffected. But Islamic revolution was far too wide in its implications. It took entire Arab society in its sweep. And soon its repercussions were felt even outside Arabia during Prophet's own time. Thus Islam brought about total change of equations. The old tribal relations were replaced by the concept of Muslim ummah. It was totally a new concept for a tribal society transcending all tribal barriers.

Also, tribal autonomy was completely shattered. The focus of power shifted from tribe to a much wider community, which soon embraced even non-Arabs. It was no ordinary change and such a change could not take place peacefully by any stretch of imagination. Quraysh was acknowledged as superior in power and material resources in the Arab peninsula. And it is for this reason that when question of successor to the Holy Prophet assumed controversy it was proposed that the successor could only be from the tribe of Quraysh.

Such a doctrine militated against the concept of ummah or Islamic brotherhood and equality of all believers, yet it was proposed by members of the Quraysh tribe and was accepted as still the centre of gravity of power in Arabia resided in the Quraysh. This also ultimately became a potential source of violence and we will throw more light on this later. Thus the nascent Islamic society faced fast changing equations of power. This became a powerful source of internal violence in the Arab society.

III

As pointed out above the Islamic revolution took entire Arab society in its sweep with far reaching implications. Before Islam the Bedouin society outside urban areas of Mecca and Madina survived by inter-tribal raids called *ghazwa*. There was no source of agricultural production in vast expanses of desert and most of the tribes survived through these raids. But now tribal raids were no longer possible as a wider community transcending these barriers came into existence. When internal source of survival dried up one had to look for certain external sources.

And this source was not far to seek. Islam had united these tribes into an ummah under one banner and they could march towards what was then known as Fertile Crescent. There was also pressure on limited sources of Arabia from the South. The famous dam in the Yemen known as Ma'arib was breached a couple of hundreds of years before Islam and the Yemen lost its primacy in rich agriculture and the people began to migrate towards north for better resources.

The Arabs divided into innumerable tribes and internecine struggle could be no match for the powerful empire either of Rome or Sassanids. The Fertile Crescent was great source of attraction for the Arabs under constantly increasing pressure on scarce land resources in the south and Southeast Arabia. But they could not take on the might of the Romans divided as they were in mutually feuding tribes.

Now they were united under the banner of Islam and could march towards the Fertile Crescent. It was not only unity but also they were armed with a cause – to take the message of Islam to other peoples. It is also important to note that there were Christian Arabs on the border of Roman and Sassanid empires. These Christians were Monophysites on and formed buffer between the Romans and Muslim Arabs. But these Monophysite Christians were highly oppressed at the hands of the Romans belonging to a different sect of Christianity.

These Monophysites were also looking for someone to liberate them from the oppressive Roman regime and the Arabs were looked upon as liberators by them. These Arabs did not impose their religion on this 'heretical' sect of Christianity nor they imposed heavy taxes like Romans. Thus these Arabs became liberator for them both in religious as well as economic sense. They enthusiastically supported these Arabs in fighting the Roman forces, which they could not have taken by themselves. .

Thus initial invasions by Arabs of Roman empire had socio-political dynamics of their own. These invasions became liberative for the Monophysite Christians who were also Arabs and also it provided much needed land and economic resources to the Arabs from the South. It became much easier for these Arabs to defeat powerful forces of Roman empire with the help of the these Monophysite Christians constituting the buffer state.

Looked at it from any perspective these invasions were certainly of liberative nature. The Romans were after all colonial power and were highly exploitative and oppressive. These Arabs, it is important to note, were not even properly armed vis-à-vis the most sophisticated and powerful army of the Romans (or the Sassanids on the Eastern border) and yet armed with revolutionary zeal provided by Islam they could defeat them. In ordinary circumstances it was impossible to defeat the Romans. Thus Islam began to spread beyond the limits of Arabia.

It should however, be noted that the intention was not to spread Islam or force Islam on these people. All the treaties entered into by the Muslims with the conquered people, which we find in the classic work of al-Baladhuri *Futuh al-Buldan.* There is no mention in these treaties, of converting anyone to Islam. Islam spread in these areas slowly and steadily for various other reasons. People were left to themselves. The conquering forces negotiated only for *jizya.* All these treaties mention how much *jizya* will be paid both in cash and kind. It is also important to note that the *jizyai* was negotiated and not unilaterally imposed and that it was much lighter than the taxes imposed by the Romans or Sassanids.

Thus the wars in the earliest phase of Islam after the death of the Prophet were part of very complex situation obtaining in and around Arabia. There were external and internal compelling factors. The internal situation in Arabia put pressure for outward movement and the situation on eastern and northern borders of the Arabian desert was inviting the newly organised Arabs charged with a revolutionary ideology to liberate the Sassanid and Roman occupied parts. The outward thrust of the Arabs was, initially at least, quite liberative.

IV

However, like other wars of liberation, these wars also had far reaching consequences on the internal situation of the Muslims. The conquests created forces, which had their own dynamics. The Arab tradition, also upheld by Islam, permitted war booty called *mal-e-ghanimat.* Since the wars on both eastern and northern fronts were fought with the two great empires of the town they yielded very rich booty. The booty, as per the tradition, was distributed among the soldiers and one fifth of it was deposited in state treasury known as *bait al-mal.*

This naturally led to accumulation of wealth – something, strongly denounced by the Qur'an. Even some of the senior companions of the Prophet came to posses great deal of wealth. Ibn Khalladun, the noted 14th century historian and sociologist has described the amount of wealth some of these companions possessed. He has quoted this from *Tabqat ibn Sa'ad.* Talha and Zubayr, the two companions of the Holy Prophet, for example, possessed so much wealth that silver and gold had to be collected with spade on their death. It was this accumulation of wealth, which led another senior companion of the Prophet, Abudhar Ghifari, began a campaign against accumulation of wealth by some companions by reciting the verse 9:34 denouncing accumulation of wealth.

Thus it will be seen that new contradictions were emerging in the Islamic society of Mecca and Madina which led towards internal conflict. The Qur'an, as pointed out above, led great stress on establishing a just society and these conquests were creating forces which brought the concept of a just society under severe pressure. And it is these forces which ultimately led to conditions of civil war in which thousands were killed in the period of thirty years after the death of the Holy Prophet.

V

It is seen in the history of all social revolutions that with the passing away of first generation of those who participated in revolutionary movement the sense of commitment to revolutionary values becomes a secondary thing and struggle for power primary. Islamic society could hardly escape this fate. With more wealth and affluence on one hand, and, expansion of territories on the other, power struggle became primary objective for many among the Muslims.

Also, with new territories conquered, more and more non-Arabs began to embrace Islam and soon these non-Arab Muslims and Arab Muslims outside Island of Arabia outnumbered the Arab Muslims from Mecca and Madina and its immediate environs. Many outside Mecca and Madina, mostly non-Arabs, embraced Islam. Many of these who embraced Islam were from low social origin, as Islam did not make any distinction between Arabs and non-Arabs and people of low or high origin. But in practice these distinctions remained and created contradictions in Muslim society.

Much of the conflict in early Muslim society originated in fast changing sociological composition of Islamic society. Now there were three distinct groups, Muslims claiming share in power and other material resources. Dr. Taha Husain of Egypt has given detailed description of these contending Muslim groups in his book Fitnat al-Kubra (The Great Insurrection). This book is full of insights into early Islamic society and the struggle within it, which caused so much conflict and violence.

It would be interesting to throw some light on these contending groups in order to understand the causes of this great insurrection. One group was of the Quraysh who were more advantageous position in as much as the first group of Muslims came from the tribe of Quraysh. This tribe, as pointed out earlier, was most influential and most experienced tribe in matters of diplomacy and international affairs. Many from this tribe had not only refused to embrace Islam but had severely persecuted the Prophet and his followers forcing them to migrate to Madina.

But all Qurayshites, including the worst enemies of Islam, embraced it after the conquest of Mecca. Of course among them also there were those who had made great sacrifices for the cause of Islam and had stood worst kind of persecution. On the death of the Holy Prophet the Quraysh claimed right to succession and rejected the claim of Ansars i.e. helpers of the Prophet from Madina saying that *nubuwwah* (prophethood) and *khilafah* (i.e. succession) should reside among the Quraysh.

When Ansar who belonged to the tribes of Aws and Kahzraj of Madina said that we have helped the Prophet and should have share in power and let there be one from you (i.e. from Quraysh) and one from us (i.e. Ansar) this was not accepted. However, many Ansar were given high position in the administration to remove their discontent. In fact there was problem within the tribe of Quraysh too which split Muslims into two sects i.e. Shi'ahs and Sunnis. The clan of Hashimites within the tribe of Quraysh was also brushed aside and Ali, the son-n-law of the Prophet became fourth Caliph though the Shi'ahs maintain he was the rightful claimant appointed by Holy Prophet himself.

The children of Ansar, the second group who came of age during the period of third caliph Uthman also began to nurse the grievance that justice was not done to them. The historians of early Islam tell us that the Umayyads, one of the clans of tribe of Quraysh, had taken major share in the higher administrative posts during the time of the third caliph Uthman. Thus Ansars and Hashimites felt completely sidelined by the time of Uthman.

The third group was of new entrants in Islam from the conquered territories who were mostly non-Arabs in origin and had client status (called mawla in *Arabic*). They embraced Islam hoping for equal treatment as the Qur'an refers to all believers as ikhwan i.e. brothers of equal status. Islam had laid great stress on brotherhood of all believers irrespective of their tribal, racial, national or social origin (30:22). This emphasis on equality had attracted large number of non-Arabs towards Islam.

But soon they discovered that in practice Arabs and Arabs of Quraysh tribe were more than equal. This caused lot of discontent among these new entrants to Islam and they rose in revolt during the time of Uthman, the third Caliph. The early Islamic society was rocked by inequalities created in the society by new forces which came into existence with quick conquests of vast territories within few years of the death of the Holy Prophet. Now no ruler, howsoever just, could control these forces of inequalities.

Ali, who was elected fourth Caliph, was very close to the Prophet and had imbibed values of Islam and was known for his strong commitment to these values. Thus the insurrectionists, knowing his commitment to Islamic values almost forced him to assume the responsibility of governing the vast Islamic Empire which was in a state of great turmoil. The insurrectionists had murdered Uthman, the third Caliph, while reciting the Holy Qur'an. Ali knew it would be very difficult to control these forces which had caused the insurrection. However, he ultimately agreed to take charge as there was no one around who could really deliver impartially.

By the time Ali took over another discontented group had come into existence known in Islamic history as *Khwarij* (seceders). Seceders were mostly of Bedouin origin for whom urban governance made no sense and were more for equality of all believers and refused to submit to any urban government. They deserted Ali at a critical stage when he was about to register victory over Mu'awiyah who belonged to Umayyad clan and refused to accept Ali as the rightful caliph of Muslims. He established his parallel regime in Syria and raised banner of revolt against him.

Ali's strong commitment to Islamic values of justice and equality was not acceptable to those powerful vested interests who came to control vast amount of wealth and power. Now the Islamic society was no more a simple society of early period. Now one had to contend with great power, which many Muslims acquired. Umar, the second caliph had followed very wise land policy. He had not allowed private ownership of the conquered lands and forced many senior companions of the Prophet to return to madina and not to settle down in conquered lands except few. Uthman, the third caliph, under great pressure, yielded and allowed rich fertile land to be exchanged with the land in Mecca and Madina thus bringing into existence powerful landed interests.

Now one had also to contend with these new landed interests to restore peace and justice in a society torn by conflicting interests. Ali tried his best but could not succeed as these powerful interests became law unto themselves and their interests were hurt by the policies of justice and equality followed by Ali. Ali refused to compromise on these Islamic values and himself became victim of violence. These powerful interests conspired to eliminate Ali so that they could have free hand to govern in their own interests. Maulana Maududi in his book *Khilafat aur Mulukiyyat* has thrown detailed light on transformation of Islamic institution of *khilafah* into *mulukiyyat* i.e. hereditary kingship.

Ali was assassinated by these forces while praying in the mosque early in the morning in Kufah whereto he had shifted the capital from Madinah. His son Hasan took over the reigns of governance but had soon to yield to pressures from Mu'awiyah who had revolted from his father. Imam Hasan had agreed to step down on certain conditions one of which was that after Mu'awiyah the question of khilafat will be left to Muslims and that he will not nominate his successor.

Unfortunately Mu'awiyah violated this condition and nominated his son Yazid to succeed him. This was the beginning of transformation of *khilafat* to *mlukiyyat*. It was not only the violation of condition on which Imam Hasan had abdicated in favour of Mu'awiyah but violation of the very revolutionary value system of Islam. Yazid had no commitment to Islam at all. He was born of a Christian mother and was given to 'good things' of life.

There was hardly any teaching of Islam he did not violate, or even ridicule.

Imam Husain, the younger son of Ali and himself an exemplary Muslim brought up in the Alid tradition of justice and equality, refused to accept Yazid as legitimate caliph of Muslims and preferred to give his head rather than his hand of support in the hand of Yazid. Thus he ıaid down his and his near and dear ones lives for the sake at keeping Islamic evolution alive and is gratefully remembered by all Muslims as the greatest martyr of Islam and is referred to as Saiyyid al-Shuhada' i.e. leader of martyrs. The Imam fought for defending Islamic values while Yazid committed aggression against him to defend his illegitimate power.

We have thrown here some light on the causes of violence in early Islamic society to show that violence was not result of teachings of Islam but far from it. Violence erupted in early Islamic society because new forces which came into existence tried to derail the Islamic value system which would have proved great boon for the mankind. Islam was the first systematic attempt to bring a just society into existence in the history of mankind.

17

Is Islam Compatible With Democracy and Modernity ?

Because of certain happenings and because there happens to be monarchy or dictatorships in most of the Muslim countries it has been concluded that Islam is not compatible with democracy and also with modernity. Some even maintain that very Islamic culture is an stumbling block and cannot permit democratic polity and modernistic society. To maintain this amounts not only to misunderstanding religion but also society, history and social forces at work.

If this logic is to be accepted then Christianity will also come under cloud as the Christian Church also opposed democracy, secularism and modernity until 18th century. A great struggle ensued between church and princely rulers on one hand, and between church and secular elements in the society, on the other. It was finally only during 19th century that democracy and modernity became acceptable to western society.

However, even some well-known scholars and orientalists have often accepted such superficial view of Islam and Islamic society. The western media partly for political reasons and partly for ignorance of social and material forces at work, also has been a great instrument of propagating such views about Islam and Islamic societies. In order to understand reality one has to bring to bear not only religious, but also sociological, political and historical view of reality. It requires deeper insight into social processes and working of societies.

Recently a debate took place on a web page and 10 questions were circulated to be replied by the participants. These questions were 1) Whether Islam and democracy are compatible; 2) Can Shari'ah laws with their harsh punishments and democracy go together; 3) Is it possible in Islamic countries to separate religion and state? 4) Can Islam support individual rights i.e. human rights?; 5) Has United States contributed to hampering democracy in countries like Saudi Arabia, Egypt, etc; 6) Is Islam opposed to modernity and refuses to come to terms with it; 7) Could religious texts be used as blueprints to structure modern society; 8) Do women hold inferior position in Muslim society? Can equality for women be ensured only through secular laws; 9) Is Islam tolerant and progressive? Islamic countries ban music and T.V., cinema posters etc.

We will try to answer these questions one by one. As stated before to understand the problem it is not enough to see what is happening in Muslim countries today and ascribe it to religion and religious teachings. Religion may appear to be a dominant cause but often it is not. Much happens behind the cover of religion and religious teachings. One who has penetrating insight into socio-political affairs would know what role religion and other forces play in a society. There are all sorts of interests, particularly political and economic which are more determinative than any thing else and while exercising ones judgement one should not ignore the role of these forces. One also has to remember that there is no single interpretation of religion. It generally has multiple interpretations. And ones interpretation is deeply influenced by ones socio-political inclination and ones bent of mind. The contemporary forces also play an important role in interpretation of religion. Contemporary Islam is being interpreted in multiple ways.

Also one should keep in mind the role of history,

historical forces and culture. Certain cultural formations also play important role. Culture, in turn, is not determined wholly by religion and religious teachings though it does play part therein. For understanding contemporary socio-political set up one can hardly ignore the role of culture as well as that of historical heritage.

With these preliminary remarks I would throw light on the questions detailed above. The first question is whether Islam is incompatible with democracy. It is certainly not. In fact even if one goes by religious text the Qur'an lays emphasis on what it calls *shura*' (consultation) (3:159, 42:38). Even the messenger of Allah is required to consult his people in worldly matters and Muslims are required o consult each other in their secular affairs.

Now it is true such consultation and modern day representative democracy may not be exactly similar. However, the spirit of modern democracy and the Qur'anic injunction to consult people is same in spirit. New institutions keep on developing and human beings, depending on their worldly experiences keep on changing and refining these institutions. The Qur'anic text not only gives the concept of *shura*' (democratic consultation) but does not support even remotely any concept of dictatorship or authoritarianism.

Some people try to use the Qur'anic verse 4:59 to justify obedience to any kind of authority including a monarch or a caliph or a military dictator. It is certainly not the spirit of the Qur'anic verse. One has to see it in historical background. The verse is addressed to Bedouins who were nomads and were not habituated to submitting to any authority. The Prophet used to send his representatives to these Bedouin tribes and they will refuse to follow their instructions. The verse thus exhorted them to obey these authorities. One cannot justify submission to illegitimately constituted authority. And, if this verse is read in conjunction with the verses

3:159 and 42:38 it would mean one has to submit to properly and democratically constituted authority. An authority has to be legitimate and properly constituted.

In contemporary world the concept of *shura*' should mean democratic process and constitution of proper democratic institutions of which elections are a necessary requirement. In Islam any authority forcibly constituted or acquired by power of swords or arms can have no legitimacy whatsoever. The institution of monarchy or military dictatorship did not exist during the prophet's time at all. These are subsequent developments and were legitimised by the 'Ulama in order to prevent anarchy. Thus 'Ulama conferred some legitimacy on monarchy, not in the light of Islamic teachings but only to prevent anarchy. Some of them also became part of power structure and their pronouncements had no Islamic legitimacy. One sees this today in most of the Islamic countries. The 'Ulama in Saudi Arabia are very much part of monarchical power structure and legitimise everything the Saudi rulers do.

Thus the absence of democracy in Muslim countries is by means on account of Islamic teachings or incompatibility of democracy with Islam but due to host of factors political, historical and cultural. The imperialist powers, firstly of Europe and then those of United States also play their own role. The early Islamic democracy breathed its last within thirty years of the Holy Prophet's death. The institution of monarchy crept in under Roman influence. It is important to note that the capital of Islam had shifted from Madina to Kufa in Iraq and then to Damascus in Syria which was once under Roman Empire. Mu- 'awiyah who siezed power without consent of Muslims was functioning from Damascus and adopted Roman monarchical ways. Thus deeper historical and cultural forces must be taken into account to understand the political institutions in many Muslim countries today. The US and British interests also play their role in shaping things in these countries. In many

Islamic countries including the Saudi Arabia, Egypt and other Muslim countries there is deep urge for democracy and popular government among the people but it is frustrated by heavy hand of authoritarian rulers. Islam in no way comes in the way of establishing democracy in these countries. It is powerful vested interests both internal and external, which do not permit democracy to be established.

The next question is of implementation of Shari'ah law in Muslim countries. Many theologians and their followers believe sincerely of course that problems confronting their countries and societies can be solved by enforcing Shari'ah laws and the punishments prescribed therein. Also, they believe these laws must be enforced as they were evolved by the early jurists (*fuqaha'*) without any rethinking.

This is certainly not the spirit of the Qur'anic injunctions. Many Qur'anic verses were revealed in a particular situation and while applying these laws that has to be kept in view. The fundamental principle is to prevent crime and crime can be prevented in number of ways. At times harsh punishments become necessary and at times reformative efforts more relevant. The Qur'anic injunctions about crimes like murder, theft, robbery, rebellion, rape and adultery are understood carefully it becomes quite obvious.

For example, the verse on cutting off of hands 5:38 is immediately followed by verse 5:39 which says, "But whoever repents after his wrongdoing and reforms, Allah will turn to him (mercifully). Surely Allah is Forgiving, Merciful." Thus emphasis is on reform and repentance, not on harsh punishment. It may be awarded only in extreme case. Also, if it is read in conjunction with the verse 5:33 where punishment for "those who wage war against Allah and His Messenger and strive to make mischief in the land is that they should be murdered, or crucified, or their hands and their feet should be cut off on opposite sides, or they should be imprisoned", it should become obvious that one must distinguish between ordinary and ultimate crime. When for mischief in earth or waging war against Allah and His Messenger could be imprisonment as well, how can the punishment for mere theft could be cutting off hands.

It could be interpreted as metaphorically as well i.e. cutting off of hands means taking measures which will prevent him from committing theft in future as cutting off tongue means silencing some one, not literally cutting off tongue. Also, one must keep conditions in Arabia at the time. This was the traditional punishment meted out at that time and also some tribes indulge in crimes for their survival. The Qur'an used prevalent punishment and also added the concept of reform and repentance and talked of Allah's Forgiveness and Mercy. A criminal, if repents and reforms should be forgiven and shown mercy. Thus the Qur'an accepts the prevalent punishment but also improves upon it. The real purpose of the Qur'an is not to give harsh punishments but to reform the criminal but not to spare him if he persists despite better opportunities in life.

Another question relates to separation of state and religion. It is true Muslims in general believe that in Islam religion cannot be separated from religion. This belief has acquired almost a status of doctrine among Muslims. However, it has no such doctrinal position in the Qur'an. In fact it has been pointed out that Qur'an does not even give any concept of state, only a concept of a just society.

However, in Arabia there was no state at the time of appearance of Islam and the Prophet laid down a bare framework of administration of newly emerging society. There was no paid police, army or bureaucracy during his time. It was during the time of 2nd Caliph Umar that a register (*Diwan*) of paid army soldiers was started. Thus it was mere historical coincidence that a state structure came into existence along with a religious movement. The Shari'ah law has such status in Islam as in Arabia as there was total legal vacuum and Islam provided, for the first time a cohesive and logical legal structure. This legal structure was provided in total legal vacuum. It was great development. Hence Shari'ah law acquired very high status in Islam.

So integration of state and religion is historical coincidence rather than religious doctrine. Over period of time Shari'ah law which was result of dynamic process became stagnant. Some modern scholars tried to infuse the principle of dynamism by invoking the institution of ijtihad but did not succeed much in view of total stagnation in Muslim countries. The authoritarian rulers in Muslim countries find legitimisation only by seeking support of the 'Ulama and 'Ulama insist on retaining the Sahri'ah law as inherited from the past. If Shari'ah law is rethought or re-interpreted keeping in view the modern conditions, the orthodox 'Ulama fear loosing grip over power structures. Thus such collaboration between authoritarian rulers and orthodox 'Ulama has resulted in total social, political and legal stagnation in Muslim countries.

Though in given circumstances it may not be possible to attempt total separation between state and religion in Muslim countries as this has become integral part of historical legacy, one should begin by taking gradual steps in that direction. There cannot be any universal recipe as much will depend on concrete conditions in each Muslim country. But an overall Islamic moral framework has to be retained as had happened in many western countries including USA where an overall Christian moral frame-work has influenced law making. There are few countries in the West, which have discarded such influence totally. Among Muslim countries Turkey has achieved separation of state from religion. It also has to be borne in mind that forcible imposition of modernisation and separation of state and religion has failed in Muslim countries like Afghanistan during thirties and in Iran during Shah's time. Such attempts resulted in Islamic revolution and imposition of Shari'ah law from above.

INDIVIDUAL RIGHTS

Individual rights are very fundamental to functioning of any liberal democracy. In fact the concept of individual rights or human rights has evolved along with evolution of democratic power structure. Since there is no full fledged democracy in any Muslim country there is no respect for individual rights and many authoritarian rulers in Muslim countries reject the very concept of human rights denouncing them as western and secular in origin.

Thus one has to struggle for democratic power structure in order to usher in the concept of individual rights in Muslim countries. The Human rights activists in Muslim countries like Saudi Arabia, Egypt etc. are dubbed as western agents, persecuted and thrown into jails. As a result of this anyone who holds different political opinion faces persecution. Some who advocate change in Shari'ah laws in view of changed conditions or attempt to re-conceptualise Islamic philosophical doctrine face severe persecution. Thus there is no respect for individual rights and individual dignity. It will be possible only when democratic culture prevails. For that there is basic need for democratic polity.

Freedom of conscience and freedom of speech has never been denied by Qur'an or the Prophet. The Prophet never suppressed individual freedom or discouraged differences of opinion. He even said that difference of opinion in Islamic ummah is matter of grace and mercy. However, with evolution of feudal and monarchical culture differences of opinion were not permitted and ruthlessly suppressed. During the early Abbasid period a controversy raged whether the Qur'an is created or co-eternal with God. The Abbasid who supported the Mu'tazilah viewpoint that Qur'an is created forcibly suppressed the other point of view that Qur'a' is co-eternal with God and flogged person of Imam Abu Hanifa's'stature for holding views contrary to those of Mu'tazilah. This authoritarian culture has not changed in Muslim countries until today. Many profound scholars of Islam had to leave for western universities from countries like Egypt, Pakistan and other Muslim countries.

It is for this reason that in no Muslim country today has good tradition of social or physical sciences. For these sciences to flourish one needs liberal democratic culture. The Muslim countries would remain far behind in these fields if authoritarian power structures are not demolished and replaced with democratic ones. Unfortunately there is no such movement in sight. The United States has always propped up corrupt and authoritarian rulers in Middle East who suppress freedom of expression and these countries remain totally dependent on the west in every respect. They cannot develop even like India has developed. No Muslim country can boast of any modern scientific discovery.

ISLAM AND MODERNITY

In fact democracy and modernity go hand in hand and one can hardly be modern without being democratic. One can say that there are authoritarian models of modernisation like China and Singapore but on deeper reflection it will be seen that democratic model is far more congenial to modernisation in all spheres including social sphere. Modern social sciences cannot flourish in authoritarian regimes though natural sciences might.

However, lack of modernity in Muslim countries is not on account of Islamic teachings but more due to its medieval interpretation. Islam can not only come to terms with modernity but its teachings were quite modernistic if one goes by the Qur'anic pronouncements. Qur'an encourages pluralism if one goes by the verses like 5:48,6:109, 60:8 etc. All these verses are quite supportive of pluralistic social structure. In fact earlier the Islamic societies were much more pluralistic than any other societies throughout medieval ages. The Qur'an not only recognises validity of other faiths but also makes it incumbent for Muslims to respect equally all past prophets and one who does not, is not true Muslim. The verses 4:150-152 are clear proof thereof.

Intolerance in Muslim societies today is more political than religious. Islam is not intolerant of any other religion including that of kufr (unbelief) if it agrees to co-exist peacefully and harmoniously. Thus Islam and pluralism always go together. In fact it was in Europe in medieval ages that non-Christians were not tolerated. Islam today of course needs to be freed from intolerant theologians who are close to authoritarian power structures, which is at the root of their intolerance.

RELIGIOUS TEXT AND MODERN SOCIETIES

It is true religious texts pose some serious problems for modern society. But it need not be so with all religious texts if they are appropriately interpreted, at least not with Qur'anic text if it is understood in its real spirit. But at the same time one should not obstruct democratic social and political structure if some text is problematic. The religious text were revealed or evolved in very different social background and one must take today's relevance into account. One need not reject religious text per se but examine its suitability or otherwise for modern societies.

STATUS OF WOMEN

It is true that Muslim countries are treated women as inferior to men and try to justify this treatment by quoting from the religious texts including from Qur'an. But they quote very selectively from Qur'an to prove women's subordination to men. Qur'an, if approached holistically promoted equal status for women. The verse often quoted by theologians to show inferior status of women is 4:34 and ignore verses like 2:228, 33:35 and several others or try to explain away them as merely promoting spiritual equality. It is far from true. The Qur'an taken as a whole is far more supportive of equality of sexes. The modern Islamic scholars are totally rejecting orthodox interpretation of the verse 4:34 which was done in an atmosphere wherein male superiority was considered as quite natural, social and biological. I have discussed this in details in my book *Rights of Women in Islam.* It need not detain us here.

But one has to wage serious struggle to promote sexual equality in contemporary Muslim societies wherein Muslim women suffer several disabilities. Again, it should be a part of democratic struggle. One can break stronghold of conservative 'Ulama only in a tolerant, pluralistic modern democracy. It is not Islamic teachings which come in the way, it is orthodox 'Ulama on one hand, and authoritarian power structure, on the other, which come in the way. Qur'an, in fact, can become a great asset for promoting sexual equality.

For that we need not only modern interpretation of the Qur'anic text but also female theologians fully conscious of their rights.

18

Shari'ah Law, Civil Society and Human Rights

Recently there was a conference in Abuja, Northern Nigeria on Islamic penal and family laws and human rights to which I was invited as a resource person. The conference was convened after a woman Amina Laval was sentenced to death by stoning in Northern Nigeria for the offence of adultery. This sentence had attracted world-wide protest from human rights groups.

In this conference convened by the International Human Rights Law Group, Nigeria, not only modern scholars but also a large number of traditional 'Ulama also participated. It was a useful dialogue. What was a pleasant surprise to me was that the Nigerian 'Ulama could speak English fluently and some of them were also fully conversant with the modern academic jargon.

Number of papers were presented from both sides and were followed by heated but not acrimonious debates which generated as much light than as heat. The issue at stake was whether there was need for change in Islamic penal and family laws. Most of the 'Ulama, of Maliki persuasion (Maliki madhhab) resisted change (with few exceptions, of course) while modern scholars of Islam pleaded for it. I was also invited for a live T.V. discussion on Islamic penal laws with an 'Alim from Abuja.

The modern society has thrown up new problems which need to be tackled within the framework of Qur'an and hadith. The great jurists of early Islam also experienced various problems and they tried to tackle them in the light of their own experiences and social background. The early jurists were as much a product of their own society as we are of our own. The early jurists tried to tackle problems they were confronted with reference to the Qur'an and Sunnah of the Prophet (PBUH). Thus an element of human interpretation of the divine word and Sunnah of the Holy Prophet was definitely involved.

The 'Ulama hesitantly accepted this fact in all discussions. Thus it was established that the Shari'ah was based on human understanding of the divine sources in the light of their socio-cultural experiences. It is true that the society remained stagnant for long throughout medieval ages and no need was felt for change until nineteenth century when colonial rule in most of the Muslim countries created conditions for social change. Most of the modern movement thus started in this century. The great thinkers and reformers like Jamaluddin Afghani, Muhammad Abduh and others began to stress need for change.

In the post colonial period the nation states came into existence and these nation states undertook programme for modernisation and nation building which included programmes for spread of modern education. The spread of modern education both among men and women brought much greater awareness of social, political, cultural and religious rights. The women also acquired higher education and modern skills and began to demand their rights. All this created need and social pressure for change.

However, the 'Ulama in general, with few exceptions, refuse to take notice of any change and maintain that no change is needed. They want to follow the Shari'ah laws as evolved by the great Imams, the founders of various *madhahib* (schools). It is said that in the early period of Islam there were more than 100 schools of which only four in Sunni Islam survived. All the imams maintained that it is their opinion and their disciples differed from them on many issues. Thus there always was space for interpretation and re-interpretation.

The principle of *ijtihad* is of course accepted by all without exception but the conservative 'ulama do not permit anyone to do ijtihad saying no one is qualified to do ijtihad. Of course every one cannot be permitted to do it unless one has profound knowledge of Qur'an, sunnah, fiqh (Islamic jurisprudence), and history of evolution of Shari'ah. No one without such knowledge would ever claim right to do ijtihad. The Nigerian 'ulama too raised such objections and maintained no one including themselves are qualified to attempt ijtihad.

In fact the question is not so much of qualification as of willingness. Unless one is ready to open ones mind to modern conditions and use divine sources to reinterpret issues in penal and family laws, it will not be possible to explore the richness and comprehensiveness of the Qur'anic teachings.

The 'Ulama in Nigeria also expressed their apprehension that this re-interpretation may lead to what is called *tafsir bi' al-ra'i* (i.e. basing the Qur'anic meaning on ones own opinion) and they quoted a hadith that one who attempts *tafsir bi' al-ra'i* his place is in hell. This hadith is undoubtedly true but this was meant for those who tried to use the divine injunctions to suit their selfish desires and were swayed by their own interests. No one can be permitted to use the Qur'anic injunctions to suit ones personal interests.

But an honest and sincere attempt to interpret a divine source to meet the given conditions cannot be equated with *tafsir bi' al-ra'i.* If it is so equated then everyone, including the founders of various schools of jurisprudence, will also be exposed to that charge i.e. doing *tafsir bi' al-ra'i.* One must distinguish between an honest sincere attempt and being swayed by personal desires (what the Qur'an calls hawa').

The Holy Prophet permitted ijtihad even if there is likelihood of committing error unconsciously. He said that for those who do ijtihad and commit error would be singly rewarded and those who do so correctly will be doubly rewarded by Allah. The Prophet was well aware that his *ummah* will continue to face new situations and ijtihad (utmost intellectual exertions to understand) will be very much needed. But with the decline of Muslim power with sack of Baghdad in 13th Century the 'ulama became extremely apprehensive and closed the door of ijtihad ever since.

Now the political situation has radically changed and nation states generally tend to be democratic and a large number of Muslims live in Diaspora in many non-Muslim countries. Each nation-state has its own problems depending on level of its development, composition of population, spread of literacy and awareness of people. What is to be borne in mind that though the Qur'anic principles and values are universal, but their application is situation specific. The early jurists tried their best to apply these values and principles according to their situation and we have to apply them according to ours.

One clarification is highly necessary here. The Shari'ah has two distinct aspects: *'ibadat* and *mu'amalat* i.e. one aspect pertaining to matters of worship and beliefs about *tawhid* (unity of God), *risalah* (Mohammad being messenger of Allah and other previous prophets), *qiyamah* (Day of Resurrection). These are most fundamental beliefs (*'aqa'id*) and cannot be subject to any debating much less any change. There is naturally no question of any *ijtihad* as far as these beliefs are concerned. This also includes prayers, fasting, haj and so on.

However, it is the other aspect i.e. mu'amalat which is under discussion for likelihood of change. This was made abundantly clear to the 'ulama in Nigeria also. *Mu'amalat* pertain to interpersonal relations, family laws *ahwal al-shakhsiyyah*), crime and punishments, etc. Here too the Qur'an has laid down certain basic principles and values which are not subject to any change.

It was pointed out by me that most stressed values of Qur'an are justice (*'adl*), *ihsan* (benevolence), *rahmah* (compassion), *hikmah* (wisdom) and human dignity. These values cannot be compromised in any law and if any law violates these values would be Islamically unacceptable. All the 'Ulama accepted this unanimously and here was a meeting point. This was stressed in final declaration also.

It is also important to note that these values could not find their fullest expression during medieval ages. The Qur'anic values were far ahead of their time and the concept of justice in democratic society is qualitatively different from that in a medieval society. What was considered just then cannot be considered just now in a democratic society. This will have to be kept in mind by the law -makers today. This becomes the main point of contention between those who resist any change and those who advocate change.

The modern concept of justice is rights-oriented and not merely duty-oriented. This is great difference. Also, modern discourse gives centrality to freedom and liberty whereas medieval society and traditional 'ulama stress *'aqa'id*, constancy of epistemology. Mr. Sanusi Lamido Sanusi, a modern Nigerian Islamic scholar pointed out, "One point needs to be made before we proceed with a discussion of modernist epistemologies. Traditional Muslim thought rejects completely the principles of modernism including "western" conceptions of liberty were alien to Islam. In most instances the rejection is based on the source of these theories and their root in Judeo-Christian and/or secular paradigms."

The democratic discourse considers liberty as quite central and no democracy can survive without its centrality. However, no one can seriously argue that liberty or libertarian critique can ever ignore values mentioned above. Freedom can never transcend limits set by these fundamental values. Modern human rights discourse is entirely based on certain values. Freedom should be contraposed to authoritarianism and not to values. What it means is that there is no single authoritarian interpretation of divine source but there can be multiple interpretations.

It is interesting to note that right from the early period of Islam multiple interpretations of the Qur'an have been in vogue. It is not later day development. Many eminent commentators wrote commentaries on the Qur'an having significant differences. Also, in Shari'ah formulations imams not only relied on different ahadith but also on different interpretations. A lot has been written on this. In nineteenth century too when colonial rule began in the Muslim countries, reformists, inspired by new vision, began to reinterpret earlier sources.

In the early Islamic period differences of interpretation were mainly a result of personal inclinations. Now the differences between the orthodox and conservatives arise more on account of modern situation and new developments. The reformists today see much better chances of unfolding of the Qur'anic values and seeing various issues in the light of unfolding of these values.

Today in a democratic social structure civil society plays an important role due to its enhanced awareness and greater empowerment. The 'expert view' is also subject to much greater scrutiny today. The doctrine of *ijma'* (consensus) was limited to only 'ulama in those days. Today the doctrine could be extended to ummah as a whole, which was the real intention behind ijma'. In those days civil society did not exist nor even a section of it could intervene in such matters. Thus ijma' remained confined to the experts (i.e. 'ulama) only.

Today the concept of human rights has quite significant role to play. One cannot dismiss human rights merely as 'western concept'. They have come to be accepted universally and most of the Muslim countries are also signatories to the declaration issued by the UNO in 1948. The universality of human rights is such that many Muslim countries and their organisations are not only accepting them but also examining them in the light of teachings of Islam. Today we have Islamic declaration of human rights.

Thus we see that Organisation of Islamic Conference adopted a declaration of human rights in Islam in Cairo on 5th August 1990. There are twenty-five articles in all in this declaration. In fact numerous Qur'anic and Shari'ah pronouncements are quite compatible to human rights concept today. In fact these pronouncements preceded human rights declaration by centuries. Unfortunately the authoritarian Muslim regimes right from medieval ages until today never allowed these pronouncements the centrality they ought to have been accorded.

Many of the Shari'ah formulations based as they were on human endeavour to apply divine injunctions in their own times were also affected by medieval ethos and thus would certainly serve divine purpose better if they are rethought and reformulated afresh, especially those about which there are is no unanimity in ummah. We would also like to deal with issues of crime and punishments.

Take punishment for adultery, for example. The Shari'ah punishment for adultery in shari'ah is stoning to death. This punishment has not been mentioned in the Qur'an. In Qur'an the punishment for zina is hundred flogs. The Qur'an says, "The adulteress and adulterer, flog each of them (with) a hundred stripes, and let not pity; for them detain you from obedience to Allah, if you believe in Allah and the Last Day, and let a party of believers witness their chastisement." (24:2)

It is to be noted here that in Arabic the word *zina* is used for fornication, rape and adultery. There are no separate words for these acts in Arabic. Thus the word *zinai* in this verse includes adultery as well as fornication and rape. The punishment for both fornication as well as adultery thus will be flogging and not stoning to death. The shari- 'ah does prescribe stoning to death for adultery. But there is no basis for this in Qur'an. Even its basis in sunnah is subject to controversy.

Stoning to death was, in fact, a Jewish punishment and we find reference to this in Bukhari (23:61). According to Bukhari the Prophet (PBUH) had given this punishment to a Jew and a Jewess according to their religious tradition. And to the Muslims it was given before revelation of this verse. That the Qur'an never intended to accord stoning to death for adultery becomes clear from the verse 4:25 wherein it is specifically mentioned that the punishment for married slave-girls is half that of free women. How the death punishment can be halved? Since it is specifically mentioned married slave-girl what is intended is a punishment for adultery and not for fornication.

Also the following verse i.e. 4:3 also make it quite clear that punishment for adultery could not be stoning to death. According to this verse an adulterer can marry only an adulteress or an unbeliever and vice versa. To marry an unbeliever has been mentioned as he/she did not really strongly disapprove of such relationship in the Arab society of that time. Thus a Muslim adulterer or adulteress was considered closer to an unbeliever than to Muslims. Where is then the question of stoning to death?

The Seceders (Khawarij) never accepted stoning to death as punishment for adultery arguing on the basis of the verse 4:25. Thus one has to seriously re-think the punishment for adultery in Islam. Amina Laval's case has made it all the more urgent. Amina is a divorcee and was in fact deceived by a man who promised her to marry. She confessed to illegitimate relationship without knowing the implications. No one informed her of the implications of her confession. She is an illiterate woman from rural background.

It should also be borne in mind that a large number of Muslims live in non-Muslim countries and hence are not subject to Shari'ah punishments. In India where second largest number of Muslims in the world live, there is common secular criminal code. Shari'ah laws regarding crime and punishment do not apply to them. The British rulers enforced secular criminal code in early twentieth century and the Indian 'Ulama accepted it unanimously. In fact Maulavi Nazir Ahmed, an eminent 'alim of the time translated this secular criminal code into Urdu and was awarded the coveted title of Shamsul 'Ulama (Sun of Islamic theologians) by the British.

It would be in keeping with the Qur'anic spirit to abolish stoning to death as a punishment for adultery. It is also important to note that the Qur'anic outlook for crime and punishment is reformatory and not merely punishment-oriented. Punishment is an ultimate measure failing all other efforts to reform an offender or a criminal. *Tauba* (sincere repentance) is a measure recommended by the Qur'an repeatedly and many verses on punishment like the one on theft are followed by the ones on repentance and reform. Thus the verse 5:38 prescribing punishment for theft is followed by 5:39, which says, "But whosoever repents after his wrongdoing and reforms, Allah will turn to him (mercifully). Surely Allah is Forgiving, Merciful."

Thus it is quite clear that emphasis is as much on repentance and reform as on punishment. One cannot inflict ultimate punishment without giving chance to reform. In connection with these punishments it also has to be borne in mind that before appearance of Islam on the scene the moral conditions of the Arab society during the period of *Jahiliyyah* (ignorance) was far from healthy. Various crimes sometimes not considered crimes at all) like *zina* and inter-tribal raids etc. were widespread and had to be brought under check. And thus certain punishments had to be prescribed which appear harsh to check those crimes.

These punishments have to be seen in the then prevailing social conditions in Arabia. Only hardened criminals refusing to repent and reform could be awarded these punishments. In general emphasis is on repentance and reform. Punishments are means and not ends. Unfortunately those not aware of social conditions, social changes taking place and philosophical ends, rigidly insist on punishments and miss the baby for bath water.

Even the punishment for flogging for *zina* (fornication or adultery) appear quite harsh to us as we do not keep social conditions then prevailing into mind. Also, the way today this punishment is inflicted is not the way it was inflicted in the Prophet's period or the period immediately following his period. The provision for a party of believers witnessing the act of flogging (24:2) suggests that it was not so much bodily punishment as disgracing that was intended.

In early period whip was not used for flogging but either stick or hand or even shoes. The intention was disgracing rather than injuring. The offender was not even asked to remove all clothes unless he wore very thick clothes. However, later on rigorous rules were laid down and intention changed from disgracing to physically torturing.

Today when, unlike medieval society, emphasis is on human dignity and right to life as sacred right (the Qur'an also emphasises right to life) one has to rethink the concept of punishment as less corporeal and more as reformatory unless all efforts to reform an offender fail. Also, one must exercise ones wisdom in assessing the circumstances, which compel one to commit a particular offence. Justice otherwise cannot be done.

19

Religion, Pluralism and Modern Society

I

Modern society, one wishes or not, is essentially a pluralistic society. The great religions of the world, on the other hand, have originated, more often than not, in monolithic societies. Thus the theologies of these religions were tailored to suit such societies. Even if a religion originated in a society with more than one religion and subsequently became a dominant religion in that society, its theology evolved as if it was the only valid religion.

In order to understand it in proper perspective one could divide religion into three related categories: 1) the revelatory aspect of religion which is contained in the compilation of revelations received by the prophet or intuitional sayings of its founder; 2) theology developed on the basis of these revelations, sayings of the prophet, and the immediate circumstances in which those observations were made and 3) popular practices, customs and traditions among the followers of that religion.

Thus most fundamental to a religion should be its revelatory aspect which lays down the principles and guide lines for its followers. However, often this part of religion is sidelined and theologies developed by eminent theologians of the faith and traditions and popular practices become more widely accepted. The real problem in accepting validity of other religions is not revelatory or intuitional aspect but the latter two i.e. theological and popular traditions. Sometimes popular practices and traditions are much more accommodative than the theological aspect.

The real problem in accepting the validity of other religions is mainly posed by theological rather than revelational aspects. Theology is more of a human construct than divine injunction though it is based on revelation. However, theological formulations are primarily based on human understanding of the revelatory text and this understanding is influenced by human circumstances. If the religion concerned becomes dominant one or is embraced by the rulers its theology often reflects this dominant, majoritarian attitude.

Christianity as long as it was religion mainly followed by the oppressed people of Palestine its dominant values were very different. The Bible is full of sympathy for the oppressed, exploited and rejected of the society. There was much more emphasis on the Sermon on the Mount than on conversion and damnation of non-Christian. However, after few centuries when it was embraced by the Roman rulers, the attitude of its theologians underwent change and it acquired the characteristics of a religion of the dominant ruling community. Now there was greater emphasis on damnation of non-Christians.

Islam too has similar history. Its Meccan phase is much more humane and full of sympathy for the oppressed and exploited. In fact Mohammad Taha of Sudan, emphasises this in his *Second Coming of Islam.* He feels emphasis should be on the Meccan practices to make modern Islam more humane and pro-oppressed. Though the Qur'anic revelations remained consistent with the Meccan revelations (there cannot be contradictions in divine revelations), the Medinese practice of Islam is more problematic.

In Madina Islam soon became religion of majority and despite its ideals of recognising Christianity and Judaism as religions brought by the prophets of Allah Moses and Jesus, it came into clash with Jews who began to resent dominant position acquired by Islam and thus the Medinese Jews began to secretly conspire with Meccan unbelievers to defeat Islam and Muslims.

The Prophet (PBUH), as long as he was alive, remained a role model for his followers and he practised the Qur'anic values like *'adl* (justice), *karamah* (human dignity) and *rahmah* (compassion). He tried to accommodate Jews as best as he could in the given circumstances and even entered into a pact with them giving them full freedom to follow their religion. They were made part of the city community of Madina. But conflict of human interests did bring about clashes between them and Muslims. And that the Muslims were emerging as a dominant community made things more difficult.

Subsequently Islam emerged as a religion of the most powerful empires of the world and this became the classical period of Islam. Most of the theologies and juristic theories and formulations came into existence during this period. These theologies do reflect the dominant position of Muslims during the period. The Qur'an had shown great respect for all the prophets and mentioned by name several of them, though not all of them. The Qur'an also made it obligatory for Muslims to show equal respect to all these prophets and those who do not are real unbelievers.

Yet, Muslims and Jews on one hand, and Muslims and Christians on the other, came into serious conflict. The crusades, though apparently religious wars were in fact, struggle for power between the two dominant communities. Both communities wanted to occupy as much political space as possible and fought to extend their sphere of influence. It is interesting to note that during the Medinese period there is clash between

Muslims and Jews and more amiable relations between Muslims and Christians. But later on main conflict developed between Christians and Muslims.

The reason is obvious. In Madina there were no Christians and the Jews enjoyed dominant position before advent of Islam. However, this position of the Jews was threatened after Muslims occupied both social and political space and Jews felt they were being marginalised. Thus conflict developed between them and it resulted in bloody battles.

However, when Islam spread to areas under Roman Empire, it clashed with Christians and this conflict with Christians continued as Islam spread to Europe where Christianity was a dominant religion. This conflict acquired the form of theological war as reflected into the Muslim and Christian theologies of the period. And since there was no Jewish empire anywhere at that time, there is no further history of conflict between two communities until the state of Israel came into existence in 1948.

Thus it will be seen that there is no real religious conflict between these religions. Yet, if one examines the pronouncements of theologians of that period one will find serious conflict and even damnation of each other. It was not really conflict of religions and question of spiritual salvation but of political domination and socio-cultural space.

In India too, there was in fact no conflict between Islam and Hinduism in religious and spiritual sense. Those Muslim theologians, who were part of Muslim ruling establishments, tended to adopt condemnatory attitude towards Hindu religion. Their condemnation was not based on close study of Hindu scriptures but on popular practices prevalent. Also, those theologians trying to go closer to the rulers or ruling establishments, tended to show greater degree of hostility towards the religion of rival community and their attitude also reflected arrogance of ruling theologians.

II

It is also important to note that there is as much inner plurality within a religious community as between external religious communities. One finds as much degree of hostility between inner plurality as among external plurality. The Christians developed several sects in its early period and leaders of one sect persecuted the people belonging to other sect, especially when these leaders happened to be in dominant position or with dominant power structure.

Thus there was serious conflict between Roman Catholics, the Orthodox Christians and Monophysites when Islam appeared on the scene. The Monophysites on the border of Roman empire who also happened to be Arabs were severely persecuted by the Roman Christians as they happened to be in dominant position. Persecution was so severe that many of these Monophysite Arab Christians preferred to adopt Islam rather than remain Christians and face persecution. The Roman Catholics also severely persecuted the Protestants later in Europe when Martin Luther rejected the sole papal authority.

Islam also developed several sects in its early period. The first schism appeared on the question of succession to the Prophet (PBUH) i.e. between Sunnis and Shi'ahs. When the Umayyads constituted the ruling dynasty the Shi'ahs were seriously persecuted. The persecution was so severe that the Shi'ahs had to adopt the doctrine of *taqiyya* i.e. dissimulation. To avoid persecution they practised the Sunni faith publicly but followed the Shi'ah faith in private.

The Isma'ilis faced similar persecution at the hands of the Abbasids for close to two centuries and the Abbasids hunted down for the Isma'ili Imams who went into seclusion and lived life hidden from their own followers. There was dissension within the Sunnis and one Sunni sect persecuted other Sunni sects. There was great conflict between those who believed the Qur'an was co-eternal with Allah and those who believed it was created by Allah. Imam Abu Hanifa, an eminent Sunni jurist was severely persecuted and lashed publicly for holding the opinion that the Qur'an was co-eternal with Allah.

This internal plurality within every religious community also became cause of severe conflict and damnation of dominated community by the dominant community.

Thus it will be seen that internal pluralism has caused as much problems as the external pluralism. Tensions and conflicts, as shown above, have not so much on account of religious teachings per se as on account of either power struggle or similar other material causes. The Qur'an does not teach disrespect to any other religion. Christians and Jews were treated as people of the book (*ahl al-kitab*) and this category was extended to other faiths such as Zoroastrians (by the Prophet himself) and Hindus by the 'ulama.

It is true that often some 'ulama would declare Christians or Hindus as kafirs but it was again for reasons other than religious. Imam Taymiyyah, for example, declares Christians as kafirs in thirteenth century when Christians and Muslims were engaged in crusades. Similarly, many 'ulama in India often pronounced the fatwa of *kufr* against Hindus in the course of power struggle. Similarly some 'ulama belonging to one school of thought issued fatwa of *kufr* against the 'ulama of another school of thought.

Also, there have been different trends both orthodox as well as liberal in the same religious community. Sufis, for example, adopted very liberal attitude and never condemned people of other religions. Muhiyuddin ibn Arabi who was founder of sufi school of *Wahdat al-Wujud* (Unity of Being) was quite open to all other faiths. In fact the doctrine of *Wahdat al-Wujud* itself, as propounded by him, is quite liberal one and implies that real being is one and all of us are His manifestations. Thus all being His manifestation, there should be no wall of separation between them.

The sufis practised another important doctrine called *sulh-I-kul* meaning total peace and by implication peace with all. Such doctrines are very helpful for a pluralist society. In India, which has been a pluralist society for centuries sufi doctrines were extremely helpful in maintaining inter-religious peace. It is important to note that the sufis maintained their distance from power structures and were not involved with power seeking rulers and hence could be more effective in maintaining religious harmony. They believed in dialogue and were not averse to cultural adaptation.

It was this sufistic attitude coupled with Bhakti movement in India that religious synthesis, rather than religious confrontation resulted. Many syncretistic religions like Kabir Panth, Sikkhism, Pranam Panth, Imam Shahi sect etc. came into existence. Also, common people in India developed respect for all religions. The Indian tradition encouraged *sarva dharma sambhava* (equal respect for all religions) and the Islamic tradition emphasised *al-khalq-u-'ayalullah* (entire creation is Allah's family). Thus both these traditions promoted adjustment with plurality. Thus in medieval India pluralism became way of life for the people.

However, Europe was not so fortunate. When India was enjoying comparative religious harmony and peace Europe was involved in inter-religious conflict of severe kind. On one hand, there were anti-Jewish pogroms, and on the other, intense struggle between Protestants and Catholics. But renaissance ushered in an enlightened era later on. It was this renaissance period, which encouraged growth of science and Europe began to change radically.

III

But modernity and scientific progress in Europe was not without problems for the Asian and African countries. These countries experienced colonialism and colonial policies were based on divide and rule. India, which had enjoyed relative religious peace throughout medieval ages, began to experience religious conflict during modern colonial period. Thus modernity came to India at the cost of religious strife. The religious plurality became a severe problem during modern period in India.

Thus as far as India was concerned modernity dawned with religious conflict partly because of divide and rule policy of the British colonialists and partly because of indigenous factors. Modernity encourages competitiveness and in a religiously pluralist society communal differences become the main fault lines. Thus the Hindu elite and the Muslim elite began to compete for scarce jobs and took the form of communal strife. This was further exacerbated by the British policies both of divide and rule and that of stifled economic growth.

Now the process was reversed. While European society began to experience greater degree of secularisation both due to renaissance and faster economic growth, the Indian society began to experience more and more communalised and the strife continues until today. Thus modern democracy, which was thought to be a great boon for its emphasis on secular governance, often became a nightmarish experience due to caste and communal differences getting exacerbated. Caste and communal identities became the main source of political mobilisation for the political elite of these caste and community elites.

In all communal and religious strifes today, religious leaders are not as much involved as the political leaders. More intolerance is shown towards other communities by communally charged political leaders than religious leaders. However, it does not mean that religious leaders do not play any negative role; they do. Either they collaborate with communal leadership or remain silent spectators of hate campaign by communal leaders. In the Gujarat carnage last year the religious leaders in Gujarat chose to remain silent and thus strengthened the hands of communal fanatics in massacre of innocent people.

A modern pluralist society cannot function smoothly unless politicians continue to exploit religious differences for political mobilisation. Unless politics is issue-based and value-based the pluralist societies will continue to experience intense strife. Also, religious leaders should shun power ambitions. Unfortunately some religious leaders choose to collaborate with communal politicians in order to fulfil their ambitions for power.

Religion has staged come back for numerous reasons. Firstly, in modern secular societies economic and political competition creates uncertainties and religion becomes an anchor for common people. The modern societies uproot people from their place of birth and force them to migrate from less developed to more developed areas in search of livelihood. This creates sense of alienation and rootlessness. Religious identities alone can provide sense of belonging and rootedness.

A modern urban society creates sense of directionlessness and meaninglessness. It is religion which can remove this sense of directionlessness and meaninglessness and thus religion becomes a very important source of intellectual certainty. All this leads to greater urge to belong to a religious tradition and a strong sense of religious identity. And in a multi-religious society this becomes a source of conflict.

It is therefore highly necessary to maintain harmony in modern multi-religious societies. This can be done only if members of all religious communities strive together to usher in a just and equitable society. No religious community should be unfairly treated. Modern societies consist of more educated and aware people and hence they are quite sensitive to injustice of any kind. This sense of injustice will always be politically exploited and would become sure recipe for strife.

Second important thing for modern pluralist societies is to treat religion only as what it is meant to be i.e. a source of spiritual and moral growth, and not as a means for fulfilling political ambitions. It is only the modern committed intelligentsia, which can evolve checks and balances to maintain inter-religious harmony. For this it is not only necessary to develop equal respect for all religions but also to shun religion-based politics. In modern competitive societies it is very dangerous to indulge in religion-based politics. It will surely lead to religious extremism, as we have been experiencing in India and Pakistan.

Religious extremism causes great deal of violence in the society and innocent people are repeatedly butchered as we have seen in the case of Algeria also. No religion permits violence against defenceless people but religious extremists are blinded by their rage against the enemy. They legitimise their feeling of revenge by invoking religion against the innocent people of other religion. The modern society has developed highly destructive weaponry, which can kill hundreds at a time.

Thus those who are committed to true spirit of religion should cultivate tolerance and respect for different religions and should see to it that religious differences are solved through dialogue rather than through confrontation. Modern urban life is far more tension ridden for ordinary people and any emotional issue can lead to religious extremism and militancy.

Thus truly committed people would always try to promote better understanding among people of diverse religions. Peace, in such pluralist societies, should be the first priority for those committed to religious teachings. Pluralism, as a *doctrine* can greatly help as it means accepting equal validity for all religions and to live in peace with people of other religious traditions. This is true spirit of pluralism as a religious doctrine.

20
Muslim World and Role of Intelligentsia

The Muslim world is undoubtedly under throes of crisis and Muslim masses in general and Muslim intellectuals in particular are deeply concerned about it. What is the nature of that crisis and what are causes of the crisis needs to be analysed and understood properly before any remedial measures can be suggested. And after the attack on 9/11 the sense of, if not the actual nature of, the crisis has deepened.

The nature of crisis has to be traced to the pace of modern changes, which are taking place rapidly in the Muslim world today. Most of the Muslim countries have still not left their feudal past behind. The mindset of Muslim peoples in these countries is still attuned to feudal era. The feudal value-system requires people to submit to, rather than be critical of, ruling and religious authorities. The Muslim world is in a state of transition and the transitory state is bound to create crisis and confusion.

All countries and peoples go through such crisis and intellectual confusion. The European countries went through it during 17-18 centuries lingering over to 19th century. It was during this period that the authority of the church was weakened, democratic governance emerged and critical mindset developed. It is also to be noted that the European countries, especially England

and France, could ease the nature of their transition through colonialism. This luxury is not available to any country of the third world. On the other hand, the nature of crisis in Muslim countries is getting worse because of further crisis being created on account of globalisation.

One cannot understate the nature of crisis in the Muslim world today. These countries for various reasons have even not been fully democratised. Either they are ruled by kings, sheikhs and military dictators or at best have strictly controlled democracy. While Gulf countries fall in the first category, countries like Algeria, Syria, Pakistan and Malaysia, fall under second category. However, the western world is particularly more worried about the nature of crisis in the Gulf countries as these are oil rich countries and the West, especially the USA wants to maintain its sole hegemony here.

Much of the crisis has to do with the hegemonic control America wants to exercise over this region. The Western, and particularly the American interests in this region has not only aggravated the nature of the crisis in the Muslim world, it has stalled the process of democratisation also. It is the irony of the situation that these very powers then blame Islam for lack of democracy in the Muslim countries.

It would be interesting to throw some light on this question, as it is also part of the contemporary crisis in the Muslim world. Some of the Muslim countries like Algeria, Libya, Syria, Iraq, Malaysia, Indonesia (and of course Pakistan and Bangla Desh) were colonised but countries like Saudi Arabia, Iran etc. were not directly colonised. The freedom struggle in some of these countries was armed struggles and that played a part in emergence of militarily controlled regimes or controlled democracy. In Egypt the struggle was democratic but the power was transferred to King Farouq rather than an elected regime and then Jamal Abdul Nasir staged a coup and captured power. He put down Islamic extremist opposition to his regime with heavy hand and before he could accomplished much died a pre-mature death and power was captured by lesser people like Anwar Sadat and controlled democracy was put in place.

In Iran again struggle against imperialist domination was not violent and Mosaddiq tried to usher in democracy and nationalised oil. However, this was totally unacceptable to Western powers and America used CIA to stage a coup against Mosaddiq and brought the Shah back to power who ruled over Iran until he was overthrown by Islamic revolution in 1979.

In Algeria the nature of struggle against French imperialism was in the nature of armed insurrection and power passed over to those who controlled arms and thus army established its control over power and is reluctant to give up power even though it was voted out in early nineties. In the Gulf countries the kings and sheikhs who wielded power were not allowed to be disturbed by the Western powers, as there was high stake due to presence of rich oil resources.

In Indonesia Sukarno came to power due to his prestige acquired during struggle against the Dutch imperialists but was overthrown in a coup by Suharto, a military general with the help of CIA due to Sukarno's 'dangerous' inclination towards China. Thus Indonesia also continued for close to four decades under military dictatorship until the people of Indonesia won democracy through their hard struggle.

Thus this brief survey shows clearly that lack of democracy in the Muslim world today is more because of imperialists machinations than because of Islam. Since the USA supports the dictatorial regimes in the Muslim world, particularly in the Gulf countries, the peoples of these countries are unable to express their grievances democratically and they resort to violence to find ventilation to their suppressed anger. The attacks on 9/11 on trade towers on New York were partly due to these reasons though there is more to it than only this.

The events of 9/11 are going to have far reaching consequences for the Muslim world as much deeper processes are involved than mere attack on the trade towers. Not only that the Muslim world will have to come to grips with new realities the Western powers also have to deal with an entirely new situation. This new situation is partly their own creation though they could never foresee it. For the peoples of the Muslim world too, this would prove to be a blessing in disguise. It has given a new impetus to the thinking process among the Muslim intellectuals.

Apart from all this there is yet another factor which is deeply impacting on the Muslim world, particularly on the countries of the Gulf region i.e. modernisation. It also has lot to do with oil resources in the region. This region until recently was quite poor in resources and it was in early seventies after the war of Yom Kippur that oil prices shot up and the region was suddenly flooded with what came to be known as 'petro-dollars' or 'black gold'. This tremendously increased the pace of modernisation in the region causing great deal of turmoil.

Social change, if it is brought suddenly and with greater pace than people can digest, leads to great turmoil and intellectual confusion. The Gulf region including Saudi Arabia was stagnant for centuries and people were content with their religion and cultural traditions and at peace with themselves. But it all changed suddenly as if they were caught in a vortex. The ruling classes in the region could hardly be expected to manage the whole situation wisely. They were worried more about their own stability and continuation than managing the change with wisdom and insight. Moreover the Islamic revolution further frightened them and added to their woes. Some of them feared they might be overthrown any time.

Also, Ayatollah Khomeini and Saddam had their own irreconcilable hostility towards each other. Saddam, under pressure from the Shah of Iran, had thrown

Khomeini out of Iraq and he had to take refuge in France. When the Ayatollah made Islamic revolution succeed in Iran, called for overthrow of Saddam and made repeated appeal to the Shi'ahs of Iraq. These repeated appeals provoked Saddam and goaded by USA he invaded Iran and the 10 year long war between these two countries created a new crisis in the region. Later Saddam attacked Kuwait too (perhaps again under direct or indirect motivation from the CIA) pluging the region yet in another crisis.

All these developments made the Gulf regimes more panicky and hence more repressive. Apart from political repression these rulers saw greater chance of their political survival in using religion for political ends. The concept of Islamic state and enforcing orthodox Shari'ah laws strictly came in handy. These measures were publicised with all fanfares to create a repressive orthodox religious atmosphere. Due to fear of Islamic revolution of Iran greatly hostile to America, the USA also adopted policies to undo Islamic revolution in Iran, on one hand, and to project Islam in bad light, on the other. It was American media, which coined the term 'Islamic fundamentalism' and gave it a pejorative sense.

It was strange irony that the American rulers strengthen the authoritative rulers in the Gulf region on one hand who depended mainly on enforcing what American media called 'fundamentalist Islam' and on the other, condemned it outright. The Americans had to play these games to serve their interests in the region. This created lot of confusion in the minds of non-Muslims dependent on the media for their information and anger among the Muslim youth from these countries.

The Gulf region has remained in great turmoil ever since oil prices have gone up in early seventies and subsequent Islamic revolution in Iran. The region has not known peace ever since. Again America attacked Iraq under the pretext of it possessing weapons of mass destruction and plunged the region in further crisis. Now a section of the Iraqi people, particularly the supporters of Saddam Hussain, has unleashed unstoppable violence. America, now fearing worst scenario, wants to quit Iraq as early as possible. Thus it is America, which is creating conditions for political violence in the region, it is Islam which is portrayed as violent by the media.

Instead of analysing the situation people blame the violence on Islam. This is further reinforced by acts of few Muslim groups who commit violence invoking the concept of jihad. The people then begin to think that Muslims resort to violence as a religious obligation and that Islam teaches violence. This impression is very widespread and it is for Muslim intellectuals to remove it. Many of us unfortunately defend use of violence out of anger and revenge and this further reinforces the impression that Islam requires its followers to resort to jihad.

The Muslim intellectuals, who understand the goings on in the modern world, have great responsibility to study Islamic teachings in the light of modern day challenges and project proper image of Islam. This task cannot be left to orthodox 'ulama most of whom often view things with a medieval mind-set. On account of their training in conventional madrasas, they are unable to develop critical thinking. They are trained only to submit to given dogmas. Often they issue fatwas in the light of their conventional learning without proper understanding of modern day developments.

The conventional centres of higher Islamic learning do not impart teachings in modern social sciences, much less in natural and physical sciences. When the Soviet Union sent a satellite to moon in late fifties, a learned 'alim (a friend of my father who was also a conventional 'alim) denounced it and called it a 'deplorable act of man to intervene in the divine functioning'. When human cloning was being discussed a Saudi 'alim issued a fatwa that the scientist who worked on human cloning is severely punished.

Such fatwas then are headlined in the media and ignorance of modern world by the conventional 'alims brings bad name to Islam. It is unfortunate that still in the centres of higher learning of Islam the theories and dogmas developed during medieval ages and which have nothing to do with the Qur'an and authentic sunna are being taught. Even those concepts borrowed from Greek sciences and philosophies remain integral part of Islamic learning.

During second and third centuries of Islam these Greek sciences and philosophies were most progressive and our 'ulama and philosophers readily accepted them and thus became precursors in the world of higher knowledge. It was through them that the European scholars came to know about Greek treasure of knowledge and hence H.G. Wells, a noted historian, describes the Arabs as 'foster-fathers' of Greek knowledge and wisdom. However, the Greek sciences are matter of history now and modern science has taken great strides.

But the Islamic institutes of higher learning have still not imbibed these scientific developments. Our 'ulama remain hooked to medieval sciences and vehemently reject modern scientific theories and discoveries and even dub them as sheer blasphemy. It is to be noted that this is doing great harm to the Muslim community as a whole as common Muslims are often influenced by the opinion expressed by them. Thus there is great need for reforms in madrasa education (also described as modernisation) no initiative is being taken by authorities in the Muslim world.

It is matter of great concern that despite great deal of oil money the Gulf countries have not taken worthwhile steps to disseminate modern scientific education. There are no institutions of higher learning and research in modern sciences. More and more Islamic universities are being opened to train theologians and Islamic jurists. Needless to say these theologians and jurists lack knowledge of modern social sciences and juridical theories. In these institutions there is no development of knowledge but only encouragement acknowledge, no process of cognition but only emphasis on recognition.

These Muslim nations will remain totally subservient to the western countries in the field of science and technologies. Mere possession of natural resources does not make a nation powerful. What makes a nation powerful is development of science and technology. The Arab countries like Kuwait and Dubai have become mere modern markets and centres of distribution, but not of production.

The oil wealth acquired by the Arab ruling classes is either transferred to western banks for safe custody or squandered only on consumption. This easily got money is being spent only on conspicuous consumption and ostentation. What is needed for technological progress of these countries is to save these precious resources and convert them into investible capital. For industrialisation one needs capital formation. These Gulf countries, however, has no will for industrialisation. They are content to become mere market places where goods produced in Japan, China and other western countries can be exchanged and sold but not produced.

Even for their defence these countries are totally dependent on America and hence the Gulf countries have become its army bases. Neither they have weapons nor properly trained army personnel. They do not have even trained personnel for various other technical jobs be they technical or managerial. They have to import human-power from other countries. There is not a single Muslim country, which can be considered in scientific and industrial developments even close to India, let alone any western country. These countries have no trained scientists, particularly theoretical scientists.

The Qur'an lays so much emphasis on studying the universe created by Allah. The true worship of Allah does not imply only praying to Him but also studying His creation. A true believer is one who meticulously studies the entire creation of Allah which include the development of theoretical and applied sciences. In Modern times the Muslim world has not even produced any astronomer or physicist of great repute. Study of astronomy and cosmic physics is so essential for proper understanding of our universe. Dr. Abdus Salam, a noble laureate in theoretical physics was also product of western universities. His services were not even properly recognised by ay Muslim country. When he proposed to the Saudis to finance him for establishing a laboratory for theoretical physics to study strong and weak forces. The Saudis turned down the proposal and Abdus Salam established the lab in Italy with the help of funds from UNESCO.

If the Muslim nations have to become self-reliant powers unto themselves the first requirement is to establish institutions of higher scientific learning and go for theoretical research in modern sciences. This of course requires training modern scientist with critical mindset. Absence of democratic culture produces only submissive minds and those who possess critical faculties run away to other safer countries. The absence of open democratic culture in Muslim countries is another obstacle in the progress of science and technology.

Though it is not desirable to go for nuclear weaponry, the Muslim countries (with the exception of Pakistan) are not even capable of developing nuclear science. America will never allow them to do so for fear of developing nuclear weaponry. Thus some of them try to obtain enriched uranium, heavy water etc. stealthily from Pakistan. Dr. A.Q.Khan is reported to have allegedly sold them technical know-how. Pakistan, though economically backward compared to oil rich gulf countries, is scientifically more advanced in the Muslim world, thanks to South Asian traditions of scientific learning.

In these Muslim countries one does not find great scholars of social sciences, much less natural sciences due mainly to lack of intellectual freedom. Any scholar who shows any sign of independent thinking faces severe persecution. This lack of culture of intellectual freedom is matter of great concern who want to see Islamic world progress and achieve great heights of knowledge in all fields of life. America will be more than happy if the Islamic world concentrates only on religious sciences as of now and neglects natural sciences. This will ensure their dependence on America and other western nations and they will continue to exploit the rich oil resources of these countries unchallenged.

It would therefore be almost suicidal for these countries to remain stagnant and adopt only outward signs of modernisation (i.e. modern buildings and infrastructure mainly built by western experts what is called hard modernism). And to suppress or neglect progress in theoretical natural and physical sciences with resultant implication of intellectual freedom and critical thinking, democracy and respect for human rights (what can be called soft and inner modernisation).

It is therefore duty of modern Muslim intellectuals to come forward, at times even at the risk of persecution from authorities, and attempt a healthy critique of modern Muslim regimes and work towards flowering of modern sciences in the Muslim world. It would be not in the interest of peoples of these countries to depend on conventional 'ulama for the intellectual resources. They will ensure backwardness of Muslim countries, if they become the sole intellectual resource for the people.

Ideally a synthesis of Islamic and modern sciences can work miracles for backward Muslim societies as the modern trained 'ulama can be a bridge between religious and natural sciences and this can have great impact on Muslim masses. It would require futuristic vision on the parts of authorities to establish such institutions of learning. No one seems to be in sight right now. But one can certainly visualise it so that it becomes a reality at some future date.

The Muslim world had witnessed such flowering of intellectual culture during third and fourth century of Islam when great philosophers and scientists were also great scholars of Islamic sciences. We need it today even with greater intensity and spread.

21
Concept of Justice in Qur'an and The Islamic World

The Concept of justice is quite central to the Qur'an. The pre-Qur'anic Arab society was governed by oral customs and traditions. The tribal society had its own ways of dealing with situations requiring justice and normally no problems arose. In Meccan society too tribal norms were sufficient as long as no institution of private property had developed. But in pre-Islamic days the Meccan tribal society was far from being static. It was undergoing fast changes and hence tribal norms or oral customs and traditions were not sufficient to deal with emerging complex situation.

Mecca, as I have discussed in details in my book *The origin and Development of Islam* (Orient Longman, 1998) had developed into an international centre of high finance and inter-tribal corporations were coming into being, weakening tribal bonds on one hand, and, tribal norms, customs and traditions, on the other. Along with finance and commerce, institution of private property had developed and new problems, often severe in nature, of injustices, began to emerge in the society.

Accumulation of wealth and aggravation of poverty and misery, as in modern society, went hand in hand. Instances of starvation and hunger were spreading. All tribal norms and practices had broken down. There was no way for the weaker sections of society to get justice. There was no government or ruler to appeal to. No courts to approach and no tribal institutions for redressal of their grievances.

When instances of injustices, oppression and exploitation increased and violence and injustices multiplied, descendants of Hashim, Zuhrah and Taim in Mecca formed an alliance of virtuous Hilf al-Fudul for redressal of grievances of violence and injustices. Muhammad was then young and later when he became Prophet used to remember this alliance with pride. According to Sir William Muir, this confederacy "aroused an enthusiasm in the mind of Mahomet, which the exploits of the sacrilegious war failed to kindle."

Thus the Prophet (PBUH) was deeply concerned with justice from his very young age. He was observing the social and economic scene of Mecca and was deeply disturbed. He also was disturbed deeply by the religious scenario of Meccan society. He found nothing but superstitious practices and no real spiritual content. Also, tribal chiefs and the powerful in the society went unchallenged. He intensely felt about them and it burst forth in Meccan surahs like 104 and 107. Both are strongly denunciatory of accumulation of wealth and of neglecting the poor and needy.

Thus 'adl (justice) became a key word in the Qur'an and also one of the names of Allah i.e. 'Adil. Also, one who is muttaqi i.e. pious must be 'adil (5:8). A true worshipper of Allah has to be just as Allah is Just Himself. Justice, as we would see shortly, is an all comprehensive concept in the Qur'anic ethic. 'Adl, in Arabic carries sense of balance and absence of excess. Thus a balance has to be maintained in life as a whole, whether it is social, economic, conjugal or spiritual life. The concept of justice requires that there should not be excesses even in spiritual life as far as an average person is concerned. It is for this reason that Islam does not encourage ruhbaniyyah (renunciation of the world) as it would disturb balance between secular and spiritual life. The Prophet, though a spiritual person in orientation and deeply revered by the sufis for this reason, never renounced the world. He lived in the world and changed it. He successfully ushered in a great revolution based on the concept of justice in all fields of life. According to W. C. Smith, it was the greatest and most systematic revolution before the communist revolution in the world.

The concept of justice is so comprehensive in the Qur'an that no field has been left out where it is not applied including, as pointed out above, the filed of conjugal relations. The permission for polygamy was not granted unconditionally and most important and most emphatic condition laid down was justice for all wives. There are two verses on polygamy in the Qur'an 4:3 and 4:129 and both verses emphatically mention justice to the wives. While the 4:3 says if you fear you cannot do justice then marry only one and the other verse 4:129 says that you cannot do justice between wives even if you wish but be not disinclined (from one) with total disinclination, so that you leave her in suspense.

Thus it would be seen that justice is an important and basic requirement even in conjugal relations. Defining the concept of justice for more than one wife the Islamic jurists maintain that the husband should not only pay equal maintenance for justice to be done but also spend equal time with each of them. But some Mu'tazilite jurists, referring to the verse 4:129 even maintained that equal maintenance and equal time are not enough, equal love for all wives would also be necessary in order for justice to be done. Otherwise ends of justice will not be met.

The Qur'anic concept of justice is also very critical of ostentatious use of wealth and accumulation of riches. The 'afw (what is more than basic need) should be given away for the needy in the society (see 2:219). To check ostentation Islam even forbade wearing of gold ornament and silk clothes for men and use of silver wares. Such ostentation throws economic balance overboard and causes grave economic injustices to the deprived sections of society.

However, in history of humanity including in the history of Islam such economic balance or economic justice could not be done except for a brief period of time. Unfortunately, as we would see Islamic history is also full of economic injustices and hence its history also remained full of violence and turmoil.

The Qur'an had repeatedly warned against accumulation of wealth (9:34 etc.) and Qur'an strongly expressed its sympathy for the weak (mustad'ifin) in 28:5 and yet history of Islam, like history of other religions, was dominated by the powerful (mustakbirin). It was, therefore, full of oppression and exploitation though of course there were short spells of justice and peace.

As pointed out above, pre-Islamic society of Mecca and Madina was full of violence, injustices and exploitation. Powerful vested interests had come into existence and it was not easy to establish justice in that society. Whatever violence and bloodshed we see during the life time of the Prophet was due to his untiring efforts to establish a just society where there would be no exploitation and oppression.

The Qur'an also denounced economic exploitation and dishonest trade practices. It greatly emphasised honesty in weights and measures and denounced weighing less. Thus the Qur'an says, "And give full measure when you measure out, and weigh with a true balance. This is fair and better in the end." (17:35) This should not be understood mechanically but symbolically.

The word used in this verse qistas is quite meaningful as it means justice. Thus the whole economic system should be based on justice whether it is trade system or system of economic production. What the Qur'an implies is exchange of commodities should be just and iriba' any excess in exchange giving less and demanding more of the same commodity is a grave injustice. In fact riba' is excess in hand to hand exchange of commodities. Qur'an strongly denounces the practice of riba'. Riba' literally means unjust growth and any unjust growth is strongly denounced. Thus all unfair practices which lead to enrichment of few at the cost of toil of others are unjust and condemned by the Qur'an.

The Qur'an wanted to establish a society free of all forms of exploitation, a society based on equality and human dignity and human dignity included dignity of both the genders. Justice is of course difficult to define and hence, as we would see later, there were debates on the concept of justice in early Islamic society. It is important to note that the Qur'an was being revealed there was no production but exchange of commodities and that too except in Mecca the whole economy was based on primitive exchange.

Yet, the Qur'an gives us highest form of moral consciousness and a very comprehensive concept of justice. For comprehensive justice one needs fulfilment of several other conditions – like freedom of conscience and freedom of conscience is possible only when one accepts human dignity and human dignity is possible only when racial, tribal and national discriminations are rejected. Thus we see there are so many dependent conditions to be established before we can have comprehensive concept of justice.

It is amazing that in a primitive society like the one which prevailed in Arabia before Islam we have such a refined system of morality through the Qur'an which emphasises all these pre-requisites of freedom of conscience (2:251), human dignity (17:70) and exhortation not to discriminate between people of different races, nations and tribes (49:13). Thus the Qur'an does not confine itself to the use of word 'adl (justice) but also talks about all associated attributes required to establish social justice. The Prophet repeatedly emphasised that an Arab is in no way is superior to a non-Arab. The Arabs were of course very proud of their arabness but the Prophet never hesitated for a moment to attack this false Arab pride. There were many people of non-Arab origins; in the then Meccan and Madinese societies who were mostly of lowly origin like slaves and to accord them equal dignity was to deeply hurt the Arab pride. But the Qur'anic teachings and the Prophet were quite emphatic about human dignity, hurt or no hurt to Arab pride. Justice cannot be established without rigorously following universal norms.

But the Arabs who embraced Islam did not put these norms into practice. The first four caliphs themselves found the situation so difficult and complex. Always people embrace any religion for different reasons. Some embrace it because it appeals to their hearts and minds and they make all possible sacrifices for the purpose. It is their inner conviction which motivate them. Several Meccans initially embraced Islam with their heart and soul and with deep conviction and made great sacrifices to uphold their convictions.

After Islam became a force, all sorts of people as usual started embracing it. After conquest of Mecca its worst enemies embraced it as there was no other way left and they could gain a lot by embracing it. What they could not gain by opposing it, now they desired to gain by adopting it, especially the Umayyads. Also, there were many Bedouin tribes who had resisted and made common cause with those Qurayshites of Mecca who fought against the Prophet of Islam. They also had no other way but to accept Islam.

But these Bedouins were not comfortable with any form of government. After the death of the Prophet a systematic government was sought to be established in Madina and the Bedouins who had always lived in desert and loved freedom would not like to submit to any authority based in urban areas. They felt no need for it. Thus though they embraced Islam but refused to submit to any authority and pay zakat. And when the first Caliph demanded zakat they renounced Islam and rebelled against the central authority. It is known as war of riddah in history of Islam.

This was first major challenge to an attempt to set up a just society in the Arabian Peninsula. To administer justice one needs a central authority, at least in a society, which is not an advanced democratic society. Also, there was need to check concentration of power and wealth as both make it extremely difficult to make justice available to each and every individual in the society. During the Prophet's time there was neither concentration of power not of wealth and prophet could be reached easily by any member of the society and hence it was easier to dispense direct justice.

After his death, Islam began to expand due to conquests and apart from Bedouins, large number of non-Arabs, especially Persians and others, entered into the fold of Islam with their own old value systems. The Arab, non-Arab conflict erupted on one hand, and the mawali (pl. of mawla client) of Arab tribes, of inferior social and economic status began to demand equality as the Qur'anic teachings. This led to a very complex situation and administration of justice became increasingly difficult.

Within thirty years the first Islamic State in history had grown unbelievably large and unwieldy and comprising bewilderingly large number of ethnic groups. This state had already incorporated into it parts of Roman and Sassanid empires. Apart from bringing large number of ethnic groups and nationalities with their own cultures and value systems, it also led to concentration of power and wealth in few hands. Thus the third and fourth Caliphs had to face very complex situation. There was turmoil all around, non-Arab Muslims clamouring for justice and equal partnership in governance. And when power went into the hands of Umayyads, they threw all Islamic norms to the wind and denied partnership in governance not only to non-Arabs but also to non-Umayyad Arabs. Naturally the cause of justice suffered greatly. They had to suppress others ruthlessly. Thus Umayyads resorted to tyranny and the first victim was grandson of the Holy Prophet Imam Husain himself who was killed in Karbala along with 72 members of his family and friends. This is one of the greatest tragedies of early Islam. And one of the governors of the Umayyad rulers Hajjaj bin Yusuf became notorious for his tyranny.

Unfortunately the Qur'anic ideal of justice and just rule was not practised by Muslim rulers whose lust for power knew no bounds. Islamic rule became dynastic and hierarchical and Islamic Empire huge and unwieldy. It was not possible to stick to Islamic norms when you are governing such a huge empire with a mix of such different ethnic groups and nationalities. Thus power became primary and justice incidental.

22
Contemporary World

The entire political scenario has changed in the contemporary world. Now there are nation states, not empires and human rights and democracy have become central for just governance. The Muslim countries are divided into nation states but many conditions for just governance are missing. Firstly, there is no democracy in most of the Muslim countries and no respect for human rights. Human rights are very central to Islam too. The concept of human dignity (17:70) is central to Qur'an and concept of human dignity central to human rights. But in non-democratic or authoritarian regimes one cannot expect human rights to be respected.

Also, there is serious problem with rights of women in Islamic world today. Most of the Muslim societies have yet to emerge from feudal or semi-feudal age at least as far as social values and ethos are concerned. External modernisation in the Muslim world (modern communication technology, roads, buildings, automation, computers and so on) has still not impacted deeply on inner attitudes, social ethos and values. Democracy, human rights, women's rights etc. are part of what can be called inner modernisation as against apparent or external modernisation.

As we have pointed out above, the Qur'anic concept of justice is very comprehensive embracing aspects like economic, social, political and gender-related. There should have been great appreciation of Qur'anic concept of justice at least in the modern age but the course of 266governance is extremely convoluted in the Muslim world and even women are not getting desired justice.

The Shari'ah laws as formulated during early centuries of Islam relating to women's rights are static and 'Ulama resist any change. Justice, as pointed out above, has to reflect the changing aspirations of people and hence what was thought to be justice during medieval ages would appear to be unjust today, particularly so in case of women. The concept of justice should not remain static but should reflect aspirations of women today. Today they cannot be satisfied with secondary status, much less as mere obedient wives and daughters. The Qur'an does not project wives to be obedient and secondary to their husbands. They have personality and dignity of their own.

Today we need new theology of justice whether it is gender justice, political justice or economic justice. The institution of zakat has to be recast. It should not be treated merely as charity to be dispensed to the poor. Zakat was very important ingredient of bait al-mal and greatly contributed to economic justice in the society. Today zakat is also a static, if not a dead institution. Zakat can play very dynamic role in Muslim societies, at least those which are poorer countries.

Firstly, zakat should be taken out honestly by the rich or those who are under that category (nisab). It should not be directly given to the poor which, is quite counter-productive. The Pakistani experiment of directly deducting zakat amount from bank account led to great complication and corruption as the empirical studies have shown. The zakat should be given to a voluntary board constituted by local residents of unquestionable integrity and this board should use zakat fund for interest free loans to small traders, vendors, small peasants and others so that they can stand on their own feet. It should also be used for scholarship-cum-loans for able students to pursue higher education.

Also, as proposed by many thinkers and scholars Islamic jurisprudence should no longer be the monopoly of conventional Islamic jurists. Modern jurists fully equipped with knowledge of Islamic jurisprudence should assist parliament to bring about changes in Shari'ah laws within the frame-work of the Qur'an. There should be no monopoly of traditional jurists on framing Islamic laws. Due to their training their minds are rigidly conditioned and for them justice is secondary and traditions are primary. This trend has to be reversed.

Also, there is great need for opening new centres of Islamic learning which would combine modern learning with traditional learning and would help create modern mindset. Also, students of such universities or Islamic seminaries should be required to do Ph.D. in modern social or natural sciences, which would greatly enhance their understanding of modern or contemporary problems. Unfortunately there are no such Islamic seminaries in Muslim countries combining higher learning in Islam with higher learning in modern social and natural sciences. This combination has become very essential to make them appreciate modern aspects of social, economic, legal and gender justice. To begin with at least one such international university be set up in one Islamic country on experimental basis. This will help create new breed of modern 'Ulama.

The Muslims should understand that Islam's centre concern is justice and this concern should be restored. This concern should be reflected in all fields particularly in socio-economic and legal field as well as in gender relations.

Index

N

O